Massive Plunder of Afghanistan's Mineral Wealth

Massive Plunder of Afghanistan's Mineral Wealth

The US and NATO burglars, Taliban, Islamic State of Khorasan, and jihadist groups of Central Asia, go-fifty-fifty

MUSA KHAN JALALZAI

Vij Books India Pvt Ltd
New Delhi (India)

Published by

Vij Books India Pvt Ltd
(Publishers, Distributors & Importers)
2/19, Ansari Road
Delhi – 110 002
Phones: 91-11-43596460, 91-11-47340674
Mobile: 98110 94883
e-mail: contact@vijpublishing.com
www.vijbooks.com

ISBN: 978-93-89620-10-8 (Hardback)

ISBN: 978-93-89620-12-2 (ebook)

Contents

Introduction

Hidden War Crimes, and Pillaging of Mineral Resources by Taliban, Islamic State of Khorasan, Criminal Militias, and the US and NATO Forces in Afghanistan

Nuclear bombs, missiles, torture and humiliation cannot undermine determination and zeal of the people of Afghanistan in their fight against international terrorism. Their verve and vehemence are as strong as they never genuflected to foreign occupation. For Afghans, it is time to spotlight their real enemy. The fact is, Afghans are being killed by Taliban, ISIS, the US drones and private criminal militias. They are being killed by bombs, bullets, fire, improvised explosive devices (IEDs), and missiles, biological and chemical weapons in their homes, markets, shops, colleges, universities, schools, and work places. It is crystal clear; however, the US army funded militias are spilling blood of innocent Afghans, destroys their houses, and kidnap their youn children and women in night operations across the country.

After 18 years of imposed war in Afghanistan, nothing has changed. On 24 October 2019, Pakistan's former Ambassador to Afghanistan, Mr. Rustam Shah Mohmand in his article described hardship, suffering, mental and physical diseases, and displacement of Afghans inside their own country at the hands of Taliban, Daesh, and US Army and NATO forces:

> "Forty years of war have devastated the lives of most of the country's residents. There is no area, sector or ethnic community that has not been exposed to varying degrees of hardship, pain, and suffering. But the physical damage to lives as well as to infrastructure has been well documented.

> Meanwhile, there is another tragic dimension to the unending agony that has not received the attention it deserves. Millions of Afghans—men, women, and children—have suffered varying degrees of psychological trauma and struggle with mental health illnesses because of the conflict. The war, relentless bombing, drones flying overhead and threatening to drop bombs anytime anywhere, people being killed in the senseless and brutal bloodbath unleashed by Daesh, the detentions of innocent people, persecution of the rank and file Afghans, growing poverty and unemployment and deepening frustration, have all taken a toll on the mental health of the population. Afghanistan today presents a dismal sight of a people who have endured agonies for two generations. There is hardly any household that has not suffered in terms of someone having been killed or wounded in a senseless war. Women and children have been the worst affected. Displacement of people adds another ominous dimension to the troubles of a beleaguered populace. Tens of thousands have sought shelter in other countries while large numbers have been forced to abandon their villages and flee to safer zones in the country".

However, analyst Mark Taliano (Global Research, 04 September 2019) argued that the United States and NATO allies support the Islamic State and Al Qaeda in Syria, Iraq, Yemen and Afghanistan. He also noted war crimes of these organizations, and their plunder of Syrian and Iraqi national resources:

> "U.S-led NATO and its allies support ISIS and al Qaeda globally. They supported al Qaeda to destroy Libya, they support al Qaeda/ISIS and their affiliates in Syria and in Iraq, and now evidence demonstrates that they are also supporting al Qaeda/ISIS in Yemen. The irrefutable evidence that the West supports these internationally proclaimed terrorists in Syria, Iraq, and Libya has been available for years. Now, thanks to the efforts of investigative journalist Dilyana Gaytandzhieva, we see strong evidence that the West supports ISIS in Yemen as well. In her September 1, 2019 article, "Islamic State weapons in Yemen traced back to US Government: Serbia files (part 1)" the evidence is available for the world to see. Tracking the

lot number of these Serbian weapons I was able to identify and trace mortar shells in the hands of Islamic State terrorists in Yemen back to their buyer – the US Government. These documents expose the biggest lie in the US foreign policy – officially fighting terrorism while secretly supporting it." Whereas Western foreign policy is on the wrong side of international law, humanity, morality, and civilization itself, the "Axis of Resistance" holds the higher ground. Whereas the West and its allies vilify and oppose Hezbollah, for example, evidence demonstrates that instead of slaughtering Christians in Syria, as the West's ISIS/al Qaeda proxies do, Hezbollah protects them".

Afghans have suffered serious human rights abuses at the hands of US backed local militias, which include a diverse array of irregular forces-ranging from armed groups working for tribal leaders to private security companies, so-called Mujaheedin leaders, criminal gangs, and insurgent groups. These militias have been involved in murder, rape, torture and extortion. They are operating outside the Afghan government chain of command-have been used by international forces. Author Bob Woodward in his 2010 book "Obama's Wars" noted: "The CIA's 3000-man covert army in Afghanistan. Called CTPT for Counterterrorism Pursuit Teams, the army consisted mostly of Afghans, the cream of the crop in the CIA's opinion". These pursuit teams, the AAN report noted were a paid, trained and functioning part of the CIA that was authorised by former President Bush.

The Afghan NDS-Unites backed by the CIA committed abuses "amounting to war crimes", according to a new report of Human Rights Watch (HRW). The report alleged that the troops "committed summary executions and other grave abuses without accountability". These include extrajudicial killings, forced disappearances and attacks on healthcare facilities. However, On 17 September 2019, the US backed Taliban's suicide attack on election campaign rally in Parwan, north of Kabul, killed at least 26 civilians and injured more than 42. The Taliban shamelessly claimed responsibility for the attack. Patricia Gossman, Associate Asia Director at Human Rights Watch said: "The Taliban's claim of responsibility is essentially an admission of culpability for a war crime.

The Khost Protection Force (KPF) is also killing innocent villagers. Allegations against the Khost Protection Force are long-standing. These include extrajudicial killing, torture and beating of civilians". As I cited above, there are prism of private militias engaged in various fronts. One of these militias is the Khost Protection Force (KPF) that committed war crimes. The Afghanistan Analysts Network (AAN) reported war crimes of Khost Protection Force (KPF) in its recent report:

> "In December 2015, US newspaper reporting alleged that six civilians had been killed during Khost Protection Force-led raids on homes in the province in the presence of American advisers and that the group was still unlawfully detaining and abusing detainees, UNAMA's 2016 mid-year report cited particular concerns about the number of civilian casualties caused by the Khost Protection Force and called for its integration into regular ANSF chains of command and accountability".In its research paper on criminal militias in Afghanistan, Afghanistan Analysts Network (Kate Clark, 26 October 2017) also documented criminal activities of NDS sponsored militias:
>
> "In 2013, there were two disastrous raids in the Shigal Valley in Kunar which brought to light the existence of the '0-4 unit', a 1200-strong force that was nominally NDS. However, then Presidential spokesman Aimal Faizy told The Guardian the force was actually a CIA proxy: "Some of them are said to be working with the NDS, but they are not armed by the NDS, not paid by the NDS, and not sent to operations by the NDS. Sometimes they only inform the NDS minutes before the operation." During two raids in Shigal on 7 February and 13 April 2013, when seven or eight CIA para militaries accompanied about 75 men from the unit, the CIA called in air strikes which killed nine and 17 civilians".

Criticism has grown over abuses, torture and killings by CIA-trained Afghan Special Intelligence Forces known as Units 01,

02, 03 and 04. All these units are under the control of CIA. At the end of 2019, they killed more than 30 civilians in Nangarhar. In September 2019, in Helmand province, a wedding party was turned into a massacre after a commando attack by the NDS killer Unit-02. These attacks were justified in the name of fighting terrorism. On 05 May 2019, the UNAMA report noted that the US army airstrikes on so-called drug laboratories in Farah province caused at least 39 civilian casualties, including 14 children and one woman.

The CIA funded militias are mainly used in night operations against residential areas. The operations typically lead to high civilian casualties. The UN mission report in 2019 warned that the Khost Protection Force carried out human rights abuses, intentionally killing civilians, illegally detaining individuals, and intentionally damaging and burning civilian property during search operations and night raids." The UN used similar language to describe the CIA-supported Special Forces of the Afghan intelligence agency, the NDS, in both its 2017 and 2018 reports. On 13 August 2019, Tolonews reported the killing of 11 innocent Afghans by the 01 Unit of the National Directorate of Security (NDS) in a night raid in Zurmat District of Paktia province:

"Most of the educated people such as students, university students and teachers are being killed," said Mohammad Osman Zurmati, a resident of Zurmat district. Mr. Hayatullah, an employee of Ministry of Education in Kabul; Mr. Mohammad Shafi, a teacher; Mr. Ansarullah, a student at Paktia University; and Mr. Akhtar Mohammad, a student at Kabul University who went to visit their families in Zurmat district were killed by the NDS terrorist unit. Moreover, Mr. Mohammad Asif, principal of Dawlat Khan School in Zurmat, Mr. Inam, a madrassa student, Mr. Rahmatullah, Mr. Hekmatullah; and Mr. Nusratullah (brothers), Mr. Fida Mohammad, Mr. Nasrullah and Mr. Fathullah, farmers in the district were killed by the terrorist Unit-01 of the NDS".

Consisting of local sarcastic elements-trained and armed by the CIA, which also has a base in the province, the militia itself, which has become notorious among locals, mainly conducts joint night raids with US forces, tracks targets for drone operations, and often appears at the scene after airstrikes. The militiamen of the KPF receive high salaries. They get thousands of dollars each month from the CIA. On 22 August 2019, Journalist John Wight, writer of Independent, Morning Star, Huffington Post, Counterpunch, London Progressive Journal, and Foreign Policy Journal wrote an interesting piece on the website of RT Television on US army and its funded militia's war crimes in Afghanistan:

> "Currently there are 14,000 US troops in the Central Asian country, along with a further 17,000 troops from 39 NATO and other countries. This it must be stressed is the official occupation force. There is, however, an unofficial element to the US presence in the country. It is a presence both sinister and conspicuous by its absence from the draft agreement, drawn up in Doha. It is here we come to the shadowy and sinister activities of an equally shadowy and sinister CIA. Calling to mind the infamous CIA-run contras in Central America in the 1980s, the notorious US intelligence agency has been running in Afghanistan what amounts to a private war with its own private army. Details of the CIA's operations in the country are highlighted in a chilling report, produced by the Costs of War Project based at Brown University's Watson Institute of International and Public Affairs in the US. The report's authors make the point that "There is virtually no public oversight of their activities or accountability for grave human rights abuses." What this describes is the conduct not only of a private war but a dirty war by the CIA, one clearly inimical to any prospect of a lasting peace in a country that has known only conflict and strife over the past two decades. Covering the story in The Intercept, the investigative news website, Alex Emmons reveals that the best known of these CIA-run Afghan militia groups is the Khost Protection Force, operating out of the CIA's Camp Chapman in Khost province".

The New York Times in one of its reports noted the origin of CIA-sponsored strike forces in Afghanistan. In January 2018, during a joint NDS and US operation, at least 20 men reportedly were dragged out from their homes at night by the NDS terror forces and summarily executed. Afghan politicians, military generals, and parliamentarians remained tightlip. On 12 April, 2019, International Criminal Court was threatened by the US government of dire consequences when it pursued war crimes investigation against the US troops in Afghanistan. International criminal court had received more than one million complaints against the war crimes of US Special Forces and the CIA funded militia. Director of Tricontinental-Institute for Social Research, and Chief Editor of Left Word, analyst Vijay Prashad (23 April 2019) in his column documented war crimes of the US army in Afghanistan:

"Almost a decade ago, on February 12, 2010, U.S. Special Operations Forces arrived at the home of Haji Sharabuddin in Khataba (Paktia Province, Afghanistan). The family of Sharabuddin was celebrating the birth of a grandson. Inside the home were close family members (including a police investigator and a government prosecutor) as well as the vice-chancellor of Gardez University, Sayed Mohammed Mal. At 3 a.m., the U.S. forces attacked the home, killing five members of the family including Sharabuddin's son—Mohammed Dawood—who was the police investigator. After the killing, the soldiers carried the bodies into the house and removed the bullets with a knife. They did not want to leave evidence of their actions. They then ransacked the home—including stealing money—and left. The U.S. military said that those whom they killed were insurgents. Both the Afghan Independent Human Rights Commission and the Criminal Investigations Department of the Afghan Ministry of the Interior found this allegation to be false. A war crime had been committed here. The killing in Nangalam was by a U.S. helicopter on March 1, 2011. The pilots fired on nine boys, killing them all. "My son Wahidullah's head was missing," said Haji Bismillah. "I only recognized him from his clothes." The U.S. apologized for the killing but did nothing other than that".

In a special report into the impact of damage to more than 60 sites in Farah province's Bakwa district, and in neighbouring Delaram district on 5 May, investigators from the UN Assistance Mission in Afghanistan verified 39 civilian casualties–30 deaths.

The toll included 14 children and one woman. On 06 June 2019, The Bureau of Investigative Journalism in its investigative report documented the unlawful killing of Masih-ur-Rahman Mubarez's family by the US army:

"It was 4 am when Masih Ur-Rahman Mubarez's wife Amina called, an unusually early time for their daily chat. When he picked up the phone, he could hear the panic in her voice. Amina was calling from the Afghan province of Wardak, where she brought up their children while he worked over the border in Iran to support them. She told him that soldiers were raiding their village. Some of them were speaking English. Amina was told to turn off her phone but Masih asked her not to - how would he know they were ok? The call ended with Masih saying he would call again when things had calmed. But at 9 am, when he dialled his wife's number, her phone was off. He tried again at 9.30 am. Still off. Through the whole of that day and the next, he repeatedly called. But Amina's phone remained off. It took another day for him to learn the truth. Relatives avoided his calls or gave vague replies to his questions, until finally, his brother broke the news. "He tried to avoid telling me the whole story, but I insisted that he tell me the truth," Masih recalled in a wavering voice. "He told me to have patience in God - no one is left." An airstrike on Masih's house had killed his wife and all his seven children, alongside four young cousins. His youngest child was just four years old. Masih's children were aged between four and 14 years old; his wife Amina was 32. The cousins, all girls, were aged from 10 to 16".

On 06 October 2018, Associated Press quoted International Criminal Court's report that uncovered the US army war crimes in its report. The AP indicated that the US armed forces subjected at least 61 detained persons to torture, and cruel treatment on the territory of Afghanistan: "US armed forces and the CIA may have committed war crimes by torturing detainees in Afghanistan, the international criminal court's chief prosecutor has said in a report, raising the possibility that American citizens could be indicted even though Washington has not joined the global court. "Members of US armed forces appear to have subjected at least 61 detained persons to torture, cruel treatment, outrages upon personal dignity on the territory of Afghanistan between 01 May 2003 and 31 December 2014," according to the report issued by prosecutor Fatou Bensouda's office. The same report says that the Taliban and Afghan government forces also may have used torture and committed other atrocities in that country's long and bitter conflict. The report says the Taliban and its affiliates killed thousands of people and are suspected of committing war crimes including murder, recruiting and conscripting child soldiers and attacking civilians and humanitarian workers". AP reported.

On 25 September 2019, analyst Oscar Grenfell in his World Socialist Website's article uncovered war crimes of Australian Special Forces in Afghanistan. He quoted some reports and civilians comments that ratified war crimes of Australian Special Forces by murdering innocent women and children in Afghanistan:

> "An episode of Channel Nine's "60 Minutes" program on Sunday night featured new details of alleged war crimes committed by Australian Special Forces (SAS) soldiers in Afghanistan. The allegations included testimony from whistle blowers within the organisation and comments from Afghan civilians whose relatives were murdered. The program followed a two-year investigation by several journalists, including from the Sydney Morning Herald and the Age, which has implicated the SAS in extrajudicial killings, the desecration of corpses and other violations of international law. The exposures resulted in an unprecedented police raid on the Sydney headquarters of the Australian Broadcasting Corporation (ABC) in June, and secretive official investigations by the Australian Federal Police and the Inspector-General of the Defence Department. Most explosively, the program alleged that Ben Roberts-Smith, one of Australia's most highly decorated soldiers and a widely-feted public figure, kicked an Afghan civilian off a cliff before he was murdered by another soldier. Nine Media publications had previously alleged that Roberts-Smith was involved in incidents under investigation without providing details. According to the program, Roberts-Smith and his colleagues were deployed to Darwan, a small village in Uruzgan province, in September 2012. They were tasked with finding an Afghan

soldier who had shot several Australian troops. The SAS troops allegedly rounded up several Afghan civilians, including Ali Jan, an impoverished farmer who had travelled to the town to collect supplies. Other war crimes previously alleged in the ABC's "The Afghan Files", included at least 10 extrajudicial killings by the SAS. Among the victims was a small boy, shot in Kandahar Province in 2012, along with a 14- or 15-year-old boy in a separate incident. Bismillah Azadi, an Afghan civilian, was killed during a raid on a house in 2013 as was his six-year-old son. SAS soldiers have also been accused of cutting-off the hands of corpses".

Now, let's highlight some aspects of Taliban, Islamic State of Khorasan, and criminal militias looting and plundering business and their illegal war on mineral resources of Afghanistan. The supervening details of pillage and looting of mineral resources are heart-breaking, and interesting. They had come to Afghanistan to fight war against terrorism, but their real and transmogrified faces were exposed by international media and research reports when they started looting resources of a poor country they occupied. A new investigative report revealed how Afghanistan's 6,500 year old lapis mines prompting corruption, conflict and extremism in the country. Global Witness has found that the Taliban and other armed groups earn up to 20 million dollars every year. Global Witness has often called on Afghan puppet government and its international partners to tackle the looting business with iron hand. David Mansfield (The Afghanistan Research and Evaluation Unit-AREU, May 2019) has also mentioned of drug trade and illegally exploitation of mineral resources of Afghanistan, and noted that this trade finances terrorism, and insurgency in the country:

"There are of course further sources of rent for armed actors in the form of licit goods that are produced and sold illicitly. Precious stones are mined in Afghanistan, including rubies and emeralds, as well as the semi-precious lapiz lazuli. There are also significant deposits of industrial minerals such as chromite, coal, and magnesium silicate. Many of these are mined illegally, without licence and smuggled across the borders into Pakistan, Iran and the Central Asian Republics. There is also a vibrant economy in the smuggling of licit goods— "the transit trade"—a range of different consumer and luxury goods imported into Afghanistan only to be smuggled out to neighbouring countries to be sold at a profit. Officials estimate that as much as 50 percent of the goods imported under the transit trade agreement are smuggled across the borders into neighbouring countries. Combined with prohibited drugs, these illicit economies represent a significant source of revenue that does not flow to the central coffers of the Afghan government in Kabul and in the case of opiates, marijuana and methamphetamine is unlikely to do so in the future. It seems most likely that the vast majority of these funds will remain in the provinces in which these goods are produced and transported or banked overseas. While the scale of the revenue generated is unknown it is clearly significant and shapes the political economy of the provinces in which these goods are produced: the patronage networks within them, cross-border relationships, and perhaps most importantly the interests of that conflict and a political settlement in Afghanistan. Developing a better understanding of the scale of these illicit economies, and in particular the illicit drugs economy, and what can realistically be done to address them will be critical to an enduring political settlement".

The Looting and ransacking of Afghanistan's natural resources by criminal militias; such as the ISIS terrorist group, and Taliban caused misunderstanding between the Afghans and International Coalition that they all are involved in looting of mineral resources of their country. The Islamic State of Khorasan controls large amount of territory in Afghanistan, and that includes parts of the country's rich mineral wealth, especially talc, chromite and marble. According to the Global Witness research report, several insurgents' groups, militias, Taliban and the ISIS are deeply involved in the plunder of these resources:

"The Islamic State in Afghanistan (ISKP) controls major mining sites in eastern Afghanistan and has a strategic interest in the country's rich mineral resources, new Global Witness research shows–a powerful example of the wider threat posed by armed groups and corrupt actors in Afghan mining. The Islamic State in Afghanistan (ISKP) controls large talc, marble and chromite mines in the Islamic State (IS) stronghold of Achin district in the Nangarhar province of eastern Afghanistan – the same area where in April 2017 the US military dropped the 'Mother of All Bombs' against ISKP-held caves. Nangarhar was the deadliest Afghan province for US troops in 2017". However, the Global Witness report (At any price we will take the mines) also documented the looting and pillaging business of these groups:

"The Islamic State, the Taliban, and Afghanistan's white talc mountains uses satellite imagery and extensive interviews to highlight this threat in unprecedented detail. But it also shows how ISKP are just a high-profile example of a much wider problem of the involvement of armed groups and corrupt actors in Afghan mining. The global talc industry is predicted to grow to around US $3.29 billion by 2021. An estimated 380,000 tons of talc was imported into the United States in 2017. On average around 35% of US imports are from Pakistan, according to the US Geological Survey. From our research we also estimated that around 80% of Pakistan's 2016 exports of talc actually originated in Afghanistan. Of those exports, 42% went to the US, and another 36% went to EU countries, especially the Netherlands and Italy".

However, in 2016, Global Witness report (War in the treasury of the people: Afghanistan, lapis lazuli and the battle for mineral wealth), exposed the importance of mining, especially of lapis lazuli, for the Taliban in Afghanistan. The report warned that armed groups including the Taliban were earning tens of millions of dollars per year from Afghanistan's lapis mines, the world's main source of the brilliant blue lapis lazuli stone, which is used in jewellery around the world. Moreover, William A. Byrd and Javed Noorani, in their report (Industrial-Scale Looting of Afghanistan's Mineral Resources, 2017, the United States Institute of Peace) warned that international community and different sectarian, militant and terrorist organization of Pakistan and Afghanistan are looting mineral resources of Afghanistan on an industrial scale:

"Based on the evidence from fieldwork and case studies, a different explanation is far more compelling. The post-2001 Afghan government from the time of its formation has been politically penetrated by networks of power holders—actors with their own access to the means of organized armed violence—whose members are involved in, or at least benefiting from, ongoing mineral exploitation. These networks, which had formed and developed during the resistance against the interests of different power holders and funding their political and security expenditures; reductions in one kind of rent may well push the political system to increase rents in other spheres of activity. The high profits that can be relatively easily obtained from mineral looting constitute a strong pull factor attracting interest groups into the mining business. These profits have become progressively more accessible as experience is gained, markets are identified and exploited (for example, lapis in China, and talc in Europe), transport channels open, and business linkages are developed. Such dynamics can result in snowballing of extraction over time, as has occurred in the case of lapis, talc, and apparently chromite, among others". Analyst Ikram Afzali (16 February 2018) argued that Afghanistan's minerals have caused prolongation of war in the country:

"Afghanistan has massive mineral reserves, even if poor infrastructure makes them less valuable than the top-line numbers suggest. But those riches have done precious little to help the Afghan people, who have seen a fraction of the revenues that they should have—even as mining has been second only to narcotics in funding the Taliban. Competition over mines among "pro-government" strongmen has turned parts of the country that staunchly resisted the Taliban—like Badakhshan province—into hotbeds of the insurgency. Locals angry at exploitation which does little to help them have backed the takeover of mines by illegal militias. Meanwhile, major concessions like the Aynak copper mines have seen allegations of large-scale bribery, and both US and Afghan officials say the Ministry of Mines lacks the capacity to manage new contracts. Any new mining project in Afghanistan is at very grave risk of falling foul of one or more of these dangers. The main threat to the sector is not lack of investment, though that is certainly an issue: it is the lack of governance".

As of mid-2017, the ISKP's presence in Badakhshan was the result of local forces of the Islamic Movement of Uzbekistan (IMU) pledging allegiance to them, and not of Taliban commanders defecting. There is a long record of cooperation between the IMU and the Taliban in Badakhshan, unlike in the rest of Afghanistan, and this seems to have continued after IMU's 'rebranding'. The Global Witness report has also documented the Taliban and Pakistan's plundering of Afghan natural resources, specifically by the Quetta Shura:

> "At the highest level, the Taliban leadership reportedly have a role through the Finance Committee of the Quetta Shura (which also gets at least a share of the revenues). On a more day to day level, one of our sources reported that the Taliban had a representative in the Arzan Kimat district of Kabul, a mullah who ran a local madrassa [religious school] and who was empowered to sign contracts for the mines. A copy of a Taliban mining contract we obtained shows what such documents might cover, including production rates and standards. Businessmen could also receive letters of introduction if needed, to negotiate directly with senior Taliban officials in the mining districts or could buy talc directly at the mines. Another source similarly reported that deals with the Taliban were either made with the shadow District Governor, or with a representative either in Kabul or in the Zakhel area of Jalalabad. But the same Taliban source also reported that the movement was itself engaging in direct exploitation, at least in less accessible mines–and that this was following the example set by the Islamic State. This would allow them to retain more profit. However, there was no indication of what proportion of mines was exploited this way".

Not only this, terrorist and criminal militias have kicked off business of Hawala system in Afghanistan to finance their terrorist operations in the country. Michael Kelvington in his Small Wars Journal has linked terrorism with terror-finance in Afghanistan, and warned that this illegal business has causing trouble in the country as several terrorist organizations have become partners in expanding Hawala system to Afghanistan's neighbouring states:

Money laundering, including the financing of terrorism, along with drug trade, criminal activity, and corruption, is devastating Afghanistan's already weak economy. The 2015 GDP for the country of Afghanistan was only $19.33 billion. With an economy suffering from a deficit in balance of trade of -$7.1 billion and current account of over -$4.8 billion, the last thing their economy needs is a rampant money laundering epidemic where illicit and often untraceable "dirty money" freely flows, further frustrating the economic instability of Afghanistan. A Ministry of Finance report indicated "only 35 percent of the financial flows within the country are legal. The main culprit is the hawala system, "an important informal institution . . . handling both financial transfers and currency exchange." If the U.S. wants to help Afghanistan stabilize its economy and attack terrorists' financial lifeblood, it must work with its government to develop an action plan to implement "a fully functioning banking system . . . sensitive to the needs of an emerging licit economy." Providing full visibility of money transfers would allow the government to manage money demand, interest rates, levy taxes and duties, and provide long-term stability for the Afghan economy and legitimacy to its government, all the while cutting off a key element of the CTF efforts against the Taliban, ISIS-K, and Al-Qaeda".

Moreover, courageous and world known author and intellectual, Prof Michel Chossudovsky (Global Research, 04 January, 2019) in his investigative research report noted that Afghanistan's opium economy caused the surge of heroin addiction in the US, and warns that this multibillion dollar hike is the result of a significant increase in the volume of heroin transacted worldwide coupled with a moderate increase in retail prices:

"Despite President Trump's announced US troop withdrawal, the Afghan opium trade continues to flourish. It is protected by US-NATO occupation forces on behalf of a nexus of powerful financial and criminal interests. In 2004, the proceeds of the Afghan heroin trade yielded estimated global revenue of the order of 90 billion dollars. This estimate was based on retail sales corresponding to a total supply of the order of 340,000 kg of pure heroin (corresponding to Afghanistan's 3400 tons of opium production) (See Michel Chossudovsky, America's War on Terrorism, Chapter XVI, Global Research, Montreal 2005). Today a rough estimate based on US retail prices suggests that the global heroin market is above the 500 billion dollars mark. This multibillion-dollar hike is the result of a significant increase in the volume of heroin transacted Worldwide coupled with a moderate increase in retail prices". Based on the most recent (UNODC) data (2017) opium production in Afghanistan is of the order of 9000 metric tons, which after processing and transformation is equivalent to approximately 900,000 kg of pure heroin". In the tail-end, I am indebted of Brigadier Pradip, and Rohan Vij for their encouragement and cooperation.

Musa Khan Jalalzai

London, January 2020

Chapter 1

At any Price we will Take the Mines: the Islamic State, the Taliban, and Afghanistan's White Talc Mountains

The Global Witness Research Report

Summary

In April 2017, the largest non-nuclear weapon in the United States arsenal, the 'Mother of All Bombs', crashed into a hillside in the district of Achin in Eastern Afghanistan, targeting a network of tunnels held by the Afghan affiliate of the Islamic State (known as Islamic State – Khorasan Province, or ISKP). But on satellite photos, craters of another sort stand out, starting just a few hundred meters from the impact area: the marks of extensive mining for minerals at sites along the length of the valley.

ISKP controls a limited amount of territory in Afghanistan, but that includes parts of the country's rich mineral wealth, especially talc, chromite and marble. There are conflicting indications about how much they have exploited the mines so far: the available satellite imagery does not appear to show vehicles in the main ISKP-controlled area around Achin's Momand valley, and several sources denied mining had taken place since ISKP seized it in mid-2015. At the same time, multiple other credible sources reported that they have indeed benefitted at least to some extent from extraction and from taxing the minerals trade, and that they had done so with a tighter grip than the Taliban.

Whatever the reality, the danger is clear. Natural resources have long had a place in ISKP strategy in other countries, and that seems to be echoed in Afghanistan. In late 2017 more than 60,000 people were displaced by fighting between ISKP and the Taliban for control of other mineral-rich districts close to Achin: a Taliban official explicitly linked the ferocity of the battle to the struggle over the mines. An Afghan police source said ISKP had attempted to build a road to smuggle minerals south over the border to Pakistan. As early as 2015 an Afghan ISKP commander described control of mines in one mineral-rich province as a key priority, saying: "at any price we will take the mines."

But the threat from ISKP is just one dramatic illustration of the much wider danger of conflict and corruption around Afghanistan's resources. In Nangarhar, our research documented the Taliban's grip on the talc trade, which generates millions for them from just a few districts. Satellite imagery shows extensive activity, including use of heavy machinery, at sites reported to be under Taliban influence, and trucks carrying minerals are routinely taxed. The onward trade is reportedly dominated by politically connected strongmen, and widespread corruption costs the government millions in revenue. Beyond Nangarhar, mining has been a key revenue source for insurgents, strongmen and illegal militias – and a key driver of instability – across the whole country.

And while talc may be the least glamorous of conflict minerals, ultimately much of its value comes from America and Europe. Our research indicated that almost all Afghan talc generates revenue for the Taliban, and almost all is exported to Pakistan. Most Pakistani exports in turn actually originate in Afghanistan: and the largest single market for them is the United States, with European countries not far behind. Consumers in those countries are almost certainly unwittingly helping to fund the insurgency.

There are no easy responses to this challenge. But there are basic measures which are realistic and could help, and which the government and its allies have yet to implement so far. Part of this is direct pressure. Minerals like talc and marble need trucks to transport and are relatively easy to interdict. Much more could also be done to increase controls on the trade in Pakistan, and further up the supply chain. A greater emphasis on security in mining areas is another fundamental step, although clearly a difficult and risky one: it is hard to deal with illegal mining if armed groups hold the mines.

Those measures would help to target the Islamic State and Taliban directly, but returning the mines to government control will be of limited benefit if abusive extraction simply continues under other masters. And durably displacing abusive extraction is difficult without filling the resulting vacuum, with a cleaner extractive sector that benefits all Afghans. That is the ultimate endgame in any case: the aim is not to close down the trade but to make it legitimate. In other words, the Islamic State's interest in Afghanistan's minerals should be an urgent wake-up call not just for the fight against extremist armed groups, but for the wider reform that the sector has been lacking so far.

And there are eminently realistic measures to implement that reform, based on the three core principles of transparency, community benefit and monitoring, and stronger oversight. They include amending the law to make contract publication a condition of validity, creating a single transparent account to be used for all payments as a condition for their receipt, and using the network of Community Development Councils to deliver a percentage of mining revenues to local communities. If ordinary traders and local communities can profit from legal mining, it will give them a reason to push back (to the extent they are able) against the takeover of resources by armed groups or corrupt strongmen, and reduce the political pressure on the government to turn a blind eye to abuses.

For its part, the Afghan government is relying on mining to help fund its budget and grow the economy and has specifically identified talc as a priority for development. But without stronger action, it is hard to see those hopes being realistic. To be fair, the government says it recognises the problem, and it deserves real credit for publishing mining contracts and making some strong commitments on more systematic reforms. But progress in actually implementing those reforms has been much more limited, with critical measures like revenue transparency and community benefit often more of an ideal than a reality, and amendments to the mining law still under discussion. A 2015 ban on the talc trade showed that the government could impose effective restrictions on illegal mining but was dropped within months under pressure from traders. As a whole, the international response has also been inadequate (with some exceptions): the key concern of the Trump administration, for example, seems to be to press the Afghan government to give US companies a greater stake in Afghan resources.

The scale of the challenge is significant – especially for the Afghan government, which faces many other problems, not least a large-scale insurgency. None of our recommendations offers a silver bullet. But even if the government and its partners cannot tackle illegal mining everywhere, they could start by making limited, key areas (like the Nangarhar mines) a particular focus for security and a showcase for reforms and put in place the higher-level changes which are within their control. Without action, as Nangarhar so powerfully demonstrates, the reasonable expectation is that Afghanistan's resources will do much more harm than good. That is a threat which must not be ignored.

1. Restrict illegal mining by armed groups in Nangarhar

a. Block the transit of talc, chromite, marble and other minerals from areas of Nangarhar under the influence of illegal armed groups, while moving as quickly as possible to create the conditions for 'clean' extraction, even if this is initially in a limited area.

b. Make it a higher priority within security strategy to protect key resource-rich areas and associated transit routes, including mining sites in Nangarhar. Prioritise political means where possible.

c. Ensure any enforcement or security actions are tied to wider measures like those outlined below, and to negotiations with local communities and protections for livelihoods –so long as this does not undermine efforts to exclude armed groups and strongmen from the trade.

2. Give local communities reasons to support legal mining

a. Create effective mechanisms for a community share in legal revenues, community monitoring of mining, and community or artisanal ownership of mines. Ensure local communities can control what projects their revenues are used for, under appropriate safeguards including transparency and community monitoring. As a first option, consider distributing the funds as supplements to the budgets of Community Development Councils.

b. Within Nangarhar, make community benefit from or ownership of mines a central element of wider efforts to reduce insurgent influence in the area.

3. Reform laws and oversight to make illegal mining harder and legal mining more attractive

Put in place basic transparency and oversight reforms to make abusive mining more difficult and create space for legal extraction that benefits the country and local communities. In particular:

a. Within the next six months, amend the mining law and regulations in order to.

   1. Make the publication of contracts a condition of their validity.

   2. Require the publication of production and payment data.

   3. Require the creation of a single transparent subaccount of the Treasury Single Account, to be used for all extractive sector payments as a condition of their receipt, and published at least quarterly The published statement must include clear identification of the relevant individual project for each payment, and information on the basis on which it was made, such as amount and grade of production.

4. Create a public register of beneficial ownership, and require companies to register and update their entries as a condition of bidding for or holding government contracts.

a. Strengthen the oversight capacity and practices of the Ministry of Mines, specifically information and contract management, cadastre, community relations, and inspection functions. Develop management capacity and mechanisms for artisanal and small-scale mining.

b. Reform contracting processes to strengthen transparency and ensure companies are treated fairly. Move towards a license rather than contract model for extractive concessions. At a minimum, mandate the use of model contracts incorporating the strongest available protections against corruption and conflict, developed in conjunction with civil society, local communities, and mining companies.

4. Use satellite imagery to monitor key mining sites

a. Systematically monitors key mining sites using satellite imagery, including both optical and radar data. Make all images at commercially available resolutions automatically available to the public to allow transparent and broad-based monitoring of the sites, and share higher resolutions with established and reputable CSOs.

5. Control supply chains

a. Work with trade partners and consumer countries to put in place strong controls over supply chains from conflict affected areas, including a requirement for due diligence by both Afghan companies and those from major importing countries.

Key actors

The Islamic State in Afghanistan is a relatively loose set of armed groups which have declared allegiance to the wider Islamic State extremist movement centred in Syria and Iraq. It grew mainly from fighters loyal to the 'Pakistani Taliban' (Tehreek e Taleban e Pakistan, TTP). Others have defected from the Afghan Taliban, and the two groups remain in violent competition.[1]

The Taliban came to prominence in 1994, during the civil war that followed the end of the Soviet occupation of Afghanistan.[2] While they lost almost all of their territory after the US-led invasion in 2001, they are now estimated to control 41 of Afghanistan's 407 districts and contest an additional 118.[3] Before 2015, the Taliban was present in areas of Nangarhar that now form the heartland of the Islamic State in Afghanistan, and they are still a major force in the province.[4] The Government of the Islamic Republic of Afghanistan and its allies are fighting both the Taliban and the Islamic State, but US forces in particular have focused attention on ISKP out of proportion to the small size of the group.[5] This includes a major offensive in April 2017, Operation Hamza.[6]

1. **Support Afghan efforts to strengthen resource governance**

    a. Provide full material and political support for government reforms of extractive sector governance, notably the mining-related measures discussed in the National Anti-Corruption action plan and the reform of the Ministry of Mines. Explicitly prioritise strengthening of oversight, governance and conflict prevention.

    b. Provide or fund the acquisition of high-resolution satellite imagery for monitoring of key extractive sites by the Afghan government as set out above, and direct your own intelligence resources to exposing and understanding links between resources, armed groups and corrupt actors.

    c. All importing countries for Afghan minerals, oil and gas should commit to requiring that companies carry out risk assessment and due diligence on their supply chains, at a minimum to the standard set out in the OECD Due Diligence Guidance for Responsible Supply Chains of Minerals from Conflict Affected High Risk Areas.

2. Make stronger resource governance a priority for your engagement with Afghanistan

a. Integrate the most important extractive governance reforms into core benchmarks for mutual accountability between the Afghan government and its partners. Agree a single common set of more detailed benchmarks for donor support to the Ministry of Mines in particular.

b. Hold the Afghan government to its existing commitments to strengthen natural resource governance and raise the need for urgent reforms through political engagement at the highest level.

c. Avoid creating any pressure for new natural resource contracts in areas that are at elevated risk from conflict or armed groups, or before basic protections (like the measures set out above) have become effective. Focus your engagement in Afghanistan on achieving these conditions as rapidly as possible.

Introduction

The involvement of armed groups in mining obviously has implications for the future of Afghanistan and illustrates wider dangers around the abusive exploitation of the country's natural resources. Yet little systematic research on the subject exits. This report aims to fill that gap, at least in part. Our findings are based both on commercially available satellite imagery, and interviews with a range of sources with credible knowledge of the local situation. Owing to security concerns around the report, especially for individuals in Afghanistan, we felt it necessary to go to exceptional lengths to ensure anonymity and have included substantially fewer details than we normally would about the nature and background of the sources. We are confident in the credibility of our information and are willing to discuss our research methodology with responsible third parties.

The report briefly covers the background of the Islamic State in Afghanistan (for more detailed accounts, see the sources cited in the endnotes).[7] It then documents the extent of ISKP's control over resources and the evidence around how far they have been able to exploit them. This is closely linked to a discussion of their broader strategic interest in natural resources, drawing on evidence from their competition with the Taliban in other parts of the province, and briefly looking at the rest of Afghanistan. This is followed by our findings on Taliban involvement in mining in Nangarhar–highlighting the wider risk of armed groups profiting from mining. We also document the supply chains which ultimately fuel armed groups in Afghanistan, before finally discussing policy responses: there are a number of realistic options, even if it there is no silver bullet.

Throughout the report the name 'Islamic State–Khorasan Province' or ISKP, is used to distinguish the Afghan affiliate of the Islamic State from the main body of the Islamic State in Iraq and Syria, which we will refer to as ISIS.[8] "Islamic State" is used when referring to the movement as a whole (although we fully acknowledge that the term is rejected in many quarters as a usurpation of the name of Islam).[9] Some Afghan sources referred to the Islamic State using the Arabic term 'Daesh', a somewhat pejorative abbreviation of the name where they did, that term has been retained.

Locations mentioned in the text can be found on the relevant maps. Some place names could not be located with the maps available: this may partly reflect the fact that mining sites are often located away from settlements, which provide the great majority of names on the available lists.[10]

Most prices cited in Nangarhar were expressed in Pakistani Rupees (colloquially known as kaldars), as the currency is widely used in the border areas.[11] For conversions in the report, a rate of 105 Pakistani Rupees (Rs) to one US dollar ($) was used, which closely approximates the rate between August 2015 and December 2017.[12] For Afghanis, a rate of 68 Afghanis (Afs) to one US dollar was used, which roughly corresponds to the rate from December 2015 to November 2017.[13] Weights are expressed in kilograms and metric tons.

Global Witness gratefully acknowledges the considerable assistance provided by Sarmap SA in obtaining, processing and analysing satellite imagery. Sarmap's contribution was particularly critical to enable us to access Synthetic Aperture Radar imagery and conduct analysis of optical imagery. We are also grateful to Digital Globe for its invaluable assistance in accessing wider satellite imagery. Finally, and most importantly, this report could not have been written without the support and work of many others. We deeply regret that we cannot list them, but very gratefully acknowledge their contribution.

Unglamorous conflict minerals–talc, chromate and marble

Our sources described mining of three key minerals in the areas under ISKP influence: talc, chromite, and marble. Other minerals like tourmaline may also be mined, but they are relatively insignificant.[14] Talc (hydrated magnesium silicate–Mg3Si4O10 (OH) 2) is the softest mineral known to man.[15] The name is of Persian origin, possibly reflecting the long history of talc mining in Afghanistan and the region.[16] Usually processed into a fine white powder, it easily absorbs moisture and oils, and can serve as a lubricant. Perhaps best known for its use in talcum powder or baby powder, it also has important applications in ceramics, paint, paper, plastics, rubber, insecticides, and other products.[17] Global output was around 8.1m tons in 2017.[18]

Afghanistan possesses talc of very high quality, with exceptionally high-grade deposits in the Khogyani/ Sherzad area, and only slightly less pure material in Achin.[19] Resources in Achin total an estimated 1.25m tons, distributed in narrow, irregular beds of one to 15 metres in width, and generally less than 240 m in length.[20] Artisanal mining has taken place there since the 1920s.[21] Chromite (iron chromium oxide – FeCr2O4) is a heavy, dark mineral, globally important as the only economic ore of chromium, which is widely used as an essential element in the production of stainless steel and other steel alloys.[22] Global production was about 31m tons in 2017.[23]

Marble (metamorphosed calcium carbonate – $CaCO_3$) produced in Afghanistan is also renowned for its quality, with significant deposits of high-grade onyx marble.[24] Its uses range from flooring and tiles to decorative objects. There are reports of substantial smuggling, especially from Helmand province, where marble is the second largest source of revenue for the Taliban after narcotics.[25]

1. The Islamic State in Afghanistan: a complex threat

The movement calling itself the Islamic State[26] established its first nascent presence in Afghanistan only in 2014, and officially launched in early 2015.[27] Since then, they have expanded to become a threat in several provinces, but have also faced resistance from both the Taliban and government forces which has frustrated or reversed their growth. Nonetheless, they retain the ability to strike – and bases from which they aim to expand their insurgency across the country.

An important affiliate

In January 2015, the leadership of the Islamic State of Iraq and Al-Shams (ISIS) declared the creation of the Khorasan wilayat or governorate–"Khorasan" being a historical term for a region encompassing Afghanistan, Pakistan and parts of other countries.[28] The group's creation was important for the Islamic State. It marked the first official ISIS affiliate outside of the Arab world, [29] had an important religious dimension,[30]and allowed ISIS to challenge their rival Al Qaeda on the territory where they have their primary base, in the Afghanistan-Pakistan border regions.[31] Indeed, ISKP's initial attacks were against the Taliban, Al Qaeda's ally and protector.[32]

ISKP quickly grew into a significant force after it was established. Government offensives in Pakistan's tribal areas helped push militants, including foreign fighters, into Afghanistan, swelling the ranks of the movement,[33] which quickly became active in a dozen provinces around the country (including a number of northern provinces beyond their original Pashtun power base).[34] In July 2015, the Islamic Movement of Uzbekistan (IMU), a significant foreign-led militant group based in Badakhshan province in northern Afghanistan, also pledged bay'at [allegiance] to ISIS.[35] In Nangarhar, the fractured nature in many areas of both tribal society, and of the pre-2015 insurgency, made particularly fertile ground for an ISKP coup.[36]

Most estimates put the overall strength of ISKP at 1,000 to 3,000 fighters, with numbers in Nangarhar specifically put at 750-2,000.[37] The core leadership from the start has been former members of the Pakistani Taliban group Tehreek-e-Taliban (TTP).[38] Afghan and international security forces in fact claim that 70-80 per cent of ISKP fighters are Pakistanis, but this may be an overstatement, given the impact of Afghans defecting to ISKP from the Taleban; a late 2016 USIP report found these made up the majority of mid-level commanders.[39] Even so, the Pakistani influence in the group could have significant implications for its ability to expand.[40] There is also a notable (and reportedly growing) international contingent (although the numbers of foreign fighters in Afghanistan are notoriously prone to exaggeration).[41]

Franchises like ISKP receive at least a nominal level of management from the senior Islamic State leadership,[42] and for its part ISKP also asserts that its Afghan operations support the larger, Levant-centred IS fight.[43] However, the extent of more practical links between the two organisations are still subject to debate. There is a good deal of opportunistic re-branding by armed groups, with operational ties both among them and to IS leaders much less clear.[44] Indeed, some groups, especially those in Ghor and Jowzjan, may essentially be criminal networks that have taken the ISKP name.[45]

Nonetheless, one senior Afghan ISKP commander asserted that he had visited the ISIS senior leadership in Iraq and received seed funding from them, and that ISKP commanders shaped their strategy in line with guidance from ISIS.[46] There are other reports of small cash transfers (see below),[47] and General John Nicholson, the commander of international forces in Afghanistan, stated in early 2017 that ISIS was exercising "operational guidance" over ISKP.[48] Overall, there does seem to be some tie, even if there is no routine command-and-control.

A well-resourced insurgency

The growth of ISKP has been helped by the allure of the Islamic State brand, but also by the resources they could offer (although the exact extent and source of their funding is very difficult to establish).[49] This may be changing now, with some observers reporting the movement is facing financial difficulties, but others indicated that their resources still appear considerable. The UN Sanctions Committee reported in January 2017 that "ISIL is struggling financially in Afghanistan, where it has resorted to extortion of the local population and has had to stop paying its fighters at times."[50] Their May 2017 report, however, cited official sources reporting that ISKP "continues to appear to be well equipped and funded, with interlocutors reporting that it pays its fighters between $200 and $500 per month."[51] Some of this funding – about $100,000 a month–was reportedly being transferred from the core ISIS group in Iraq and Syria, despite the substantial declines in their income.[52] Whether this has changed with loss of almost all ISIS territorial control by late 2017 remains to be seen.

ISKP 's substantial propaganda work[53] and continued ability to launch operations certainly suggest that they have an independent source of funds.[54] Their fighters also appear to be paid relatively well, with several other sources supporting the UN's findings, including Global Witness interviewees from two provinces.[55] They have reportedly been burning poppy fields rather than financing themselves from narcotics – another reason to think they would be particularly interested in minerals.[56] Taxes on locals (the ushr and zakat of Islamic tradition),[57] as well as cruder extortion or theft from individuals are thought to be a key income source,[58] as are donations from sympathisers.[59] As we shall see, natural resources are another source of funds, even if their precise contribution is unclear.

Stalled but dangerous

Since 2015, ISKP has carried out a number of high-profile operations, including a string of attacks in the cities of Jalalabad and Kabul (although they may not have carried out all the operations that have been attributed to them).[60] Their methods have often been brutal even by the standards of the Afghan conflict,[61] which has alienated at least some potential supporters, and could be another factor limiting their growth.[62] They are also exceptional in the way they have explicitly targeted the Hazara ethnic minority, who are largely Shia Muslims, in an apparent attempt to foment sectarian conflict–a deeply worrying development.[63]

However, ISKP's initial growth quickly created a sharp backlash, as the movement found itself the enemy of all–the Taliban, the Afghan government, and international forces. By the end of 2015, the group had been rolled back from several provinces.[64] In February 2017, General Nicholson estimated that operations since early 2016 had reduced the number of ISKP members by half, and their territory by two-thirds.[65] A series of ISKP leaders have also been killed.[66]

Yet as of late 2017, the movement was thought to have significantly rebuilt its numbers, with no sign of a let up in their recruiting.[67] There are fears these are being boosted by fighters displaced from lost Islamic State territories in Syria and Iraq,[68] and even that the safe haven of Afghanistan may be being used to plot attacks in the Unites States.[69] Groups claiming loyalty to ISKP are active in a clutch of provinces[70]–notably Logar, Kunar, and Nangarhar in eastern Afghanistan, but also more distant territories like Jawzjan in the north.[71] These are all mineral rich areas, even if it is not clear how far that has driven the pattern compared to other factors.[72]

Nangarhar is the heartland of the remaining ISKP presence. The movement had a "comfortable position" in eight districts of the province by mid-2015,[73] after brutal clashes with the Taliban.[74] While they quickly lost many of these gains, the movement remained strong in Kot, DehBala, and Achin, especially their stronghold in the Momand valley.[75] This position lasted more or less intact until March 2017, when the government and its international allies launched a sustained campaign, including 'Operation Hamza', which dislodged ISKP from Kot district and put them under serious pressure in Achin.[76] (This may be why Nangarhar was the deadliest province for US troops in 2017)[77]

Nonetheless, they were still able to hold part of their territory, and even to relaunch renewed efforts in other parts of the province shortly afterwards.[78]

ISKP have faced major setbacks after their impressive initial expansion. Their brutality and lack of local roots, and the strong opposition they face, mean that the threat they pose to the country as a whole is limited at present. But they have shown resilience, retain a powerful brand and significant resources, and are still able to mount terrorist operations, as the attacks in Kabul show. Even as the Islamic State deals with the loss of its territory in Iraq and Syria, the danger of renewed expansion of the movement's affiliate in Afghanistan should not be discounted.

2. The threat on the ground: ISKP's hold on the mines of Nangarhar

Even in their reduced state, ISKP control a rich swathe of mineral resources. Although there is mixed evidence on the extent to which they have been able to exploit them, there are some grounds for the Afghan governments concern that: "The mines of Afghanistan can be a good economic source for [the Islamic State]."[79]

Riches in their hands: The resources ISKP controls in Achin

Achin district of Nangarhar is where the ISKP first emerged in Afghanistan, and is the heartland of their current presence.[80] They are under substantial military pressure from US and Afghan forces– including the use in April 2017 of the American military's largest nonnuclear bomb, the Massive Ordinance Air-Blast (MOAB) device, popularly called the 'Mother of All Bombs'.[81] Nonetheless, the movement has so far proved resilient despite its setbacks.

In late 2016 a source described how ISKP was particularly present around the mining areas: "Before, Daesh (…) were only in the hills (…), where the mines were. Now they have come to the villages – it is a sign that they are stronger."[82] The source said sites under ISKP control included Nargesai and Ai Tang in Achin, and Sangorai just over the border in Kot, which they said produced talc (shawkanai in Pashto) and chromite (sangina).[83](Locations of the corresponding place-names are shown on our map, although the mining areas may not be immediately adjacent to them).

According to the source, all these areas held both talc and chromite, and might each have more than a dozen individual mines. They said other minerals were also occasionally mined, including transparent and green precious or semi-precious stones (the first of these could be possibly quartz, while the other seems likely to be tourmaline, although it was referred to as emerald).[84] Another informed source confirmed that there were ISKP-controlled sites at Nargesai, Ai Tang, and Sangorai, with between 5 and 20 individual mines at each site.[85] This source said all three sites produced both talc and chromite, adding that tourmaline could also be found at Ai Tang.[86] "Everywhere that has the mines, [ISKP] now has a lot of focus that they take [them]," the source noted in mid-2016. "The local people (…) say that today (…) they have got more mines. (...) They take them from the people, from the Taliban, from whoever has them."[87]

A third informed source had knowledge of four different sites in the area where he said ISKP was mining.[88] They said Nargesai had talc, but also white marble and what he called lapis lazuli (there appear to be no confirmed reports of lapis being found in the area, and it is possible this is nephrite or some similar coloured marble).[89] The source noted that there was a place where talc was stockpiled in Nargesai, something which may be visible on the satellite imagery. As of late 2016 the source was also aware of other sites at Shne Kanda in Achin district, and Lagharjo and Yanak in Kot; and said the first two of these held marble, while Yanak had both marble and chromite.[90] All the sites had been held by the Taliban before ISKP took them over in late 2015: "There was a little fighting between Daesh and the Taliban–the Taliban gave up to the mines to the people [when they fled] and the people gave them to Daesh."[91]

Despite all the military pressure, ISKP's hold on these mining areas appears to be enduring, and may be expanding.[92] "It is propaganda that they are getting weak," one source said in mid-2017: "they are getting stronger day by day." [93]Local elders issued a similar warning in late 2017.94 In mid-2017 the movement claimed to have captured the district of Chaparhar from the Taliban,[95] and they at least temporarily captured the strategic Tora Bora area (in PachirWaAgam district, less than 30km from Achin) – an area that includes a valuable marble mine.[96] In early 2018, two traders mentioned that ISKP held Tora Bora at least for the moment, though one said the mine "is not very active."[97]

At the end of 2017, major ISKP/Taliban clashes were reported in Khogyani, likely partly around the control of mines (see below). In early 2018 two traders independently reported that the WaziroTangai area of the district was under ISKP control, and that the mines there were active, although a third said their control (and presumably any income) was limited to just a more distant part of the valley.[98] If it spreads, it could allow the movement to significantly increase its revenues.

There is doubt over the significance of the MOAB bomb in particular. The insecurity and lack of access on the ground makes it difficult to confirm claims of significant ISKP casualties, and one detailed analysis found much less damage than initially reported.[99] One informed source Global Witness spoke to was sceptical that the MOAB had done much harm.[100] Indeed, one local rumour was that the crater conveniently left by the bomb was being used for mining.[101] While that is almost certainly false (or at least distorted), it is telling that satellite imagery shows the existence of mines just a few hundred metres from the bomb site.[102]

A more intense exploitation

Several of our sources indicated that ISKP's exploitation of the mines was a step change above the normal practice of the Taliban both in terms of investment in machinery and expertise, and of the degree of security and control the exercise over the sites. That would be another sign of the importance of extractives to the movement – although it should be noted that the satellite data raises questions about how significant recent mining activity has actually been.

One informed source described how the level of extraction increased at the mines in Achin as the hold of ISKP strengthened. "The people of the village work with them – the number of workers has become a lot," he said in late 2016. "Before it was from 20-40 people [at one mine, in different shifts], now it is from 50-100."[103] He said a munshi [secretary or administrator] kept the books at the mines. In mid-2017 he reported that activity had further increased, and that ISKP had opened an office in Suriya Bazaar, near Sayed Akhmad khel village in Kot, where they would pay and recruit workers, and deal with traders.[104]

The source reported that heavy tracked machinery was used at some mines, with extraction mainly carried out with large pneumatic jackhammers mounted on excavators, and wheeled excavators used to load the trucks.[105] This equipment would be brought over from other mines when demand was high. While machinery had been used before ISKP took over the mines, "they brought more."[106] A different source similarly said that after ISKP took over another site they knew of, ISKP brought in more machinery and intensified exploitation: "now the number [of machines] has increased. (...) Extraction has gone up."[107] The source said most of the mine sites had an excavator and a loader. In mid-2016 a third source said that the rent for an excavator would be $5,000 a month, with driver.[108]

The reports of machinery being used at the mines may be linked to the confiscation of vehicles that were already at the site. One source reported that ISKP took "the private excavators by force."[109] A researcher told Global Witness that the Bilal Musazai company, which has a contract for talc mines in the Momand valley, lost "around 100" vehicles when the Islamic State took over.[110] Even if that number was exaggerated, this may explain the reports of ISKP bringing in machines. That could in turn imply that the extraction was only as mechanised as before, not more.

ISKP had also brought in foreign engineers to help extraction, one source claimed: [111] he said locals believed they came from Pakistan, Arabia, and possibly even Western countries (although the basis for their belief was accents and appearance rather than anything more definite, and sightings of 'Chechens' and other foreigners are notoriously unreliable).[112] The engineers were not constantly on the site but visited on rare occasions "to show people where to mine."[113] A second source similarly claimed that more skilled professionals–the machinery drivers for example–were brought in from outside, while a third also noted the presence of "foreigners" as well as Pakistanis.[114] (Several sources actually reported that foreigners were working as ordinary labourers, which may be significant, as the lack of local labour was one reason a number of observers said that ISKP could not be extracting significant amounts.

A tighter grip

The sources also reported that ISKP imposed substantially tighter security around the mines they controlled, with phones banned, and workers searched and monitored. In late 2016 one source reported that workers were only allowed in the mining areas when it was time for their shift: "They work in a very disciplined and strict way."[115] The source said security was even higher around one other mining site, not far from Ai Tang, where they claimed ISKP were extracting stones with a 'colour like emeralds.'[116] Whether this is indeed emeralds, or just tourmaline, it is a much more precious stone by weight. "Local people are not allowed in there at all. The workers are foreigners, they do the mining themselves and take it away themselves (…) even [having] a mobile phone [in that place] is a crime."

A different source told Global Witness that when the Taliban controlled the mines, they would take a share of the mine revenues, as well as taxes in the form of ushr and zakat–but the actual exploitation was done by local entrepreneurs. "The mine was in the hands of the people–of the maleks [local elites]," the source said.[117] When ISKP took over, they changed the system, to directly exploit the mines themselves.[118] Locals were still employed as labourers, but they were "their people," linked in some way to the Islamic State. Work was much more closely controlled, the source claimed, and again, locals were not allowed to be in the area when they were not on their shift.[119] But the source also said that unlike other sites, at the Yanak marble mines "now the local shura is extracting, but the Islamic State has half share" – with a local businessman providing machinery in exchange for a share of the stone.[120]

A third informed source similarly reported that in the past "the big people rented the mine."[121] Now that ISKP had taken over the mines, they said in mid-2016, "the Maliks [local powerbrokers] and commanders are finished. (...) These people are so upset that they cry."[122] But the source claimed ordinary people had benefited from the change. Under the Taliban, the local businessmen who exploited the mines paid labourers a flat rate of Rs 2,500 (about $24) for a ton of production – however many people were involved. Now people were happy, as the ISKP would pay a $400 monthly salary "whether you work a lot or little."

Contradictory evidence

A number of indirect sources support the testimony set out above.[123] Matt DuPée, an author and Afghan expert with the US Department of Defence, told Global Witness that sources from Achin had reported that ISKP was controlling mines and profiting from the talc trade as of late 2017, and he had also heard that ISKP was extracting minerals directly.[124] Separately, Borhan Osman of the Afghanistan Analysts Network reported that a credible source in Nangarhar had mentioned ISKP taxing talc trucks in mid to late 2015, and that local elders said the movement was exploiting 3-4 mines.[125] A June 2017 USIP report also noted that ISKP reportedly had taken control of talc mines in Achin and was "directly extracting and selling it to traders."[126] Finally, in April 2017 the governor of Nangarhar warned that "Nangarhar's regions which have forests and mines are insecure. Taliban and Daesh militants are mining illegally and destroying forests in those areas. This is an income source for their war which has to be rooted out."[127]

However, a number of other sources cast doubt on this narrative. In mid-2017 a purported ISKP source denied that the movement was making money from minerals, saying that "no one can touch the mines in (...) districts which are under the control of the Islamic State."[128] The journalist Franz Marty also reported a conversation with a former ISKP commander (albeit a low-ranking individual who appeared unaware of the location of the mines), who said the movement's leaders had ordered a stop to all economic and social activities (not only mining, but also schooling and other services) in order "to put their whole focus on their armed struggle."[129]

Of course, such individuals might have an inventive to conceal any activity. But Marty also cited a former miner from the area who said Daesh closed the mines.[130] A senior trader Global Witness interviewed in mid-2017 also said that ISKP "are not allowing us to work in the Achin mines."[131] And an elder with strong links to the area said "Daesh does not extract" the mines (though he claimed they were profiting from illegal logging): "Daesh never stopped people from mining (...) but since this area was insecure and people left the area, so the mining stopped."[132]

The researcher David Mansfield found that mining briefly continued in the immediate aftermath of the ISKP takeover in May 2015, but had been essentially dormant since the exodus of locals caused by the Taliban counteroffensive in July.[133] Finally, a senior Afghan police officer with recent experience in the province said that the Islamic State had not allowed extraction (he thought to avoid security risks, and possibly to deny the government the benefit of the trade) and that in any case access to the ISKP-controlled areas was too dangerous and too restricted by the government for mining to be possible: "Since Daesh came not one kilo was extracted."[134]

On the question of the lack of workforce, it is worth noting that some of the sources reported the presence not just of technicians but of ordinary workers from Pakistan: "they have their own labourers," one said in late 2016.[135] ISKP "gives a good salary but people do not want to work there – they are afraid. (…) very few [locals] work there. This is I think why they brought people from outside."[136] In mid-2017 the same source reported that: "now they have changed, so they are inviting [local] people (…) before it was their own people from Momand and Pakistan (…) it was people who had relations with them. Now it is not – they are using locals as well" (although they said the majority were still from outside

– including "people from Sindh" in Pakistan).[137] A second source said that "locals that are now with Daesh" worked the mines, as well as foreigners,[138] while a third said that: "Both locals and themselves [ISKP] do labouring."[139] In theory, this could provide at least a partial explanation of how the mines could have been operational even with most locals having fled.

Smuggling Routes

One question around any possible ISKP extraction is how the stone would travel out of the area. There appears to be no passable route for trucks south over the Spinghar Mountains to Pakistan, although there are certainly smaller paths through which weapons and other less bulky goods are regularly smuggled.[140] A leading talc trader in the province said ISKP "cannot take it through the mountains, they have to transport it through main roads, so they cannot mine for themselves."[141] Again, the former senior police officer said traffic from ISKP controlled areas would be restricted by government check posts on the roads.[142] This seems plausible given the limited number of exit routes, the relative ease of interdicting large talc trucks, and the clear strategic urgency of blocking a trade which could help fund the Islamic State.

But there is some evidence that material may be finding a way out, nonetheless. In early 2018, a credible firsthand source described one trader buying chromite from Ai Tang and taking it out of the area on a small truck through "a smuggler road."[143] This involved quite small quantities (around 4 tons a load), and it is not clear how many trucks travelled that route, but it could be enough to represent significant extraction. While the source did not reveal who he bought the chromite from, Ai Tang was mentioned by several other sources as within the ISKP area of influence.

Two of our other key sources similarly referred to talc leaving the area by smuggling routes – although the extent of their first-hand knowledge was unclear. "There are hundreds of roads," one said– possibly even including the long route west through Paktia province Kurram Agency, one of Pakistan's Federally Administered Tribal Areas.[144] Another reported that "it goes on the official road through

Torkham," before adding that the "smuggler road (...) is through Kot" – presumably meaning the initial part of the exit route before the main Jalalabad-Torkham highway.[145] Overall, while the route south seems out of the question, it is at least possible that there could be a route west of the main mining area, exiting through Kot rather than Achin district.

The satellite evidence: Extensive mining but recent activity unclear

The satellite evidence is a key part of this debate. The available imagery very visibly confirmed the presence of a substantial number of mining sites in Achin, some of them quite large. We identified at least seven significant mining areas: multiple sites in the Momand valley to the south of the villages of Nargesai and Sangorai were particularly prominent, showing extensive mining over large areas. The Islamic State clearly controls very substantial resources.

However, the images do not make clear how much these resources are actually being exploited and how much the marks are signs of earlier mining. Global Witness viewed around 25 images of the main talc mining area in the Momand valley, but all but four of them were from 2017 or early 2018 (with the most recent in April 2018), with the others from December and September 2016 and August 2014.[146] This means there is a gap of more than a year in the imagery after ISKP took over the mines in mid-2015.[147] A comparison of the August 2014 and September 2016 imagery shows clear signs that extensive mining took place in this period – but it is impossible to eliminate the possibility that this extraction took place in the last year of Taliban control, rather than in the first year under the Islamic State.

Satellite monitoring of Afghan mines

One key piece of evidence in the debate over mining in Nangarhar is the satellite imagery. The extraction of talc, marble and chromite offers particular potential for remote observation, as it involves the removal of significant quantities of material in open quarries:

talc especially is easily visible against the darker background soil, sometimes from very high altitudes. These methods have considerable potential as a way to monitor illegal mining in environments across Afghanistan where access on the ground is dangerous and difficult. They are not a silver bullet, and in practice the data answers some questions while raising others – but they provide useful points of reference, which we refer to at various points in the report.

Global Witness partnered with SARMAP, the Swiss-based imagery specialists, to acquire and analyse satellite photos from Achin districts. These were commercially available Pleiades visible spectrum images, with a 50cm resolution. A more extensive selection of commercially available optical satellite imagery with a resolution of between 50cm and 30cm was also obtained from Digital Globe, covering all parts of Nangarhar. Finally, with the assistance if SARMAP, both 1.5 metre resolution stereoscopic SPOT images and Synthetic Aperture Radar (SAR) imagery were used for volumetric analysis – documenting selected areas where there had been significant changes in surface levels which could indicate that mining had taken place, and estimating the quantities of material involved. However, in the time available for this report, this was only done for a small area of Achin and over a relatively small period – about two weeks in late August 2017.

After September 2016 meanwhile there are few obvious signs of large-scale extraction – in that the surface area of the mines appears to be roughly unchanged, and there appear to be no visible vehicles or other direct signs of extraction, not only at mines but on the roads in the Momand valley.[148] The SAR imagery failed to show significant removal of material in the mining area it covered, although it only measured over a 10-day period, and the resolution and terrain meant that its ability to highlight small differences was limited.[149]

There are a number of factors which might explain this situation. The first is that issue of timing: violence around the Momand valley escalated sharply in March 2017, and this could have deterred otherwise active mines from operation.[150] Against this, the half-dozen satellite images before this, from September and December 2016, and January and February 2017, do not show any more activity than the others (although only one of them is the highest 30cm resolution). It is still possible that mining was largely concentrated in the year after ISKP took over, but there is nothing in particular to indicate that was the case. While the information from our sources is somewhat skewed towards mid and late 2016, one of them in fact reported as late as mid-2017 that extraction had increased.[151]

Our analysis may have missed signs of activity, either because activity was hidden, or because it took place outside the areas we concentrated our search, or simply because it was less intense and more scattered than expected, and trucks were not present during the time of the satellite overflights. (The output described by our sources who claimed mining was ongoing would only amount to around a dozen trucks a day, though diggers would also be present.)[152] Given the insecurity in the area, it is plausible that mining could have been irregular. And it is important to note that, with the exception of a single blurry and uncertain identification of a possible truck, we could find no vehicles in the one image we viewed from 2014, before ISKP took over – a period when the mines where certainly likely to be active.[153]

One source indicated that mining did take place outside the main sites, with corroborating evidence of chromite extraction using a single digger and men working with basic tools along the side of a road in mid-2017.[154] That sort of activity might well be difficult to spot, especially where there was tree cover. Having said this, some small sites are quite visible in the imagery, at least for talc. Extraction of existing mines may also have dug deeper rather than expanding their area in a way that is relatively easy to spot. It is even possible that IS could be mining at night or otherwise discreetly, given the level of conflict and the possible threat from US drones. However, one would expect there to have been some mention of this from our sources (one spoke of mines working at night, but as part of additional shifts to maximise production.)[155] The Achin images were all acquired in a narrow window, between about 1030 and 1115 local time (0600-0645 UTC), but there seems no particular reason why activity would not be taking place at this time of day.

Finally, the resolution of the images does make it possible that activity is missed: only six of the images were of the clearer 30cm class, and atmospheric conditions also have an impact. But it is useful to compare the Momand valley images to the mining site in Ghunday in Sherzad district, presumed to be under Taliban influence. Changes in surface area are noticeable, and there are multiple trucks visible in images from August 2014 to April 2018, also taken around 1030 local time. While they are blurry, trucks can be identified, including at 50cm resolution. The task is made easier in Ghunday by the presence of several vehicles in a single site, and one might be harder to spot on its own (especially the smaller '6 wheel' trucks mentioned by our sources). Overall, Ghunday is exceptional in its level of activity: the Achin mine would have fewer trucks to see, and they may work more intermittently, over a larger area. Nonetheless, it is certainly notable that none have so far been identified.

The shadal stockpile

Another possibly valuable indicator of the activity in the area is the stockpiles where talc was stored before being taken onwards to market, of which there are at least four that we could find, including two a few kilometres to the east of the Momand valley.[156] By far the largest is at Shadal, near the mouth of the valley, with its many talc mines: the village itself was reportedly held by ISKP until around March 2017–which would coincide with the start of Operation Hamza.[157] It seems certain that the talc there originates from Momand. The images clearly show a large talc stockpile at the site in late 2016–and that it had significantly increased in size from August 2014. In January 2017, that stockpile was systematically removed, with many large trucks visible in two separate images, from January 11 and January 16. This could certainly indicate an ongoing trade through Shadal. However, because of the same lack of imagery from 2014 to 2016, it is unclear when the stockpile originates from. This makes it difficult to eliminate the possibility that the talc was mined before the ISKP takeover in mid-2015 and remained at the site until January 2017.

It seems unlikely that traders would wait so long to move their goods. But multiple sources indeed reported that ISKP had prevented any movement of talc from Shadal since they had taken over the area, and that eventually a deal was struck with ISKP which allowed the talc to be exported. One local source said traders paid Rs 6,000 (about $57) per truck, while an elder gave a figure of Rs 7,000 ($67).[158] It is notable that a third source told Borhan Osman that ISKP were charging Rs 7,000 per truck back in 2015 (significantly less, they said, than the Taliban had charged when they controlled the mines).[159]

David Mansfield's sources meanwhile reported that in "the spring [of 2017] the traders had come in to ask the Islamic State for the inventory [stored in Shadal] and agreed a payment. The Islamic State agreed and that stuff was shipped out."[160] It should be noted that the images taken after January 2017 appear to show some minor changes in the distribution and number of the stockpiles, and at least one mid-size truck appears to be visible in the area, as well as occasional smaller vehicles. More noticeably, in April 2018, around a dozen small trucks are visible in part of the site, and there are changes in the number of small, darker mounds, which could possibly be chromite. This may be evidence of new extraction, but it is difficult to be sure.

So how much mining?

The overall picture from the available satellite data is somewhat uncertain, and it is worth remembering that there is no guarantee of spotting signs of activity, especially with a limited number of good images. Nonetheless, the data clearly suggests a more cautious view of what mining was taking place in the period it covers. This contrasts sharply with some of our other key sources: as set out above, three credible direct sources and two from other researchers independently spoke of mining taking place at various dates between mid-2015 and late 2017 (including three that reported extraction after late 2016), and another source reported a truck picking up minerals. At least one set of images of extraction are in circulation and support this testimony.

So, what is the reality? On balance, it seems unlikely that so many independent sources are completely mistaken or deliberately misleading (though it is not impossible). However, it is important not to ignore the significant question marks that the satellite data and some of the other sources raise. The most likely explanation is that some extraction did take place, but was significantly less intense and regular than suggested by our five sources alone and possibly less concentrated in the Momand valley. It is not difficult for sources to be honestly inaccurate to this degree, especially on figures and questions of the overall scale of extraction which might go beyond their direct experience.

The revenue that would result from this extraction is correspondingly difficult to estimate. Just about the only element about which there is a good level of certainty is that ISKP made something from allowing the removal of the Shadal stockpile. Our local source estimated the number of trucks at no less than 300, but at Rs 6,000 ($57) a truck the income generated could be as low as $17,000. It seems certain that they made something more than this from actual extraction – and the estimates range into the millions of dollars, especially if we include possible revenue from beyond Achin. But the low end of the range is in the tens of thousands. Given the uncertainty, it is probably better not to cite a single more specific figure. In any case, the extent of current extraction is not the only measure of ISKP's interest in the mines.

3. A strategic interest

Whatever ISKP's current income from the mines, the extent to which they have fought over them strongly suggests that they consider them of strategic interest? The researcher Matt DuPée noted that: "If you were to overlay the patterns of violence [between] Daesh and the Taliban, it really overlays where the natural resources are."[161] This appears to reflect the strategic priorities of the wider Islamic State as well.

The bigger picture

In 2015, one senior ISKP commander described mining as a priority, along with transit routes (for drugs and other goods). Speaking of one particularly rich mining area, he said: "The mines are in the hands of the mafia (...) At any price we will take the mines."[162] Afghan armed groups have a long history of exploiting minerals: ISKP is not unique in this respect. But this statement echoes the pattern of Islamic State activity in Iraq and Syria (see below), and their strategic doctrine, which discusses the use of extractives as a source of income.[163] ISKP would likely have targeted mining in some form without outside guidance, but the fact that the wider movement has put such emphasis on the sector is another reason to treat the activity that has already been visible as a serious concern.

The fight is over the mines

According to one source interviewed, ISKP's expansion from the Momand valley to Kot district and other parts of Achin, which he dated to late 2015, was around the mines.[164] It is unclear how much this reflected a deliberate targeting of those sites, or the need to use the cover of the mountains, or a mix of both. But the source believed that: "The real fight [between the Taliban and ISKP] was over the mines – because there are no villages there. (...) The [local] people say [that] wherever there is a mine, [ISKP] go there first."[165] More recently, Khogyani district, around 30km west of Achin, has become a key battleground for the struggle between the Islamic State and the Taliban.[166] There have been multiple clashes, with fierce fighting reported from October 2017:[167] as of December more than 60,000 local residents had been displaced.[168] Clashes were also reported in neighbouring Sherzad district and (earlier in 2017) in PachirWaAgam, both part of the wider Khogyani area.[169]

Much of the fighting has taken place in the Waziro Tangai valley in Khogyani district, around a dozen kilometres from the exceptionally high quality Ghunday talc deposits in Sherzad in one direction, and the notorious caves (and marble mines) of Tora Bora in the other.[170] The area has been described as "an important economic corridor used by militants for smuggling of Afghan mineral supplies to neighbouring Pakistan,"[171] although again the only plausible route for that seems to be via Torkham. In early 2018, ISKP appeared to have actually taken over some mines as a result of the fighting, as least temporarily. One local source reported that "the mines of Ghunday and [of] WaziroTangai (...)– they were in the hands of the Taliban and the Daesh took them" in late 2017 (although around two months later he said they were not yet being exploited – and our other sources reported Ghunday as still under Taliban control).[172] In early 2018 two other Kabul-based traders reported that the WaziroTangai mines were both under ISKP control, and active.[173] A third source however reported that the ISKP presence was limited to just part of the valley.[174]

One source, the former senior police officer from Nangarhar, was sceptical that the battles between ISKP and the Taliban were in fact over the mines, suggesting instead that ISKP was following a natural route to extend its influence west towards Logar, from where it could threaten Kabul.[175] That is certainly likely to be at least a secondary motivation. But while ISKP and Taliban strategy is difficult to know with certainty, there is a strong case that the rich mineral deposits in the district are indeed a key factor driving the two sides to this exceptional violence.

Perhaps the most powerful evidence of this comes from a Taliban official with direct knowledge of Nangarhar, who described how the mines were important enough to the movement that one of their groups alone had been forced to sacrifice 16 men in the battle with ISKP. "The fight is over the mines, the fight is over the profits," he said. "What can we do – we have expenses, we don't get much from the Arabs [unlike ISKP]. If we don't have this source [of funds] we will be defeated."[176] The importance of the Sherzad and Khogyani deposits as a source of income for the Taliban is confirmed by our own investigation. At the very least, it seems highly probable that depriving the Taliban of this resource is of considerable interest to the Islamic State–an objective of great value even if they were not able to subsequently exploit the mines themselves.

Finally, it is notable that the same former police officer also exported that around the end of 2016 ISKP: "had a plan that they would extract [talc] themselves – they began a road from [the] Tirah valley of Pakistani to Achin district [to allow minerals to leave by that route]."[177] He said they were not successful, but even starting such a major undertaking would be a powerful indicator of ISKP's interest in extraction.

4. ISIS and extractives in Iraq and Syria

A focus on oil and mining has long been an established part of the Islamic State playbook in their home ground. One of the few published ISIS strategy documents stresses the importance of the "Wealth of the State" as the principal source of financing – including "oil and gas and what the land possesses."[178] It calls for using accounting and oversight to control production, and forbids anyone who has not pledged allegiance to ISIS from having a stake in extraction.[179] In line with this focus, ISIS reportedly formed special armed groups in Syria and Iraq to control the oil fields, escort oil traders, and help with smuggling.[180] As in Afghanistan, extractives have also been a significant focus for competition between ISIS and other insurgent groups, 181 and used for political leverage.[182]

The use of oil for funding follows the established practice of Al Qaeda and other groups, [183] but it has been particularly important for ISIS.[184] By 2015, oil was generating up to $550m a year by some estimates,[185] a significant sum, even if it was likely only a fraction of the income from ordinary taxes.[186] The oil revenue was managed under an official diwan [Ministry or Bureau] of Resources–often simply referred to as the 'Ministry of Oil'.[187] ISIS requires its franchises to mirror their organizational structure, so in principle mining should also fall within such an office in Afghanistan.[188]

ISIS has now lost almost all its territory in Iraq and Syria.[189] By early 2017 the UN described them as operating a "crisis" budget due to their reduced territory and thus tax base, as well as coalition attacks on oil infrastructure.[190] Nevertheless, as late as October 2017 a report put their oil-related revenue at $4m a month.[191] (The

UN report also found another natural resource, gemstones, were an important source of Islamic State funding in South East Asia.)[192]

The Islamic State is of course using whatever resources it can find: the focus on extractives in Iraq and Syria to some extent merely reflected the local environment. But the fact that the Islamic State does have so much experience and interest in the sector certainly increases the threat of their affiliates exploiting extractives in another resource-rich area like Afghanistan.[193] For the movement as a whole, extractives are a part of the core playbook–and Afghanistan is fertile ground to apply that strategy

5. ISKP and mining beyond Nangarhar

Global Witness concentrated its research on Nangarhar, but a limited number of sources in other provinces also confirmed ISKP's interest in mining.

Paktia and Logar

In Zurmat district of Paktia, an informed source told Global Witness in mid-2015 that ISKP had raised the black flag of the movement and taken over four local mines from the Taliban[194] This source described seeing fighters from the group in a local bazaar, wearing cloths covering most of their faces, and said it also had a substantial foreign contingent, allegedly under an 'Arab'.

One of the mines, in Tukur, extracted magnetite; two others at Gawyan and Surkai had chromite, while one at Landaiyawara had coal and abrak (mica). Locals were excluded even from gathering firewood in the area around the mines in Tukur when ISKP controlled them in 2015.[195] "Because of fear people cannot go [to the mines]," a source reported. "[Daesh] take out the [stone]. They bring the workers themselves. They don't show the place. They do not allow us to go close.[196] The materials were allegedly smuggled out on camels to Miranshah in Pakistan (a trade large enough that the source claimed the price of camels had increased by several times).[197] However, the mines are no longer under ISKP control today, another local source said.[198]

In Logar province, ISKP appears to have limited control but a growing presence, which overlaps with a stronger Taliban control. The first reports of fighters in the district date from January 2015, and by April ISKP released propaganda photos which they said showed a training camp they had established in the province.[199] In late 2016, their hold on territory was still relatively limited, but seen as expanding: one senior official in the provincial government claimed that there were more than 200 ISKP fighters in Charkh district, with around 150 in Azra and others elsewhere.[200] There were further reports of ISKP activity in Azra in late 2017.[201]

In late 2016 one source with knowledge of Mohammad Agha district (home to the massive, though dormant, MesAynak copper project) said that ISKP visited villages where the Taliban were weaker to preach and spread propaganda: "This place is slowly going to Daesh – [they have not taken it] yet but it is moving that way. (…) when the Taliban become less [present] Daesh come and (…) force people to come together for the preaching."[202] The source claimed ISKP were offering up to 70,000 Afghanis a month ($1,029) as initial salary to attract fighters to the cause (although such a high rate was likely only for an initial period).[203]

The same source reported that ISKP already controlled two mines in the Kamalkhel area, where they extracted a "very expensive stone," probably chromite, again showing the movement's interest in mining.[204] The source described how an ISKP member had been ordered to "go to the elders and others (…) Ask about the mines–where they are, who has them, how much do they produce, what share does the Taliban take, what share do the local maleks [powerful local individuals] take."[205]

Other provinces

Badakhshan is one of the most mineral-rich provinces of Afghanistan, and there is some evidence that the Islamic State has an interest in the mines. As of mid-2017 ISKP had a close if murky relationship with the Taliban in the province (in contrast to the violent competition between to the two groups elsewhere).[206] This probably reflects the fact that ISKP's presence in Badakhshan was the result of local forces of the Islamic Movement of Uzbekistan (IMU) pledging allegiance to them, and not of Taliban commanders defecting. There is a long record of cooperation between the IMU and the Taliban in Badakhshan, unlike in the rest of Afghanistan, and this seems to have continued after IMU's 'rebranding'.[207]

In 2016, the Taliban appeared to be deriving significant benefit from the lapis lazuli mines that are one of Afghanistan's greatest treasures (as documented in the Global Witness report War in the Treasury of the People).[208] It could be argued that the Islamic State received an indirect benefit from this as they were helped by the Taliban's increased fighting strength, and local security sources reported that they also received some transfers of captured military equipment. Since 2016, however, the scale of extraction at the lapis mines appears to have dropped very substantially.[209] The Islamic State remains a threat in Kunar and (to lesser extent) Nuristan provinces.[210] There are multiple reports of ISKP profiting from mines and timber in Kunar, where they have reportedly opened a 'customs office' in the Mazar valley of Sawkai district.[211] The Taliban and local power-brokers have long profited from illegal extraction and smuggling of the same resources.[212]

In February 2016, a media report cited local officials and tribal elders claiming that the Islamic State had imported timber equipment and been cutting trees in the Achin, Naziyan and DehBala districts of Nangarhar province, with truckloads sent to Pakistan and local markets daily.[213] As noted above, an elder with links to Achin actually reported in mid-2017 that "Daesh does not extract [minerals] – they only cut the forest. They get a lot of profit from this extraction [of timber]."[214] And a former senior police officer also said that in late 2017 ISKP had exported timber from DehBala district: he estimated they made a profit of Rs 100,000 ($952) from each of about 40-50 small truckloads sent out before a government operation ended the trade.[215] Finally, ISKP forces are reported to be present in Jawzjan province in the far north of Afghanistan, and in December 2017 the Afghan Ministry of Mines and others expressed deep concern about the possibility of them exploiting minerals there, although there is no indication yet whether this is taking place.[216]

6. "The Islamic State is crueller"-ISKP and human rights abuses

In the areas that they control, ISKP has carried out a number of serious abuses – a particularly stark aspect of the danger they pose. They are not alone in this, but as one report noted, the group's tactics "have been beyond the pale, even by the standards of the current Afghan conflict, which can be very brutal. Beheadings and public executions have become ISKP's trademark, with victims including elderly civilian men."[217] A source reported abuses including four people killed in one village and three in another in early 2016. He said the militants would extort money from individuals with slightly greater wealth, and sometimes arrest them: "there is a lot of zulm [cruelty]." The source also said that one person who was arrested by the Islamic State (and subsequently released) reported that his captors had "slaughtered and tortured people."[218]

There are numerous reports of civilians executed for spying, often on the basis of very slight suspicion.[219] The United Nations has documented nine such cases in the last three years.[220] A source told of one such execution in Achin district in early 2016, and also said a 12 year old boy had been killed in early 2016 for having a mobile phone: "The Taliban were cruel, and the Islamic State are crueller."[221] Another case also allegedly involved the killing of a child.[222] The impact of ISKP on women is also especially pronounced, even compared to the Taliban. ISKP has reportedly imposed harsh restrictions on the movement of women outside the home, and on female education.[223] "ISIS [sic] made women sit in the home," one woman told Human Rights Watch. "If you go out they will kidnap you."[224] There are several reports of ISKP fighters demanding widows either marry or otherwise serve them.[225] One man from BatiKot district said that when ISKP arrived in 2015 they said: "'We heard there are widows here. Give them to us, they will serve our mujahids.'"[226]

A source alleged that in Achin ISKP would hang a flag on a house where a widow or eligible unmarried woman lived. "They make her marry by force. [They say that if] your husband died you should go to someone else. You should not lose the honour of your daughter."[227] The source also claimed that 40 women from families accused of supporting the government were taken from Lagharjo village around late October 2017, after ISKP defeated a local state-sponsored militia. "They took all the women from them and burnt their houses."[228] However, since their early days in the area, ISKP appeared to have consciously softened their approach to the local population. One informed source reported that when the local ISKP leader "first came, there was a lot of cruelty–he terrorised the people. (…) Now he is become very soft."[229] Whether this represents a real change is unclear.

7. Not just ISKP: the Taliban and other armed groups

The relationship between the Islamic State and mining is worrying, but it is only a case study for what is a much larger problem. Not just insurgent groups but also a host of other illegal, semi-legal and legal armed groups across the country benefit from mining. The Taliban in Nangarhar province demonstrate this with particular force.

The Taliban and mining: Achin

The Taliban clearly profited from the Achin mines now controlled by ISKP well before their takeover – presumably from their arrival in the Momand valley in 2011.[230] We have already mentioned how the movement would reportedly take a share from local producers. A source described how local elites would control extraction and employ people mainly from their own families, paying a set amount to the Taliban, which the source estimated at Rs 200,000-Rs 500,000 ($1,900$4,770) a month, depending on the site.[231] Another source similarly estimated the Taliban would collect around Rs 200,000 a month ($1,900) from each mine however hard they were (or were not) worked."[232] This rate seems low given how much a single mine could produce – but that perhaps partly reflects the Taliban's roots among local communities, and their need to make a profit in the talc trade.[233] (It roughly matched some of the rates reported for mines in Sherzad. But the Taliban would also collect the Islamic taxes of ushr and zakat. Another source reported that "people said the Taliban took a third" of the value of the output this way[234] There are indications that the Taliban would also tax vehicles carrying the minerals:[235]Borhan Osman cited a credible source who reported that the Taliban took Rs25,000 ($238) per truck in this period.[236] As set out above, the satellite data, while incomplete, also supports a picture of extensive and ongoing exploitation while they were in control.

The Taliban and mining: Elsewhere in Nangarhar

The Taliban may no longer control the Achin mines, but in other districts, especially Khogyani and Sherzad, they have even greater resources under their control – which our research indicates are generating significant income. Again, it is reasonable to assume this is one reason the area has become a battleground between ISKP and the Taliban. Global Witness interviewed a wide range of relevant sources, including a number from Khogyani and Sherzad and individuals with direct knowledge of the trade. The most direct of these sources was the Taliban official cited above, who described the revenues from the mines as critical to the group's survival in the district.[237] He put the total daily income just from the major mining area of Ghunday at Rs 500,000 to Rs 1.2m ($4,760-$11,430). It is possible this is an exaggeration, but if not it would amount to a maximum of more than $4m a year, assuming it actually was paid every day.

Some support for this account came from one credible source who reported that two local maleks controlled separate talc mines in a location called Abdulkhel (located within or close to the Ghunday/Markikhel mining area, although its exact position could not be positively identified on the map), and that they together paid a total of at least Rs 3m ($28,571) in rent to the Taliban every month, whether or not there was any extraction.[238] The source alleged that a former Minister of the pre-2001 Taliban government was a partner in one of the projects: if true, this would imply another income stream for the movement (or at least for that individual).

A second source with direct knowledge of the Ghunday mines gave a similar picture, but mentioned a substantially lower rent: just Rs 100,000 to Rs 150, 000 ($952-$1,428) a month, which he said was paid by the heads of the 8-10 large mines there.[239] (The source said there were also many smaller mines, but was unable to estimate how many.)[240] Unlike the first source, he said this rent was based on the level of production, and might be less if it was disrupted by bad weather or fighting. It already seems low given that the source estimated a mine paying Rs 100,000 produced perhaps 10 large truckloads a week – worth at least $64,000 a month, making the rent less than 1.5% of the value of the talc (compared to a rate of about 20% in the Taliban onyx contract we obtained – see Annex D).[241] On the other hand, Matt DuPée gave a roughly similar figure.

At the highest level, the Taliban leadership reportedly have a role through the Finance Committee of the Quetta Shura (which also gets at least a share of the revenues).[242] On a more day to day level, one of our sources reported that the Taliban had a representative in the Arzan Kimat district of Kabul, a mullah who ran a local madrassa [religious school] and who was empowered to sign contracts for the mines.[243] A copy of a Taliban mining contract we obtained shows what such documents might cover, including production rates and standards. Businessmen could also receive letters of introduction if needed, to negotiate directly with senior Taliban officials in the mining districts, or could buy talc directly at the mines. Another source similarly reported that deals with the Taliban were either made with the shadow District Governor, or with a representative either in Kabul or in the Zakhel area of Jalalabad.[244]

But the same Taliban source also reported that the movement was itself engaging in direct exploitation, at least in less accessible mines – and that this was following the example set by the Islamic State.[245] This would allow them to retain more profit. However, there was no indication of what proportion of mines was exploited this way. Other sources suggested the mining was generally carried out by locals, albeit as part of a trade dominated by strongmen.[246] Multiple sources also confirmed that the Taliban were collecting revenue from the trucks carrying minerals out of the district. Two sources independently reported that a fee of Rs 35, 000 (about $330) was the standard for the large tractor-trailers that haul the heaviest loads –between 40 and 50 tons.[247] (The first of these individuals specified that the minerals were loaded from Markikhel and Abdulkhel.)[248]

It appears that in principle, those renting a mine with the Taliban should not have to pay this transit tax to export their own production, but in practice something might still be extracted, even if at a lesser rate, perhaps Rs 10,000 ($95).[249] Either way, the traders in return received a letter or receipt which allowed them passage as far as the beginning of government controlled territory in Surkhrod.[250]A third source reported that a smaller 'Mazda' truck, which carried 4-5 tons, would be charged Rs 5,000 ($48).[251] A fourth source separately gave the same figure, and specified that it would be charged at the same if it was carrying stone, no matter of what kind (though they cited a lower capacity, of up to 3 tons).[252] A fifth source put the fee for a Mazda at between Rs3,000 ("if I am lucky") and Rs6,000 ($29-$57), although they said it could sometimes be as high as Rs8,000 ($76), for a 4-5 ton load.[253] A sixth source said that the Taliban would take Rs 20,000-Rs 25,000 ($190-$238) for a '10-wheel' truck carrying talc from WaziroTangai, with a load of 14-20 tons.[254]

Two other sources gave significantly higher figures. The first of these, a well-informed former senior police officer from the province, said interviews with people involved in the trade indicated that the Taliban were charging as much as Rs 100,000 ($952) per trailer of talc – generating a total of around Rs 30m ($285,714) every month, equivalent to $3.43m a year.[255] The other put the figure at Rs 80,000 ($760) from each tractor-trailer, but also claimed they could carry up to 70 tons of minerals – which is implausibly high even given the chronic overloading common in Afghanistan. From smaller trucks they said lesser amounts were taken.[256]

While the higher figures justify some scepticism over these sources, it is interesting that for this eighth source the amount per ton works out as similar to the rates given by other witnesses, which conservatively averaged around Rs 750 ($7.14) per ton (though they vary between about Rs 700 ($6.67) and Rs 2,220 ($21.16).[257] That figure is incidentally broadly in line with the royalty rates in the government's own talc contracts, perhaps an argument for its plausibility.[258] The source said traders rented the larger rig at a cost of around Rs200, 000 ($1,800) per trip (this compares to about Rs30, 000 – $286 – for a Mazda).[259] He said trucks often carried a mixed load, and might conceal the more expensive minerals: the government permitted trucks to carry wood, talc or marble, but not chromite. He gave the location for the tolls he was aware of as the village of Tutu, which he described as being under Taliban control, but said the mine that he knew of was under local powerbrokers, at least one of which had an informal militia.[260] It is significant that even where a mine was not Taliban controlled, minerals were apparently still unable to escape road tolls.

An eighth source also mentioned a Taliban check post in Tutu: they estimated that around 60 trucks a day passed through that area in a single day (mostly Kamaz, Mercedes or '6-wheeled' trucks, but including 4-5 large tractor-trailers) and that the Taliban collected a lucrative toll from each of them.[261] It was not clear what loads they were carrying, but a significant number are likely to have had minerals of different kinds. The source reported that Tutu was one of three Taliban toll posts in the area, which they estimated together provided between Rs 400,000 and Rs1m ($3,600-$9,000) in revenues every day, depending on the season.[262] The basis for this estimate was such that, while although it was credible, the exact figures should be treated with a certain amount of caution. But again the general picture is broadly consistent with the other sources.

A ninth source reported that most of the trade he knew of was organised by mine owners and so paid little or no rent on the road, but added that if trucks "don't have a road pass they will pay."[263] He guessed this might amount to Rs 5,000-Rs 20,000, to whatever Taliban check posts were on the way, "village by village." An influential local elder with links to the minerals trade in Khogyani also asserted that mines paid a tax to the Taliban,[264] while two mineral traders we interviewed separately mentioned ISKP as well: "no one can extract talc and marble without paying to Taliban or Daesh," one said.[265] The other confirmed that "Taliban and Daesh are controlling the mine areas, no one can extract talc without paying to the Taliban." They specifically mentioned Ghunday and Ladabagh as being under Taliban control, and said that dealers contracted with locals who in turn had contracts with the Taliban or gave them "a percentage."[266] (Ladabagh is another significant mining area, which our other sources confirmed was active).[267]

None of the three gave a figure for how much was paid. The two traders did however say that the Taliban were taking only Rs 6,000 ($57) per truck in road tolls, which would imply much less revenue from this source.[268] (One of the sources was referring to talc transported by a mine owner, the other to talc transported by a trader who bought from the mine.) That testimony may not outweigh the multiple sources cited above, but it is notable that it matches the figure one source reported for Islamic State taxes on the talc exported from Shadal.

Supporting sources

Findings from elsewhere further back up the picture from our own sources. A Le Monde investigation for example found that truck drivers would receive a "payment ticket" which would allow them to cross the checkpoints controlled by the Taliban insurgent groups, although they found that payments were made in Peshawar: "The transactions take place in a public place, in broad daylight, just next to the famous and majestic Speen Jumat Mosque."[269] Le Monde cited a Ministry of Mines official complaining that members of the Taliban sometimes visit the mines to try to improve the production methods, and that Ministry inspectors were unable to visit the area: "The talc trade enriches the Taliban and the Islamic State in the region," he said.[270] Matt DuPée reported from his sources that the Taliban were known to tax talc trucks at a rate of Rs 850 ($8.10) a ton.[271] He also found that taxes charged by the Taliban on marble in Helmand were substantially higher.[272] Meanwhile, a June 2017 USIP report found that in Khogyani and Sherzad districts:

Talc has been extracted by local residents and mine operators and exported to Pakistan, from where it is further exported to Italy, Saudi Arabia, France, and Japan, according to one talc trader. (...) Mine operators in Sherzad district reportedly pay $10 to local officials per ton of talc and $12 to the Taliban. Any private company operating a talc mine needs to pay "rent" to the Taliban and reportedly in some cases to ISIS as well. (...) Senior officials of the provincial mining department admit that most of the talc-rich districts of Nangarhar have come under the influence of the Taliban or ISIS. Residents have complained that the Taliban and ISIS may have started to engage in direct extraction of talc. Local elders recently stated that "the Taliban shadow governor of Nangarhar province visited the talc mines in Sherzad district to assess them, and NATO aircraft bombed his location, but he managed to escape unhurt, though several Talban died. In Achin district of Nangarhar, ISIS reportedly had taken control of talc and was directly extracting and selling it to traders.[273]

In December 2015, the Sherzad district governor claimed the Taliban earned Rs12m ($113,200) a month from the extraction of "precious stones and marbles" from mines under their control in the Markikhel area (close to Ghunday) and in Kadikhel (likely in the Tutu area – which would confirm the other mention of Taliban check posts there).[274] "The government has no control in these areas and people who know Taliban leaders get the extraction contracts," MualemMashooq said: "These minerals are extracted in an unprofessional way and 70 percent of the profit goes to Taliban." While the basis for his estimate was unclear, both areas show signs of extraction in recent satellite images.

Finally, the satellite imagery confirmed intensive mining in other areas under Taliban control or influence. The renowned talc mines around Ghunday and Markikhel in Sherzad are the most visible: the imagery shows numerous excavators and dozens of trucks. Other mines around Ladabagh also show clear signs of activity. In total we identified at least 16 mining areas with significant signs of mining in the Ghunday/Markikhel and Ladabagh areas, and some of these were large enough that it is possible they host more than one mining operation.

Millions in mining revenue to the Taliban

Both Sherzad and Khogyani districts are reported to be almost entirely under the control or influence of the Taliban, and have been for some time – as have a number of other key mining districts in Nangarhar.[275] Given the strong evidence from our sources about the prevalence of mine rents and transit fees, it is reasonable to assume that all, or nearly all, of the minerals mined in these districts contribute in some way to funding of the Taliban. For talc, that covers almost all of Afghanistan's production.[276] The precise extent of this benefit is difficult to calculate. Available estimates are mixed. A report from "an international organisation" cited in Le Monde put the total revenue of the Taliban from the province's talc trade alone at around $22m in 2014, although the basis for the calculation is unclear.[277] One civil society report alleged that the Taliban and the Islamic State were making $46m in total from the Khogyani area alone, but the credibility of the estimate is subject to question.[278]

Our own calculations range from around $2.5m to more than $10m a year, depending on the methodology and assumptions used (see Annex C). The task is complicated by the mix of revenue streams, the likely variations in arrangements for individual traders, and inevitable ambiguities in the testimony (for example over what was counted as a tax on trucks and what as mine rent). Our best estimate–very rough, but titled firmly towards the conservative side–would be in the mid-single figures of millions of dollars: somewhere around $4m a year. Given it comes from one mineral and just a few districts that is a significant sum.

A problem across Afghanistan

Again, this problem is not limited to Nangarhar, or to the Taliban. In Badakhshan, the Taliban made millions over several years from the illegal trade in lapis lazuli, much of it apparently in payments from local power-brokers (although extraction has diminished since 2016).[279] In Logar, our sources also described how the Taliban profited from local mines.[280] At a national scale, author and Afghan expert Matt DuPée found that: "The Taliban exploit mining sites in at least 14 of Afghanistan's 34 provinces and now earn as much as $200 to $300 million annually."[281] A UN report citing "various Afghan officials" gave a lower figure, "at least several dozen million" US dollars.[282] It should be noted that both these estimates are likely to be based on partial and sometimes unreliable data. But even so, it is clear mining is a major source of Taliban funding: certainly the higher figure would make it their second-largest revenue stream after narcotics.[283]

Finally, the 'pro-government' armed groups and powerbrokers that also draw strength from this trade are in many respects as much of a threat to Afghanistan as the insurgency. In Badakhshan for example, the payments to the Taliban are linked to wider abuses around mining by a local militia and the official Mining Protection Force that have caused huge damage to stability and development.[284] The problem of illegal mining goes not just beyond the ISKP, but beyond the insurgency as a whole: it is an integral part of a wider problem of rule of law in Afghanistan.

8. Implicating us all: supply chains and corruption

The value of Afghanistan's minerals to armed groups like ISKP and the Taliban ultimately depends on consumers in the rest of the world. While the supply chain is only partially documented, it is all but certain that individuals and companies in Europe and the USA in particular are effectively, if inadvertently, funding insurgent groups. And those supply chains are only possible because of the subversion of government controls.

Government corruption

It appears certain that the vast majority of minerals from insurgent-controlled mines in Nangarhar openly go through government-held territory on the main roads to Pakistan, and in particular via the border crossing at Torkham. Our sources consistently said trucks used the Torkham route to the Pakistani city of Peshawar, and other reports agree.[285] Imagery sources also support this: long lines of tractor trailers are visible lined up by the border in multiple images, as well as in video footage. The government banned the talc trade in early 2015 (though the dates are somewhat unclear),[286] but by September traders were able to successfully lobby for a one-off exception to export 100,000 tons: one researcher reported that "since then the talc has been flowing freely," with some reports even suggesting up to a million tons may have been moved by April

2016.[287] However, in theory export of unprocessed talc is still not allowed. A Ministry of Mines official confirmed that: "Companies can export processed and semi-processed talc."[288]

Capturing more of the talc value chain is a perfectly legitimate goal. But progress even towards this aim has been mixed. Talc processing centres have been established, and a late 2017 government report claimed the "highest level of export has been (...) in semi-processed (bulk) form."[289] But a former senior police officer claimed that corruption allowed 90% of talc to leave without processing, while trade data from 2016 shows crushed talc as an insignificant fraction of overall exports.[290] Meanwhile, the transit of minerals to Pakistan from insurgent-controlled areas of Nangarhar is closely linked to and enabled by corruption of Afghan government officials, as well as the payments to insurgents. This appears to take place both on an informal level and more systematically.

Three sources reported that truck drivers would buy documents at the gumruk [customs] office attesting that tax had been paid on the cargo, which allowed them to transit as far as Torkham.[291] The first of these sources put the cost at Rs 6,000-Rs 7,000 ($57-$67), adding that Rs 2,000 ($19) would go to the tarezo [weighscale] and Rs 5,000 ($48) to the gumruk office itself; those without experience of the system might pay a little more.[292] At the Torkham border crossing itself, this source said Rs 8,000 - Rs 10,000 ($76-$95) would be paid to ensure passage.

The second source put the gumruk figure at Rs5,000 ($48), but mentioned that the Pakistani "militia" also needed to be paid on the road from Torkham to the depot on the outskirts of Peshawar: in total, the expenses for a Mazda would be Rs 10,000-Rs15,000 ($95-$142).[293] The third spoke of payments of Rs6,000 ($57) for the gumruk but just Rs 2,000 ($19) at Torkham, and said the total payments to various authorities would never be in excess of Rs 20,000 ($190).[294] The similarity in the figures is more notable than the variations, given the unofficial nature of the tolls and the likely differences in the traders' individual relationships with those taking the payments. Finally, a fourth source we interviewed, a minerals trader, confirmed in general terms that 'We have to pay bribes to the police check posts on the way from Khogyani district to the Torkham border, as well as to customs staff."[295]

But this business is not just a matter of informal bribes. One of the sources described it as "a much organised system–a system of the mafia."[296] They said traders could organise transit in advance: "They call from Pakistan and say 'it is organised, show this sign' [to the authorities]." Le Monde wrote that: "Illegal extraction is protected by the provincial authorities and the insurgents, with the support of the local population."[297]

A former senior police described in more detail a system where the mines were allocated by the local tribes, but in practice the trade was dominated by zurmanda [strongmen] who had the corrupt government connections needed to get minerals out without paying unsustainable amounts in bribes or taxes along the way.[298] They were often directly involved in the trade as well. "Most of the [Afghan] companies belong to the mafia", the source said: "they make the company in someone else's name, or the companies give a share to the mafia."[299] He said the trader's 'union' could also help arrange the necessary illicit payments to get talc out of the country. Either way, many of the key political, security and administrative officials in the province, he alleged, got a cut from the trade: "the leadership of the province all has a share."

The majority of mining was done by locals, the source said, but the real profits were made by the strongmen. Locals sold talc at a low price – a reflection of the low cost of extraction (beyond a few excavators) and the abundance of the resource, but presumably also of the dominance of more powerful actors in the onward trade. "Either [the locals] independently extract and ask the mafia to [arrange for the] transfer of their vehicle and they pay them," the source said, "or they sell [the minerals] to the mafias who then transfer it for themselves. (...) If they are not with [the strongmen] these people cannot transfer a single kilo."[300] At least one of these strongmen was reported to control a small private militia.[301]

The effect of this corruption is evident. The average value of the talc declared by traders for customs is just $14/ton, compared to an average price of $60 a ton for talc bought in Afghanistan on the open market – and $150-$200 for talc being sold onto the global market from Pakistan.[302] That represents a massive loss to the Afghan treasury. From all talc production in the year from March 2017, the government's 5% export duty raised just $315,393, which is equivalent to about 450,000 tons of export at $14 a ton: that amount would have brought in $3.38m if it was valued at $150 a ton, and $1.35m even at $60 a ton, so the losses are in the millions.[303] What other revenue the Afghan government is losing is hard to say: the Ministry of Mines could not provide figures for royalty or other revenues from talc, which in itself is a deep source of concern.[304] In any case though, it seems clear that the total is only a fraction of the revenue collected by the Taliban.

This fits into a broader picture of the talc value chain in Afghanistan. If margins are tight, it would imply that large taxes or bribes would make the trade economically unviable. Indeed in early 2015 David Mansfield noted a report that traders in Achin had declined to pay a contribution to the Taliban from talc "on the basis that there are insufficient profit margins in the business."[305] But if talc is bought at $60 or less at the mines and sold at $150 that should in principle allow enough margin for the level of taxes and bribes described above, and still leave a profit for the traders.[306]

The link to international market

Minerals mined in ISKP or Taliban controlled areas almost all end up on the international market. One source put it that the stones mined in Achin "don't just go to Pakistan – they go abroad as well, they go to Italy and Australia."[307] The evidence for this is especially straightforward for talc. First, it appears that almost all Afghan talc production produces revenue for armed groups. Although the mineral is found in other provinces, there seem to be few if any active mines outside of areas of southern Nangarhar where the Taliban likely have the leverage to collect taxes – keeping in mind that this extends outside the areas they fully control.[308] While most of them lacked exact coordinates, as far as can be determined the government's own talc contracts are all in these districts (the fact that most of them are nonetheless still active is itself a cause for concern).[309]

Essentially the entirety of these productions exported by Afghan traders via Pakistan.[310] From there, much of it is re-exported as Pakistani talc: as the most recent USGS assessment explicitly noted: "Large quantities of crude talc are mined in Afghanistan before being milled in and exported from Pakistan."[311] One Pakistani company openly boasted on its website that: "We are well placed to supply/export SOAPSTONE (TALC) LUMPS in big quantity available in and around Pakistan & Afghanistan border area, which is known as world best quality and it is in demand all over the world."[312]

In 2016 (the most recent year for which figures are available), Pakistan reportedly produced 125,330 metric tons of talc, but exported 305,970 tons, worth $57.6m.[313] Pakistan has no significant talc imports from any other country.[314] From the available data, it appears Pakistan consumed around 120,000 tons of talc in 2016.[315] It is unlikely that this domestic consumption is only fed by Afghan talc, but even if it was, so that every bit of Pakistani-produced talc went into that overall export figure, it would only account for about 40% of it – meaning that the other 60% actually originated in Afghanistan.[316] A more reasonable assumption might be that domestic consumption is equally supplied by Pakistani and Afghan talc – in which case Afghan talc would make up about 80% of the total.

And the largest part of this talc in turn ends up on the US market. In 2016 the US was the destination for 42% of all Pakistani exports, 128,542 tons, worth $23.6m.[317] In turn, Pakistan is the single largest source of talc for the United States, providing more than a third of imports from 20132016: that would mean that around a quarter of the talc imported into the US is actually from Afghanistan.[318] European countries like the Netherlands (accounting for 13.2% of Pakistani exports) and Italy (12.8%) were also major buyers of Pakistani talc.[319] In total, the US and EU account for almost 80% of Pakistani exports.[320] All in all, this implies that a substantial proportion of the revenue the Taliban gets from talc – likely between a third and two thirds–ultimately comes from US and EU consumers (though of course all buyers bear responsibility to some extent).[321]

The limitations in the available data create some uncertainty around these calculations. In particular, if you add Afghan exports to Pakistan of 561,286 tons in 2016 to Pakistani production of 125,330 tons, then the total (686,616 tons) exceeds the combined total of Pakistani exports (305,970 tons) and Pakistani consumption (120,000 tons) by some 368,790 tons.[322] Unless there is major stockpiling in Pakistan, which seems unlikely, these figures should roughly balance out – meaning there must be an error somewhere. While this uncertainty affects all our calculations to some extent, it seems reasonable to think that exports from Afghanistan would if anything be understated rather than exaggerated, given the prevalence of corruption on that border. And in any case, it is clear that the US and EU are very major markets for the talc that ultimately helps fund the insurgency.

Chromite shows a similar picture, with production in Pakistan around 230,000 tons in 2016 but exports of almost 350,000 tons.[323] Resourcetrade.earth lists Afghan production in 2016 as just 4,500 tons, and exports just 29 tons: these figures are very low, and would be consistent with reports of substantial illegal extraction and smuggling of chromite from Afghanistan[324] There are no obvious reports of chromite smuggling or indeed legal imports into Pakistan from other countries which could make up the difference of 120,000 tons between Pakistani production and exports, and it seems likely that at least this much is being mined in Afghanistan and exported via Pakistan – although since it comes from a number of different areas it is harder to say what proportion is funding particular armed groups.[325] We could find no reports of chromite being consumed within Afghanistan. Finally, the data for Afghan marble exports also appears to be unreliable, with only small amounts registered: again, production is from multiple different areas.[326]

European multinationals and the talc trade

There have been more direct links between Nangarhar and the Western market. Notably, reports in Le Monde highlighted at least two European companies purchasing talc in the past through intermediaries from Afghanistan, the major French supplier

Imerys, and an Italian company, IMI Fabi.[327] Imerys suspended its purchases of talc from Pakistan or Afghanistan in mid-2017 in reaction to the Le Monde report, but it appears IMI Fabi has not.[328] Imerys sells talc on the global market, including to the United States and many European countries.[329] Their Pakistani intermediary North West Minerals reportedly bought talc from a number of sites in Afghanistan, including at least one in the Khogyani area, controlled by the Shamshir Zamir company under the influential trader Dost Mohammad.[330] The Ministry of Mines lists two possible contracts for Shamshir Zamir in the Ghunday/ Markikhel mining area (a third is in the Momand valley of Achin),[331] and the company appears in the latest EITI report, though the data raises some questions.[332]

A senior official with North West Minerals said "you have to pay taxes to the local tribe and the village."333 That of course does not answer the question of payments to insurgents, and there is no direct evidence to show that ISKP, the Taliban, or other illegal armed groups are benefiting from these specific sites. But we have already documented how routinely the Taliban appear to tax minerals in the Ghunday area: it would be strange if the Shamshir Zamir areas were exempted.[334] Meanwhile, the other Afghan mines supplying North West Minerals in Nangarhar remain unknown. Imerys for its part reacted to the Le Monde report by commissioning an independent external review, based on which they suspended their sourcing of talc from either Afghanistan or Pakistan. Prior to this, however, the company was "unsure of the exact mines from which NWM was sourcing its talc in Afghanistan." In a statement to Global Witness, they said:

Some talc coming from various sources seemed to be combined in a trading bazaar where purchases were made by suppliers of NWM. (...) NWM was contractually required to adhere to Imerys business standards, and to provide the required assurances that talc sold was not ethically or otherwise compromised. Imerys undertook a number of assessments through audits carried out by external and independent audit firms whose conclusions were confirming compliance of the supply from NWM in Pakistan. However, following the assessment by the external independent organization hired by Imerys, we decided to discontinue the purchase from NWM since we could no more ensure the compliance of the local supply chain with Imerys business standards.[335]

That statement highlights the wider problem of international companies sourcing minerals without certainty over their origin – and the weakness of current global supply chain due diligence standards. It is open to question whether the initial audits which Imerys carried out failed to identify the risks involved.[336] The company was unaware of the Afghan government's reported ban on the talc trade from early 2015, but was aware of the later ban on unprocessed talc, and said purchases after it was imposed were crushed.[337]

IMI Fabi agreed a joint venture in 2012 with the Omar Group, a major Pakistani talc company, under the name IMI Omar Private Limited. The joint venture reportedly held licenses for talc extraction in Nangarhar,[338] although the Director of Omar Group, Nadeem Omar, only acknowledged sourcing talc from "3 or 4 local concession holders," whose identities are unclear.[339] He said that production was 100,000 tons in 2014 before it dropped to around 25,000 tons, following the Presidential ban on exports in 2015. The production was processed in Karachi and part then exported to Italy for further refinement before being sold across Europe.[340] IMI Fabi CEO CorradoFabi said that "all the big global producers supply themselves now from Pakistan and Afghanistan."[341]

As of April 2018, the joint venture was still active, with Pakistan listed as a "mining and manufacturing" site "able to supply customers in the long term and on a global scale."[342] This suggests that their previous arrangement still continues. If so, it would be despite IMI Fabi being aware of the risk reported by Le Monde, which our own research for this report suggests would likely have been confirmed by serious independent inquiries. It would be a stark contrast to the reaction from Imerys (whose own inquiries apparently confirmed enough issues of concern for them to suspend operations).

CorradoFabi declined to provide responses to questions submitted by Global Witness, citing ongoing defamation proceedings against

Le Monde,[343] although he said that "we were fully aware of the Afghan government's ban on talc exports. This led IMI Fabi to heavily invest in Brazil and Australia."[344] The company's website describes corporate social responsibility as "the core policy of the IMIFABI Group."[345] Of course, Imerys and IMI Fabi are far from the only companies active in the Afghan talc trade, and may simply be more visible than others whose actions we have not been able to scrutinise.[346] But either way, two things are already clear: Nangarhar's talc production is not isolated from the international market – and greater transparency and controls are desperately needed to ensure these supply chains do not fund armed groups.

9. Policy implications and recommendations

The threat posed by the interest of ISKP and the Taliban in mining is clear. It should be seen as a red flag warning of the powerful and direct link between illegal mining and instability, not just in Nangarhar but across Afghanistan. This is not just an issue of development or economics, but a matter of national security both for Afghans and for their international allies.

The problem is all the more urgent as the government and donors are explicitly relying on mining for "the economic development and prosperity of Afghanistan," as President Ghani put it.[347] Talc is a particular priority, [348] and the High Economic Council has ordered the Ministry of Mines "to create the conditions for award of competitive tenders for large-scale development" of the mineral."[349] Our research shows just how difficult that will be. So what can be done? These problems are often thought of as intractable part of the violence and corruption supposedly inherent to Afghanistan. There are certainly no easy answers, and the government will need support. But the challenge is less a shortage of effective measures than it is the will and capacity to implement them.

Restrict illegal mining

The fundamental problem of ISKP and Taliban control over mining areas inevitably overshadows this debate. It is difficult to avoid the need to address this – and mining areas and transit routes should indeed be a higher priority within security and intelligence strategy. But military action in itself is only a vehicle and can be deeply damaging if it is done badly – especially if it is not in the service of a coherent approach to underlying problems. Other means of influence should be prioritised wherever possible.

One of these is to target supply chains. The government has shown it can block the transfer of talc, at least for a period: they should restrict the trade in minerals to areas where extraction is not significantly funding armed groups (for talc, these areas need to be created first). While a selective ban is always at greater risk of being undermined by corruption, this could still help to create pressure against illegal exploitation, not least from traders.

At an international level, the Afghan government can help bring the leverage of the market to bear by working with importing countries to develop traceability systems and by requiring any company operating inside the country to apply established standards of due diligence to their supply chains. The major importers such as China, the EU and the USA have a particular responsibility to require that any companies buying minerals in Afghanistan and Pakistan meet those standards.

Blocking the trade would create significant political pressure on the government as well. To some extent this just has to be confronted, but it means there are practical as well as a moral reason to do everything possible to avoid putting the costs of action on ordinary Afghan civilians. Measures to restrict trade, for example, should be part of an urgent wider effort to establish areas where legitimate extraction, that benefits the community and local traders, can be carried out – so long as that does not become an excuse to perpetuate corruption or the control of armed groups. This highlights the point that any effort to restrict the trade is only likely to be effective in the long term if it is tied to wider reforms – to ensure that people have a direct reason to support legal mining, and that the alternative to control by armed groups is not control by corrupt strongmen.

Give communities a stake in illegal mining

One of those reforms is to give the local population in mining areas a stake in legal mining, with the aim of bringing the weight and legitimacy of the community to bear against the incursion of illegal armed groups or corrupt strongmen of all kinds. This has its limitations – no community is going to be able to stand against the full force of the Islamic State (and in the Momand valley the "local community" has been largely displaced, at least temporarily).[350] Social and tribal structures are also fractured after so many years of conflict.[351] But they still carry significant clout, and that can be a vital leverage in the fight against abusive armed groups and corruption. Involving local communities in places with greater security also has the potential to create a demonstration effect, as more difficult areas see practical evidence of what they are missing.

Three key elements are needed: a viable channel for fair redistribution; transparency and monitoring at a local level; and in some cases, community ownership or legalised artisanal production. Firstly, for community participation to work effectively, the benefits they receive must be real enough to set against the incentives available under a strongman or insurgent group and insulated enough from corruption to reach their intended target. This is not a simple task, but it is not impossible. The existing structure of the Community Development Councils (CDCs), which manages development money at village level under the National Solidarity Program (NSP), offers one obvious path for distributing funds equitably and relatively insulated against abuses. [352]

Transparency is also essential to allow a reliable estimate of how much is owed to communities – just as it is to know how much is owed to the national treasury. Top-level transparency reforms can help here. But these should also be linked to community monitoring of mining so there is a channel for locals to flag evidence of untaxed production or breaches in contract terms relating to the community. Integrity Watch Afghanistan has already created a pilot monitoring project building on the success of similar mechanisms for aid projects.[353] Finally, another option to consider is community ownership of mines, or reform of artisanal mining, to allow small-scale miners to operate within a legal framework while ensuring some government revenue – although safeguards would be needed to prevent these mechanisms being hijacked or abused.

Clear up the wider industry

These local reforms need to be part of a systematic effort to reform Afghan mining more widely. It is difficult for example to imagine communities benefiting from mining if contracts are acquired through corruption, or the Ministry of Mines has no capacity to oversee them. Even if they did, the country as a whole would still suffer serious harm. For this wider reform, three basic transparency measures are critical (and indeed the first two would be worth applying across all government procurement). First is contract transparency. Making extractive contracts publicly available is critical for accountability. But while the government has made multiple commitments on publication, and released many contracts, at least one possibly abusive deal was not among those released and there is uncertainty about what remains hidden.[354] A simple and effective way to deal with this would be to amend Afghan law so government contracts only become valid after they are made public.

Secondly, much of the corruption in Afghanistan's extractive sector allegedly involves well-connected figures using illegitimate influence to control contracts, often secretly through third parties.[355] The government has made a very welcome commitment to creating a public register of the true, 'beneficial' owners of all companies contracting with the government, but it should go further and make this a condition of applying for or holding a mining license.

Perhaps most importantly, lack of transparency on extractive payments and production greatly undermines efforts to prevent corruption and tax losses. The government should amend the law both to require the publication of this information, and to establish a single transparent account for all-natural resource payments.

Use of the account should be a condition for funds to be registered as received. The sub-accounts already used by Afghan ministries provides a model for how to do this without undermining the central state revenue account, which could open up avenues for abuse.

These are particularly critical measures, but there are many others that could help. The government could move towards a licensing rather than bidding system to award concessions, and meanwhile reform contract allocation processes and mandate the use of model contracts (developed with public consultation and incorporating strong protections against corruption and conflict). Medium and large companies (especially SOEs) could be required to undergo annual public audits. Royalty rates could be more carefully calibrated to maximise revenue while ensuring legitimate companies are able to realistically apply for contracts. Making Afghanistan more attractive for investors can actually help the battle against corruption – if it is done the right way.

The flip side of this is that governance reforms can help attract legitimate investment, not deter it. To benefit from its resources, Afghanistan wants to attract established international mining companies – precisely the ones who have a reputation to lose and are likely to be deterred by abuses or links to armed groups. Imerys for example stated that they could consider re-engaging in Afghanistan "if a transparent and responsible supply chain for talc extraction, processing, and transport could be assured."[356] There is no conflict between better governance and the development of Afghanistan's extractives: on the contrary, the second is unlikely without the first.

Underlying all of these measures is the need for capacity and above all political will within the Afghan government. The Ghani administration has shown it understands the dangers of illegal mining. It has made a number of laudable commitments to reform and has taken initial steps in some areas like beneficial ownership. It deserves support to continue these efforts. But the test is action, rather than words, and for now these critical reforms have not been put into practice: the upcoming revisions to the mining law will be a critical test. Three years into the Ghani administration, there are no more excuses for delay.

The role of the international partners

While the Afghan government has the first responsibility for safeguarding its resources, Afghanistan's partners can play a crucial role. Donor governments have supported the Ministry of Mines in the past and some (notably the European Union) have raised extractive sector abuses at a political level. These efforts deserve recognition. But as a whole international engagement still does not reflect the seriousness of the issues at stake. The US and UK both at one stage sent ambassadors to push for the government to speed up decisions on contracts: a level of engagement that would have been welcome on governance issues.[357] US President Trump's first concern appears to be to secure a greater share for American companies in Afghanistan's mineral wealth.[358] Donors have occasionally agreed broad benchmarks on extractive sector reform with the government, but have lagged on harder-edged measures, based either on results (like increasing mining sector revenue) or specific reforms.[359]

The issue is not resources: donors have invested around half a billion dollars in developing the sector since 2001.[360] But commercial development has been the priority, in a way that addressing corruption and conflict risks has not.[361] Almost 17 years on from the US intervention, the result of this approach is that commercial development has stalled, Afghan oversight capacity is extremely weak, and revenues are a fraction of what they could be–leaving donor country taxpayers to cover the gap.[362]

Afghanistan's partners should make the reform of the sector not just a development goal but a first order political priority, embedded at the heart of the relationship with the Afghan government – ensuring strong support to their efforts, but also holding them to their (very welcome) commitments. They should continue practical support to the Ministry of Mines, but agree a common approach which prioritises oversight capacity and related processes (including information management) and sets hard-edged mutual benchmarks for reforms. As noted above, they should actively require their own companies to apply due diligence to resources imported from Afghanistan and Pakistan, and otherwise help the Afghan government control these supply chains. They should also use their intelligence and security resources to help monitor and prevent abuses.

Final word

These are all fairly obvious steps that could have a material impact on abuses that are major driver of conflict in Afghanistan, a major resource for the Islamic State and the second largest source of funding for the Taliban. The lack of action on these issues in the past is striking given how much they threaten to undermine the vast investment of international manpower and money since 2001.

Again, the scale of the challenge is significant, and none of these recommendations offers a silver bullet. But even if the government cannot tackle illegal mining anywhere, they can move the ball. It is not hard for example to imagine a focus on security in a limited area – say the Ghunday mines – which can be used as a showcase and laboratory in which to implement reforms for transparency and local benefit. At the same time the government could restrict the trade from other areas, backed up by independent monitoring. This could even be linked to an outside or even international investment, so long as it did not undermine that local benefit.

The point is that while it is impossible to solve the problem of illegal mining overnight, there are ways forward. For both the government and its partners, it is time to confront the challenge so starkly embodied in the 'white mountains' of Nangarhar. These recommendations should be considered in conjunction with more detailed proposals set out in other Global Witness documents, including the policy briefing Avoiding the Resource Curse,[363] suggested amendments to the Mining Law developed in conjunction with Afghan and international civil society groups,[364] Global Witness technical notes (notably on the Mandatory Single Transparent Subaccount for Extractives), and other documents.[365]

Recommendations to the Afghan government's President and Chief Executive

1. Restrict illegal mining by armed groups in Nangarhar

    a. Block the transfer of talc, chromite, marble and other minerals from areas of Nangarhar under the influence of illegal armed groups, while moving as quickly as possible to create the conditions for 'clean' extraction, even if this is initially in a limited area.

    b. Work with traders and communities to minimise and compensate for disruption to livelihoods as far as possible – so long as this does not undermine the effort to exclude armed groups or strongmen from the trade.

    c. Make it a higher priority within security strategy to protect key resource-rich areas and associated transit routes, including mining sites in Nangarhar but also other areas with a strong presence of ISKP, Taliban, or other armed groups (including 'pro-government' armed groups). Ensure security forces involved in these tasks have appropriate training and oversight and are rotated to reduce the possibility of involvement in abuses, and that security actions are strongly linked to governance and development measures like those outlined below.

    d. In general, tie enforcement and security actions to wider reforms and to negotiations with local communities and prioritise political means where possible. If necessary, consider piloting reforms and security measures in a limited area before extending elsewhere.

2. Give local communities reasons to support legal mining

    a. Create effective mechanisms, embedded in law, for community share in legal revenues, community ownership of mines, and legalised artisanal mining.

b. By spring 2019 put in place a mechanism to provide a share of the proceeds from legal mining to local communities in a given mining area. The level of funding and method of calculation should be developed with the aim of ensuring a sufficient benefit to have a realistic prospect of countering the attraction of illegal mining.

c. Ensure local communities can control what projects their revenues are used for, under appropriate safeguards including transparency and community monitoring. As a first option, consider distributing the funds as a supplement to the budgets of Community Development Councils.

d. Within Nangarhar, make community benefit from or ownership of mines a core element of wider efforts to reduce insurgent influence in the area.

e. This should be linked to community monitoring of mines as a way of preventing abuses. The Afghan government should facilitate and empower an appropriate mechanism in consultation with local communities and civil society, building on the work Afghan civil society organisations have already done with community monitoring of mining and aid projects.[366]

f. Explore mechanisms to legalise artisanal mining on a license basis to increase government revenues and create incentives for the exclusion of armed groups.

3. Strengthen laws and oversight to make illegal mining harder and legal mining more attractive Put in place basic transparency and oversight reforms to make abusive mining more difficult and create space for legal extraction that benefits the country and local communities.

a. Within the next six months, amend the mining law and regulations in order to:

a. Make the publication of contracts a condition of their validity

b. Require the publication of production and payment data

c. Require the creation of a single transparent subaccount of the Treasury Single Account, to be used for all extractive sector payments as a condition of their receipt and published at least quarterly. The published statement must include clear identification of the relevant individual project for each payment, and information on the basis on which it was made, such as amount and grade of production. The sub-account would remain subject to the same control and oversight mechanisms as any other part of the Treasury Single Account.

d. Create a public register of beneficial ownership and require companies to register and update their entries as a condition of bidding for or holding government contracts.

e. Require regular (at least annual) audits of medium and large extractive companies, including all State-Owned Enterprises.

f. Provide a legal basis for community monitoring, benefit and ownership.

g. Require all contracts to contain precise coordinates for the mining area under license.

i. Strengthen the oversight capacity and practices of the Ministry of Mines, particularly for information and contract management, cadastre, community relations, and inspection functions. Develop management capacity and mechanisms for artisanal and small-scale mining.

j. Reform contracting processes to strengthen transparency and ensure companies are treated fairly. Amend the Afghan Mining law to require a transparent, fair and rigorous bidding process, in line with the Open Contracting Global Principles.[367]

k. Move towards a license rather than contract model for extractive concessions. As an interim measure, mandate the use of model contracts incorporating the strongest available protections against corruption and conflict, developed in conjunction with civil society, local communities, and mining companies.

4. Use satellite imagery to monitor key mining sites.

a. Systematically monitor key mining sites using satellite imagery, including both optical and radar data. Make all images at commercially available resolutions automatically available to CSOs and the public to allow transparent and broad-based monitoring of the sites, and share higher resolutions with established and reputable CSOs, including members of the EITI Multi Stake holder Group. Allow CSOs to flag particular sites for monitoring based on field research.

5. Control supply chains

a. Tighten controls over movements of minerals through Torkham and other border crossings.

b. Work with trade partners and consumer countries to put in place strong controls over supply chains from conflict affected areas, including a requirement for companies to carry out due diligence, at a minimum to the standard set out in the OECD Due Diligence Guidance for Responsible Supply Chains of Minerals from Conflict Affected High Risk Areas and in the United Nations Guiding Principles on Business and Human Rights.

c. This requirement should cover companies linked directly or indirectly to supply chains carrying minerals from Afghanistan, or minerals that risk originating from these regions (regardless of where the seller claims they are from) – for example because they are traded from known hubs for the illegal trade such as Peshawar.

d. Responsibility for due diligence should include local as well as international companies, and extend to significant investors and financial backers of extractive projects. Due diligence efforts should be publicly reported.

e. Work with the international community to develop strong traceability systems to ensure the integrity of the minerals export trade.

Recommendations to Afghanistan's international partners

1. Support Afghan efforts to strengthen resource governance.

   a. Provide full material and political support for government reforms of extractive sector governance, notably the mining-related measures discussed in the National Anti-Corruption action plan and the reform of the Ministry of Mines.

   b. Make the strengthening of oversight, governance and conflict prevention the explicit strategic priority for this support to the Ministry of Mines and the Afghan government. Coordinate programs across donors to ensure that all aspects of this agenda are adequately covered without duplication.

   c. Provide or fund the acquisition of high-resolution satellite imagery for monitoring of key extractive sites by the Afghan government as set out above, and direct your own intelligence resources to exposing and understanding natural resource flows linked to armed groups.

d. All importing countries for Afghan minerals, oil and gas should commit to requiring that companies carry out risk assessment and due diligence on their supply chains, at a minimum to the standard set out in the OECD Due Diligence Guidance for Responsible Supply Chains of Minerals from Conflict Affected High Risk Areas and in the United Nations Guiding Principles on Business and Human Rights.

2. Make stronger resource governance a key priority for your engagement with Afghanistan.

a. Integrate a limited set of the most important extractive governance reforms into core benchmarks for mutual accountability between the Afghan government and its partners.

b. Agree a single common set of more detailed benchmarks for donor support to the Ministry of Mines.

c. Hold the Afghan government to its existing commitments to strengthen natural resource governance, and raise the need for urgent reforms through political engagement at the highest level.

d. Avoid creating any pressure for new natural resource contracts in areas that are at elevated risk from conflict or armed groups, or before basic protections (including the transparency and community measures set out above) have become effective. Focus engagement in Afghanistan on achieving these conditions as rapidly as possible.

Annex A: How big is the trade?

Data on mining in Afghanistan can be difficult to obtain and can be unreliable, given the presumed scale of the illegal trade and the incentives to under-declare the value and amount of exports. That certainly applies to the trade in talc, chromite and marble.

TALC A Ministry of Mines study on the talc supply chain found around 500,000 tons were exported in from March 2017-March 2018 (the year 1396 in the Afghan calendar).[368] This was supported by a well-informed leading member of the Nangarhar talc traders, who reported that "in general we export 400,000 to 500,000 metric tons per year."[369] Another trader said that 45 registered talc companies exported about 100 trucks per day through Torkham (a figure echoed by Matt DuPée's sources, though there was a more mixed picture from our few data points on production at individual mines)[370] This would amount to almost 1.5m tons a year if the traffic was always consistent. That seems unlikely, but the source also put the total extraction of talc at 2000 tons a day, which would give a more modest total of about 730,000 tons a year. If that applied just two days in three it would be equivalent to about 486,000 tons.

Meanwhile Chatham House's resourcetrade.earth database lists Afghan talc exports to all countries at 561,430 tons of talc in 2016, the most recent available year.[371] The figures for earlier years are much lower, apart from 487,256 tons in 2014, but this could be due to deficiencies in the data (as well as the temporary 2015 ban): one source put the total at possibly in excess of 300,000 tons as early as 2012[372]

In terms of production, a Ministry of Mines questionnaire to mining companies indicated a figure of around 1.5m tons over the 3-year period of March 2015-March 2018 – and the Ministry said companies were "conservative" in their answers. As the report noted, this number "is clearly different from the figures of exported talc during this specific period," which officially totalled just 715,000 tons.[373] Some difference between production and exports may be understandable: the government's 2015 ban on unprocessed talc exports for example reportedly led to significant stockpiling.[374] One would expect this to have corrected itself after the ban was effectively lifted (and to have bumped the 2016 figures for exports above actual production), but it is possible the formal ban on unprocessed exports is still pushing some talc to the stockpiles. But a stronger explanation may be that the amount of export is significantly understated, given the bypassing of government weighing stations and the incentives for traders to minimise the volume on which they pay tax. Indeed some reports talk of as much as a million tons of extraction in less than a year.[375] Given all this, a figure of around 500,000 tons of production in each of the last two years (2016 and 2017) seems a reasonable estimate, although a clearly conservative one: it is possible the true figure is significantly more.

Prices for talc cited by our sources vary very significantly. The Ministry of Mines reported that the average purchase price for talc inside Afghanistan was around $60 a ton (although the average price for customs receipts was just $14 – a clear red flag for corruption).[376] The price of unprocessed talc in the data from resourcetrade.earth is just $46 a ton for 2016 (the most recent available figures), although it is unclear if this might be affected by the same issue of under-valuing.[377] In previous years back to 2012 the official record varies from $65 to $80 a ton. Le Monde reported mine-gate prices of $40-$60 a ton.[378] All these contrasts sharply with the figures for 2016 unprocessed talc exports from Pakistan, which vary from about $110 to $275, with an average of just under $190.[379] Internationally, Afghan talc is advertised on the trading website Alibaba.com at around $150-$300.[380]

CHROMITE

The average price for chromite exported from Afghanistan between 2012 and 2016 was $262 per ton, according to the resourcetrade.earth statistics, with variance between $189 and $330.[381] The same source gave an average of $236 per ton for exports from Pakistan: it is unclear why it would be less, although it is possible that Pakistani chromite is of lower purity.

MARBLE

The average price for crude marble exported from Afghanistan to Pakistan in 2016 was $115 a ton, according to resourcetrade.earth. But overall crude marble exports were valued at $259 per ton – a reflection of the much higher value of the Afghan marble going to Italy. However, it should be noted that the data appears to be incomplete, with only 3,300 tons of exports noted.

Annex B: Funding ISKP

Estimating the total revenue that ISKP earns from mining with any accuracy is difficult. While a rough indication of the scale of the trade can be calculated from our sources, the uncertainty created by the satellite data in particular makes it harder to fix a definitive figure. One element of revenue over which there is little doubt is from the liquidation of the stockpile at Shadal in early 2017. One local source reported that ISKP took Rs 6,000 ($57) per large truck, and estimated that "more than 300" truckloads were loaded, with 80-100 leaving per day and an average load of 40-50 tons.[382] This certainly seems possible given the number of trucks visible in the satellite imagery. Another put the figure at Rs 7,000 ($67).[383]

That level of taxation is modest: just $57-$67 per truck. If there were indeed around 300 truckloads, that would mean a little over $17,000-$20,100 in revenue – not a significant amount. The local source claimed that the Talban collected a similar amount when they controlled the area (in addition to rent from the mines). But another source with direct information said the Taliban had charged Rs 25,000 ($238) per truck, and it is interesting how this matches the taxes collected by the Taliban in Sherzad and Khogyani, which averaged about Rs 750 ($7.14) a ton, with Rs 35, 000 paid for the largest loads of 40-50 tons (see main text above).[384] But even this would imply a revenue of no more than about $100,000, from the one-off liquidation of a significant stockpile.

It is highly likely that the Islamic State have made at least something from the actual extraction of talc, marble or chromite since they took over in May 2015. If we simply take the sources who claimed active extraction was taking place, the total would be in the millions of dollars a year. As noted above, our sources mentioned half a dozen mine sites around the Momand valley in Achin and nearby areas of Kot: Nargesai (talc and chromite) Sangorai (talc and chromite), Ai Tang (talc, chromite, and marble), Shne Kanda (marble), Lagharjo (marble), and Yanak (marble and chromite). Of these only three were mentioned by at least two sources, so we will focus on them.

One source was able to obtain information that an estimated overall total of eight to ten trucks a day were going from the 15-20 individual mines at one of these three sites when it was active, carrying talc and chromite in roughly even quantities – so at least four truckloads of each.[385] These were six-wheel trucks, with a load which the source put at eight to ten tons. Another source gave a more conservative figure for the same site, of a minimum of 24 trucks for talc and chromite combined over 10 days from 8 mines.[386] These were also 6-wheelers, though the source put their average load at six to seven tons, with talc accounting for a little more than chromite overall. Part of the difference may reflect the fact that the names of the sites refer to general areas rather than clearly defined concessions. (It is also not entirely clear which of the multiple mining areas visible on the satellite images would be referred to under which name, as different villages are usually close enough to be potentially associated with several of them.)

Meanwhile, a third source reported that talc extraction at a second mining area was four six-wheel trucks a day, with a load estimated at seven to ten tons.[387] He did not make clear how many individual mines this was from, but this is broadly in line with the others' estimate for the first site.[388] For a conservative approach to our estimate, we will take the lower end of the range of figures and apply a further discount to allow for inadvertent exaggeration and possible gaps in production. A reasonable rough assumption might be an average of 2.5 trucks a day of talc and two of chromite from the first site, with a load of 6 tons. If we assume the mine is active on average just 4 days a week,[389] this gives us a total monthly production of 260 tons of talc and 208 tons of chromite.[390] If we assume a 6-ton load and four trucks a day from the second site, that is another 416 tons of talc a month.[391]

That accounts for two of the three mining areas for talc and one of the three sites for chromite. If we take the average of the two figures for talc output from the first two sites (338 tons) and apply it to the third talc site, this would give us just over 1,000 tons a month in total. But the number of mines at the third site was reported to be less than at the first two. To reflect this, we reduce the estimate for the third site by a third, to 225 tons a month, giving us an overall total of around 900 tons of talc a month, or 10,800 tons a year. For chromite, if we conservatively assume that the two sites we have yet to account for produce only half as much mineral per day, this gives us another 208 tons a month, for a total of 416 tons of chromite a month (4,992 tons a year).

The value of this cargo at the mine site also needs some thought. The average price for talc exported from Afghanistan according to the Ministry of Mines is $60 ton, although the resourcetrade.earth website produces an average of around $46 per ton.[392] We will conservatively assume a mine price of $40, in line with the lower end of the Le Monde estimate.[393] For chromite, we will take the average resourcetrade.earth price of $262, and halve to $130, to very conservatively account for the price likely being significantly lower at the mine. This gives us overall ballpark figures of $432,000 a year for talc (10,800 tons at $40 a ton) and $648,960 for chromite (4,992 tons at $130 a ton), for a total of $1.08m.

This leaves out marble, which a source reported was also extracted in significant quantities in at least one of the three mining areas, roughly 60-72 tons a day.[394] Reducing this by a third to allow for natural variation gives 40-48 tons a day. At four days a week that would mean something like 700 tons of marble a month or 8,320 tons a year, if we take the lower end of the range. Afghan marble exported to Pakistan is valued at $115. If we take a price of $60 a ton to reflect mine-gate prices this would mean revenues of about $500,000 a year. Given this is from one site, and the source reported marble mining in four sites in total, it seems reasonable to assume that total revenue from marble might be at least in the region of $1m a year. That would bring overall revenues a little above $2m.

This ignores the cost of production borne by the Islamic State: unlike the Taliban's franchise model, it is presumed that ISKP's direct control would generally leave them to bear the burden of production themselves (even if there are occasional exceptions, as noted above). Those costs are hard to quantify, but it seems fair to assume they are not more than 50% of revenue. That would still leave the Islamic State with around $1m in profit over the course of a year.

This estimate leaves out the possibility of other talc sites, along with timber and mines reported to exploit more expensive minerals like tourmaline. The real revenue could plausibly be significantly higher. We have also left out revenue from other districts and provinces, of course, where some sources indicated that active mines were under ISKP control. And we have not attempted to account for ushr and zakat taxes on non-ISKP individuals or companies profiting from the mines – which could be significant. In other areas, the Taliban have been known to tax the trade at a rate of up to 20%.[395]

However, given the uncertainties around the calculation, and the ambiguous evidence from the satellite data, it may be best, even with our cautious assumptions, to simply state that ISKP revenue from mining in Nangarhar could be anywhere from the high tens of thousands to the low millions of dollars a year, with 'somewhere in the hundreds of thousands' a plausible mid-range. That may not seem like much, but given that the lowest estimates suggest the movement may have fewer than 1000 fighters across the whole country, even this could represent a significant source of funding.[396]

Annex C: Funding the Taliban

It is difficult to calculate just how much revenue the Taliban make from extractives in Nangarhar with any accuracy, but we can attempt to define a likely range. Existing estimates offer one starting point. One CSO report of $46m a year is impossible to verify, and so has to be discounted. A report from an "international organisation" cited in Le Monde put the total revenue of the Taliban from the province's talc trade alone at around $22m in 2014, but again the basis for the calculation is unclear.[397] The Sherzad District Governor's estimate amounts to a much more modest figure, around $1.36m from his district alone: if one assumes income from Khogyani and other districts would be at least this much, this would amount to about $2.7m a year.[398] An Afghan researcher reported an estimate from the head of the

Nangarhar office of the Ministry of Mines of Rs 400,000 ($3,809) daily just from talc, equivalent to about $1.4m a year.[399] Finally, a former senior police officer from the province reported that the Taliban were making around Rs 30m ($285,714) a month from talc, generated by a toll of Rs 100,000 on each trailer-load.[400] That is equivalent to $3.43m a year (that figure is very conservative if the toll was really that high, although it fits well with a toll closer to the average from our other sources - see below).[401] None of these estimates are ideal, but coming up with an alternative is not straightforward. Our Taliban source might be the best bet. His figure of Rs 500,000-Rs 1.2m ($4,762-$$11,429) a day put the movement's income at $1.74m-$4.17m a year for the Ghunday mines alone. Again, as a very rough rule of thumb one might assume that the movement would at a minimum receive the same again from other mines in Sherzad and Khogyani (like Ladabagh), for a figure of $3.48m-$8.34m a year. The lower end of the range would take into account that the "daily" revenue may very likely not have been collected every single day.

Another route is to consider the data on the three main forms of Taliban revenue: direct mining income, mine rents, and transit tolls. First, as noted above, the Taliban are reported to have extracted talc directly. It is impossible to say what percentage of mines would be exploited this way, but if we assume that they account for just 10% of production, then this would mean 50,000 tons. If this production is sold at a price of $45 a ton (close to the minimum figure we saw of $40 a ton), it would generate $2.25m. Of course, the Taliban would have to bear production costs, but if we assume they are no more than 50% of revenue that would still leave them with $1.125m from talc alone (rounded to $1.13m).

For mine rents, our figures from Ghunday give us a starting point. But they are quite far apart. One source alleged $28,571 a month from two mines, another reported $952-$1,428 from one.[402] The second of these figures seems low compared to the rate seen in the purported Taliban contract (see Annex D). But given Matt DuPée also reported a figure for talc mine rent of $10,000 a year, we will nonetheless weight our estimate strongly towards the lower end of the range. If we take the average of the three figures (using a mid-range where needed), we get $5,436 a month per mine. If we give the lower figures five times as much weight as the higher one, this comes down to $2,218.[403]

Without reliable data on the size or the overall number of such mines, it is difficult to extrapolate what that means for overall income. Our rough satellite analysis of 16 mining areas in Ghunday/Markikhel and Ladabagh does not account for mines in other areas, or for multiple operations at the larger sites, and includes all visible mines, not just talc.[404] The number of unregistered mines is unknown. The sites may be of different sizes, but if we assumed that at a minimum there is the equivalent of 40 talc sites in Nangarhar paying this level of rent, that would generate annual revenue of a little over $1m.

Finally, the tolls charged varied, but it seems defensible to assume an average rate of about Rs 750 ($7.14) per ton. This is based on a conservative average of our data on the tolls (as set out in the main text above), but it is also closest to the figures we got from two sources for the largest trucks. (Two other sources mentioned a higher toll for these trucks, as did other sources in relation for smaller vehicles; while only a couple of sources suggested lower rates).[405] Of course, some trucks may have avoided tolls (though those would be mainly the ones carrying production which was extracted by the Taliban or by miners directly renting the mines, which would mean that the Taliban income on it was not zero). But if we simply take our assumption of 500,000 tons of annual production of talc, we get total revenue of $3.57m, for talc alone.

The difficulty is that the balance between these three forms of income is very difficult to assess. We do not know how many mines exist in total, or how many are Taliban operated and how many rented (or how many might avoid paying rent at all, given the one mine a source claimed was out of their control – though from the testimony we have discussed above it is very few if any). We don't know how much talc the businessmen who rented mines sold to other traders and how much they shipped themselves, or how much road toll was paid on their own production.

Despite this, perhaps it is possible to suggest a reasonably plausible scenario. If we assume that just 10% of production comes from mines the Taliban exploits directly, this gives us $1.13m a year in revenue, as set out above. We then assume the remaining 90% of production is divided over the equivalent of 36 remaining mines that pay an average of $2,218 in rent each a month. This accounts for about another $958,000 a year. We then assume that 50% of the production of these mines pays road tolls, at the estimated rate of Rs 750 ($7.14) a ton, which seems reasonable given the number of sources that reported trucks paying the fees. That makes a total of another $1.6m. All in all, this would amount to $3.7m. If we allow a margin of plus or minus a third to reflect the uncertainty in the data, this gives us a range of about $2.5-$5m. This of course leaves out any revenue from ushr and zakat on individuals involved in the mining (which is potentially significant), as well as even nominal road tolls on talc from mines either controlled by the Taliban or paying rent to them. Given this, and the broad assumptions involved, it seems appropriate to round to the nearest million, and simply say we estimate the Taliban are making somewhere in the region of $4m a year.

As a final gut check, this figure appears plausible against the wider picture of the talc industry: it would amount to a little over 10% of the total value of talc produced in Afghanistan (albeit based on official statistics which may understate the trade), which is less than some reports of the Taliban take from other resources.[406] Again, other methods could produce significantly higher totals. If for example we simply accepted the report from a former senior police officer that the Taliban made Rs100,000 ($952) from each truck, this would give us more than $10m a year in revenue (or even more if we take higher estimates of the size of the trade). But given the uncertainties involved, it is probably better to be cautious.

Annex D: A Taliban mining contract

This is an anonymised and annotated translation of a purported Taliban mining contract. The contract was received from a Taliban source, although we were unable to otherwise independently corroborate it. It is thought to be for onyx marble, which is valued at up to $3,000 per ton.[407] This would make the tax rate ($571 per ton) around 20%, which is high to raise some questions, but seems within plausible limits, given reported Taliban tax rates charged elsewhere.[408] It is unclear which location the contract covers.

Mining commission

Annex D: A Taliban mining contract

Date: XX/XX/2015 [Date anonymised]

1) Per ton: 60,000 [likely Pakistani rupees, around $571]

2) This contract is only for a period of one year only. The contract for next year will belong to the [Taliban] mining commission despite their [the mining company's] work, whether they have done a large amount or fewer amounts.

3) The contractor cannot cancel the contract before the expiry date

4) The contractor at first pays (?) rupees, however this amount is going to be calculated within the main revenue

5) The work will need to be started in a month time; if this is not done the commission has the ability to cancel the contract

6) The responsibility of the contract is upon the contractor, indeed all the shareholders must agree to the [Taliban] mining commission and if the shareholders get into a dispute then the commission has the right to take the contract away from them and give it to someone else

7) The contractor cannot give a part of the mine or the entire mine to someone else in order to make extra profit

8) Extraction should be done in an appropriate and suitable way and no waste should be made

9) The extraction should be done in the specific area where it is supposed to be, and no right is given to extract any other mines in any other areas

10) The contractor is responsible for extracting at least 20 tons or more per day. If there are no security issues or natural disasters they can extract more

11) The extracted mines revenue should be paid in the current month whether the goods have been sold or not

12) The goods will get weighed in a city that is closest to the area in Pakistan with the attendance of both sides

13) The contractors need to vacate all their equipment from the mine before the end of the year and should clear all their accounts

14) Those goods that are transferred are the responsibility of the contractors and not the mining commission

15) In the case that the area is taken over by the government, the contract will be in its place but before starting the work the agreed contract amount should be paid to the commission.

16) The responsibility of contractor is to deal with Pakistan and Afghanistan governments, commission has no responsibility.

17) Mining Commission has the right to add any shareholders to the mine and the traders do not have the right to complain.

18) The Islamic Government Mujahedeen will support the contractors by not causing any harm to their goods, equipment and personnel.

19) If the contractor disobeys from rules and regulation of the contract, the commission has the right to terminate their contract

20) Both sides will commit to their contract and not cause any issues.

Signed by XXXXXX [Taliban official, name anonymised] (responsible for the contract).

And responsible person of the mining [company]

Courtesy: I am highly indebted and would like to thank for the permission and reproduction of the Global Witness this research report. Global Witness protects human rights and the environment by fearlessly confronting corruption and challenging the systems that enable it. It wants a better world - where corruption is challenged and accountability prevails, all can thrive within the planet's boundaries, and governments act in the public interest. When founded in 1993, the organization was pioneers in seeing the link between natural resources, conflict and corruption. Since its very first campaign to shut down the Khmer Rouge's illegal logging industry they also uncovered the truth about blood diamonds and helped bring trillions of oil, gas and mining revenues into the open. Global Witness has over 100 staff, and offices in London, Washington DC and Brussels along with a global network of partners and allies. Its campaigns encompass oil, gas and mining, conflict resources, forests, land and environmental defenders, and corruption and money laundering. Its investigations are known for meticulous attention to detail and months and sometimes years in the making. Moreover, Global Witness use an ever-evolving variety of skills and techniques to uncover evidence including: Secret filming: for a 2016 investigation Global Witness went undercover in New York to reveal the role lawyers can play in discussing how potential clients could move suspect money, Satellite imagery and drone footage: Global Witness used these tools to expose illegal logging in Papua New Guinea and talc mines funding the Taliban in Afghanistan. Data analysis: working with partners like Open Corporates Global Witness used artificial intelligence and cloud computing to analyse the real owners behind UK companies. Phone:4402074925820.Email: mail@globalwitness.org https://www.globalwitness.org/en-gb/about-us/

Chapter 2

The Sun cannot be Hidden by two Fingers: Illicit Drugs and the Discussions on a Political Settlement in Afghanistan

David Mansfield

Foreword

AREU is pleased to present its readers with an in-depth research paper "The Sun Cannot be Hidden by Two Fingers: Illicit Drugs and the Discussions on a Political Settlement in Afghanistan" by AREU consultant, Dr David Mansfield, and with the generous financial support of the European Union. This paper is part of the European Union funded project: Three-pronged research effort into essential areas of Natural Resources Management. The paper is based on a combination of modern technology and field research and has come up with a detailed analysis of the prospect of a ban on the production of illicit drugs in Afghanistan. The paper emphasises that some of the gains of the last two decades will be forsaken in pursuit of a political settlement.

The current debates on peace and reconciliation have largely ignored the challenge of illegal drugs production. The risks that illicit drug crop production – opium, opiates, marijuana and increasingly methamphetamine—might pose to a political settlement is not raised at all. The implications of narcotics production for an enduring peace are overlooked as is the lootable and illegal nature of the products that limit the state's ability to regulate and monopolise taxes on production. The problem of narcotics is further exacerbated due to the vested interests of different armed actors including those working for the state and those engaged in the insurgency that earn significant sums of money from the production and marketability of these illegal substances.

It should be kept in mind that illicit drugs production and trade currently make the largest single economic sector in Afghanistan. Opium poppy is the country's most valuable cash crop worth US$863 million and employs more people than any other industry in Afghanistan, over 500,000 Full-time equivalents. The crop occupied an estimated 263,000 hectares of land in 2018; three times more land than it did in 2000 when the Taliban imposed an outright ban. Conservative estimates suggest that opiates alone made up more than 10 per cent of Gross Domestic Product in 2018 and that different armed groups earned over US$40 million in taxes along the value chain. The paper recommends that given the economic and political importance of the illicit drugs economy in Afghanistan it is unwise to assume the problem away or look to resolve it with wishful and simplistic policy responses – or as the Afghan proverb says the sun cannot be hidden by two fingers.

AREU acknowledges the significant amount of contribution of the Organization for Sustainable Development & Research's help with field research, the anonymous peer-reviewers for their insightful comments and Dr Mansfield for his continuous commitment to systematic research in this field and producing such rich papers.

Sincerely,

Dr Orzala Nemat[1], Director, AREU

Executive Summary

Much of the current discourse regarding Afghanistan is focused on a political settlement and reconciliation. Talk of an end to the conflict is a welcome development for many, regardless of whether some of the current momentum is due more to political expedience and the Trump administration's desire to withdraw from Afghanistan prior to the next US presidential election.[2] There is however, a growing list of concerns that those in civil society, politicians and activists have rightfully raised. Apprehensive that some of the gains of the last two decades will be forsaken in pursuit of a political settlement, some even fear a collapse of the government and its institutions. While the most prominent concern is the rights of women, particularly given the Taliban's history in this regard, there are also questions regarding the future of elected assemblies, the right to vote, free media and expression, and human rights in general. These are all topics subject to considerable debate in a variety of fora both within Afghanistan and internationally, as well as in discussions with the Taliban themselves.

An issue largely ignored in the current debates on peace and reconciliation is that of illegal drugs production. When it is mentioned, the discussion tends to be curt, focusing largely on the possibility that the Taliban would repeat the ban on opium that it issued in the summer of 2000, culminating in cultivation falling from an estimated 82,000 hectares to only 8,000 hectares in 2001. As such, the debates centre on political power and the Taliban's assumed ability to once again coerce the rural population to refrain from opium production. There is a nominal discussion about what may be required to offset some of the negative economic effects of such an initiative, such as in the United States Special Inspector General for Afghanistan Reconstruction's (SIGAR) "High Risk" report,[3] but little consideration of the likely success of such an effort. The risks that illegal drug crop production - opium, opiates, marijuana and increasingly methamphetamine—might pose to a political settlement is not raised at all; the lootable and illegal nature of the products that limit the state's ability to regulate and monopolise taxes on production, and the amounts of money earned by different armed actors—those working for the state and those engaged in the insurgency - and the implications this has for an enduring peace are overlooked.

And the amount of money is significant. It should not be forgotten that illicit drugs production and trade is currently the largest single economic sector in Afghanistan. Opium poppy is the country's most valuable cash crop worth US$863 million[4] and employs more people than any other industry in Afghanistan, over 500,000 Full Time Equivalent. The crop occupied an estimated 263,000 hectares of land in 2018; three times more land than it did in 2000 when the Taliban imposed an outright ban. Conservative estimates suggest that opiates alone made up more than 10 percent of Gross Domestic Product in 2018 and that over US$ 40 million in taxes were earned by different armed groups along the value-chain. The value of the illegal drugs economy would be significantly higher were estimates to include the marijuana economy and an incipient methamphetamine industry-which includes what could be wide scale cultivation of an ephedra-based plant and an indigenous capacity to process increasingly larger amounts.

Given the economic and political importance of the illicit drugs economy in Afghanistan it is unwise to assume the problem away or look to resolve it with wishful and simplistic policy responses - or as the Afghan proverb says the sun cannot be hidden by two fingers. By their very nature illicit drugs are difficult for governments to tame, particularly for those governments in or coming out of protracted conflict and violence. Past efforts at banning opium in Afghanistan have proved short lived, ineffective, and counterproductive. These bans ignored the diffuse and decentralised nature of political power in Afghanistan; neglected the agency of rural communities; and led to rural dissent and contributed to violent resistance. Regulation—the production of drugs under a controlled system—is unrealistic in a country where the writ of the state in the rural areas where the crop is concentrated has always been limited, and where there is significant risk of leakage into illicit markets. Most importantly, small farms, inefficient production and poor technology render Afghanistan uncompetitive in an international market for licit opiates that is increasingly contested and where prices continue to fall.[5]

Illicit drug production in Afghanistan cannot be wished away and how it impacts, and is impacted by, a future political settlement and will need to be prioritised in ongoing discussions. The political situation in many of the provinces where drugs are produced is complex; made up of multiple armed groups and fluid alliances it is shaped as much by economic interests as they are by political ideologies and affiliations. In these areas local power brokers - some of who have official positions in the central, provincial or district authorities—reach accommodations with insurgents over rent extraction on the production and movement of illicit drugs. It is unrealistic to assume these local powerbrokers and the factionalism that has beleaguered these areas for years would come to a stop were a deal struck between the Afghan government and the Taliban. It is in these provinces where the deepest fault lines in any political settlement will become most apparent, and where a future conflict may be more a matter of groups vying for control over revenues, rather than looking to undermine peace.

Yet, confronting the illicit drugs economy in Afghanistan cannot just be more of the same. Past efforts have shown just how divisive the issue has been both within and between the different governments involved. The failure to understand and agree the nature of the problem and how it might best be managed, as well as a policy process that focuses on countering problem metrics–such as the area under cultivation—rather than addressing underlying causes, led to multiple and competing strategies and priorities that proved wasteful and counterproductive. Boundaries counter narcotics interventions that were not part of a wider development strategy proved ineffective and unsustainable. All too often narrow institutional mandates and interests ruled out the kind of cross sectoral and interdepartmental cooperation that was required to deal with a complex phenomena such as illicit drug production. In the event of a political settlement, the priority would be for a future Afghan government to be in the lead; for it not to develop a counternarcotics strategy per se, but to define the harms caused by illicit drugs as a development priority and make it a cross-cutting issue for all branches of government to explicitly address in their policies and interventions. Realistically, it will be a matter of managing the most deleterious effects caused by the production, trade and use of illicit drugs and not eliminating these problems altogether.

1. Hidden the sun with two fingers

At times, drug production and counternarcotics have been at the forefront of the development agenda in Afghanistan.[6] This has not been helpful; it has driven short-term targets, and the pursuit of action in areas such as eradication and poorly considered development interventions that have served to undermine economic and political stability and fuelled antipathy to the Afghan state and its international backers.[7] Today the reverse is true; currently no one wants to talk about drugs. This is despite the fact that the illicit drugs economy and the funds it generates are one of the most intractable problems facing Afghanistan and will ultimately shape and be shaped by the conflicts to come.

The size and significance of the illicit economy in Afghanistan is easy to ignore from Kabul and western capitals, and as such is often underestimated. For example, in 2018, the Afghan government estimated that illicit opium poppy cultivation was worth US$ 863 million; the equivalent of 4.4 percent of Gross Domestic Product (GDP).[8] This might appear relatively small given that 263,000 hectares of opium were grown in 2018 and the opium economy provided full-time-equivalent (FTEs) employment for as many as 507,000; making it one of the country's largest employers, considerably more than the total number employed by the Afghan National Defence Security Forces (ANDSF).[9] However, this estimate does not include the value of the production and sale of opiates (morphine, heroin base and heroin hydrochloride), marijuana and an incipient methamphetamine industry.

If these higher value products are also included, the contribution of illicit drugs to total GDP would rise still further. For example, including estimates of heroin and heroin hydrochloride production adds a further US$ 1.2 billion[10] to GDP, an increase of 5.6 percent.[11] The inclusion of marijuana, a significant summer crop in some provinces, methamphetamine and the services industries that support the drugs economy, such as the smuggling and transport of precursor chemicals used in processing and the growing technology that surrounds the production of opium in the former deserts of the south west, would add yet more value to GDP.

Aside from the contributions made by illegal drugs to the overall economy and employment outlook, it is also worth considering the rent extracted by various armed actors during the various stages of the production process. Even a relatively crude estimate indicates that the tax on the farmgate production of opium in 2018 would have generated US$ 25.9 million in taxes, with a further US$ 5.1 million collected in tax for cooked opium and a further US$ 8.8 million in "powder" - morphine base, heroin base and heroin hydrochloride - making a total of US$39.9 million. Of this total, US$ 30.9 million is generated in the south-western provinces of Farah, Helmand, Kandahar, Nimroz, Uruzgan and Zabul; equal to the amount of customs duty earned in the province of Kandahar in 2018, one of Afghanistan's five primary official border crossings.[12] The tax on the opiate production in Helmand alone would have been worth US$ 19.7 million in 2018.

These are just the payments on production. There are other irregular payments – bribes – referred to locally as "gifts" or "charity" made to officials, law enforcement personnel and armed actors, including insurgents. These payments are not a function of the quantity of drugs grown or processed but are facilitation fees designed to gain favour with local powerbrokers– "safe passage"–that allow the drugs business to continue. For example in GandamRaiz in northern Helmand where there is a concentration of drug processing facilities, lab owners report paying up to $400 to the local Taliban commander on a 'seasonal' basis in addition to more regulated payments of $2.40 per kilogramme for cooked opium and US$ 5.40 per kilogramme on "powder."[13] As such, whoever gains control over Helmand – most probably the Taliban – or any of these other major opium producing provinces has a valuable source of rent from which to pay its officials, provide services or indeed arm their soldiers, if so required.

There are of course further sources of rent for armed actors in the form of licit goods that are produced and sold illicitly. Precious stones are mined in Afghanistan, including rubies and emeralds, as well as the semi-precious lapiz lazuli. There are also significant deposits of industrial minerals such as chromite, coal, and magnesium silicate.[14] Many of these are mined illegally, without licence and smuggled across the borders into Pakistan, Iran and the Central Asian Republics. There is also a vibrant economy in the smuggling of licit goods— "the transit trade" —a range of different consumer and luxury goods imported into Afghanistan only to be smuggled out to neighbouring countries to be sold at a profit. Officials estimate that as much as 50 percent of the goods imported under the transit trade agreement are smuggled across the borders into neighbouring countries.[15]

Combined with prohibited drugs, these illicit economies represent a significant source of revenue that does not flow to the central coffers of the Afghan government in Kabul and in the case of opiates, marijuana and methamphetamine is unlikely to do so in the future. It seems most likely that the vast majority of these funds will remain in the provinces in which these goods are produced and transported or banked overseas. While the scale of the revenue generated is unknown it is clearly significant and shapes the political economy of the provinces in which these goods are produced: the patronage networks within them, cross-border relationships, and perhaps most importantly the interests of that conflict and a political settlement in Afghanistan. Developing a better understanding of the scale of these illicit economies, and in particular the illicit drugs economy, and what can realistically be done to address them will be critical to an enduring political settlement.

2. Debunking the policy defaults

Many of the debates on illicit drugs in Afghanistan vacillate between polar extremes. There are those that believe that drugs can simply be banned–prohibited–and the problem will disappear; this is despite numerous examples of past failures. There are others that think the solution lies in regulation – a framework for producing opium and possibly opiates under controlled conditions; where the economic benefits can be accrued by the Afghan state and farmers. The so-called middle ground is more of the same, the kind of boundaried counternarcotics interventions, like alternative development, that have served so poorly in the past. As this section explains none of these options are realistic for the foreseeable future and belie the importance of addressing drug production within the wider socio-economic, political and environmental context in which it occurs in Afghanistan.

A. Past prohibition by the Taliban and the prospect of imposing another opium ban

Taliban 1.0

There are some who hanker for the old days and believe the Taliban may place bans on opium production, as they have done in the past.[16] The Taliban themselves suggested this during discussions in Moscow in November 2018.[17] There is even a view that, unlike issues such as human rights and women's rights, this is an area in which the Taliban and US, and possibly other western donors, could reach agreement. While there might be a desire within parts of the Taliban movement to prohibit opium production–for religious reasons, to limit the flow of funds to potential breakaway groups within their midst, and to appeal to donor nations–it is clear that their ability to do so is, significantly curtailed. This is not the Taliban of the 1990s which succeeded in banning opium outright. Those suggesting that such a policy is possible require better understanding of the lessons of the past and their relevance to the current situation.

Try, try, try, try and try again

It has to be remembered just how protracted a process the Taliban ban was; this was no overnight proclamation; it required the right conditions and circumstances to be aligned before it could be imposed effectively. It is particularly important to note that by July

2000, when an effective ban on opium cultivation was imposed, the Taliban had issued statements prohibiting opium on no less than five separate occasions and not one of them had been heeded.

The first Taliban statement prohibiting opium poppy was in late 1994 and has been viewed as a demonstration of the Taliban's capacity to dramatically impact opium poppy cultivation, even in the early years of their rule.[18] The reality is that the Taliban did not impose a ban on opium poppy cultivation in 1994 only to rescind it 1996. The 1994 ban was a statement of intent, no more; and the rise in cultivation in 1996 attributed to the Taliban lifting the ban did not occur. In fact, much of the discussion of this initial prohibition is built on a misunderstanding of the estimates of opium poppy cultivation and their veracity at the time.

Firstly, the UNODC survey of 1994 was a pilot; a first stab at a visual estimate of opium poppy by surveyors on the ground and one that was recognised internally as flawed; an exaggerated account of cultivation, in part, to attract funding for the survey and programs in the future. Any decrease in cultivation in 1995 was as much the result of errors and methodological changes; UNDCP considered the 1994 and 1995 surveys not comparable and gave them "restricted circulation" (UNDCP 1995:ii and 2).

Secondly, while estimated levels of cultivation did decrease between 1994 and 1995, the bulk of this – 15,089 hectares of the 18,181 hectares reduction-took place in the eastern Afghanistan where the Taliban held no sway at the time. In the south, where the Taliban gained their first foothold cultivation rose marginally in Helmand (+8%) and fell in Kandahar (-38%) and Uruzgan (-66%) but from relatively low levels of cultivation. Furthermore, UNODC reported that farmers attributed reductions in the South primarily to falling opium prices and rising wheat prices, and only in part to statements by the Taliban.[19] Thirdly, the Taliban did not vanquish their opponents in Helmand – even then the primary opium producing province – until January 1995, some months after the planting season had begun. As such the Taliban were not in a position to ban cultivation even if they had wished to.

Finally, there is a further challenge in that the USG reported an increase in cultivation in Afghanistan between 1994 and 1995 from 29,190 ha to 38,740 ha, with rising levels of cultivation in Kandahar (from 2,666 ha to 3,050 ha), Uruzgan (from 3,293 ha to 3,640 ha) and dramatic increases in Helmand (from 12,529 ha to 22,700 ha);[20] and neither the USG nor UNODC estimates show a dramatic increase in cultivation between 1995 and 1996 that would suggest the Taliban's ban "was lifted".[21]

After the "ban" of 1994 there were four further statements by the Taliban prohibiting opium: one in November 1996,[22] a further statement in September 1997, followed by a clarification a month later,[23] and then a call by Mullah Mohammed Omar for a one-third reduction in cultivation in September of 1999.[24] Each of these so called bans stand in stark contrast to the effective prohibition imposed by the Taliban in 2000/01; this was more than just a statement of intent. Between 2000 and 2001 cultivation fell from 82,000 to 8,000 hectares, a move that was extolled by the UN and donors alike. But beneath these headlines lay a much more protracted political process that says much about the Taliban's authority over Afghanistan at the time and how it had the diffuse nature of political power in rural areas, even at the zenith of the Taliban's rule.

Sixth time lucky

In 2000 things were different from these earlier efforts to ban opium by the Taliban. Most importantly, the ban was imposed at a time when wheat prices had almost doubled[25] and opium prices were at an all-time low. In 2000 Afghanistan was experiencing a protracted drought and the Government of Pakistan (GoP) had banned the movement of wheat flour from the Punjab to what was then North West Frontier Province (now Khyber Pakhtunkhwa) for a further season in the spring of 2000 in an attempt to limit smuggling to Afghanistan.[26] Consequently, farmers in Afghanistan were increasingly concerned about their food security and whether wheat would be available to purchase with diminished proceeds from their opium crop. Under these circumstances – as we have seen time and time again–farmers switch from opium poppy to wheat, fearful that they will not be able to buy wheat in the local market and feed their families. Opium prices were as low as US$30 per kilogram in June 2000 and combined with a drought that was having a significant impact on yields, farmers were increasingly conscious of the risks of planting an input intensive crop like opium poppy, when they would need higher incomes with which to purchase ever more expensive wheat flour.

Politically the Taliban were a pariah regime and despite the widespread effects of the war and drought the country faced significant shortfalls in humanitarian funding. Recognised as the government of Afghanistan by only three nations–Pakistan, the United Arab Emirates and Saud Arabia – less conservative elements of the Taliban pressed for wider recognition by the United Nations and the member states. Their attempts to recast the regime–such as negotiating the release of hostages in Kandahar from a hijacked plane from Kathmandu, the trial of members of a Christian NGO for proselytizing, and even an offer to try Osama Bin Laden under Islamic law–were undermined by the destruction of the buddhas in Bamian and the Taliban's record on human and women's rights. A ban on opium was positioned by the Taliban as a humanitarian act of universal appeal, something that western countries would not be able to question and would need to be seen to support politically and financially.[27]

With the right economic conditions for a reduction in levels of opium poppy cultivation, and the incentives to implement, the Taliban, drew on its political and military position, as well as the religious leadership of Mullah Omar–Amir ul-Mumineen (the leader of the faithful)–pushed for a wide scale ban. By this stage the Taliban had gained traction in the countryside, consolidating their position in many of the village's areas where opium poppy was grown. They started by negotiating with some of the more influential and powerful tribes, those who might offer resistance to a ban on opium production if they were not in agreement and could influence other tribes to comply if they were seen to adhere to it. In the east the Shinwari were instrumental. A relatively cohesive tribe that dominate five strategic districts in the southern part of Nangarhar bordering Pakistan and heavily involved in cultivation and trade. The elders were alleged to have received payments to support the ban, and been provided unfettered access to a high profile mission of western donors sent to review the ban and its effects, where the Shinwaris solicited projects directly. In the southern region, elders from the district of Nad-e-Ali, in Helmand–a district that often cultivated up to a quarter of the country's entire opium crop in given year-were also given access to Mullah Mohammed Omar to make their opposition known and solicit support.

With potential powerful opponents neutralised or co-opted the Taliban then undertook a strategic campaign of crop destruction. Initially they targeted some of the higher valleys just after the crop had been planted. These where areas where the elders and tribes were already on side; where in the past there had been resistance to prohibition efforts. Targeting these particular areas served as a demonstration effect, convincing farmers in lower lying areas that the Taliban were serious in their plan to ban opium poppy and encouraged the rural population not to plant opium poppy in the first place. By striking early in the growing season farmers had not expended considerable time and resources on their opium crop only to see it destroyed; they also had the opportunity to plant something else prior to the onset of winter. This strategy served to manage the risk of widespread dissent, something the Taliban were keen to avoid as it could undermine the image they had projected – particularly to the outside world - of having complete control of the countryside.

The reality of course was something rather different. When the Taliban expanded from their base in the South across the country, they defeated some of their opponents militarily but reached political settlements with others. Tribal and military elites may have acquiesced to Taliban rule but they were often given varying degrees of autonomy depending on the political and military capital at their disposal.[28] Moreover, these settlements were not static but were constantly evolving, particularly in the late 1990s, as the Taliban faced growing dissent and increasing financial difficulties.[29]

While the Taliban ban gave an impression of consolidated territorial control, informed accounts stress a different reality, arguing that the administration was dysfunctional and inconsistent.[30] Ministries were largely a facade, they lacked budgets, policies and an effective bureaucracy. Instead, the regime largely relied on the development community (e.g., NGOs, UN) to deliver social services and in many cases infrastructural projects. Furthermore, policy positions adopted in Kabul would often be undermined by those in Kandahar with a far more conservative agenda. In the countryside there was considerable scope for pragmatism with nongovernmental organisations and the United Nations continuing to deliver education services to women and girls in those parts of the country where local leaders and communities were more supportive and pragmatic than the edicts of Mullah Mohammed Omar would suggest. Even the claims that the population had been disarmed were overstated with rural communities, particularly those in the mountainous areas retaining their weapons but consenting to withdraw them from public space as long as the Taliban maintained security. As Maley (2002: 217) notes: "The claim that the Taliban 'controlled' large tracts of Afghanistan were misleading, since the Taliban presence in rural areas was light."[31]

In reality, the Taliban regime, as with Afghan governments before it, ruled through a combination of coercion and negotiation. In lowland areas, located along the main trading routes and river valleys, the Taliban regime could easily impose its will on a population that was more accessible and consisted of a multitude of long-settled tribes–this can be understood as the 'state space' that previous regimes had also governed with relative ease. However, in the more mountainous areas the population is more cohesive, often consisting of a single tribal group, and have historically been given greater autonomy. In these hinterlands there was little evidence of Taliban presence beyond a few armed militias located in the district governor's office. In these areas the Taliban regime, like its predecessors, adopted a strategy of containment working with the rural elite to co-opt and neutralise dissent.[32]

The opium ban was also implemented amidst a backdrop of growing resentment and dissent against Taliban rule even in

Pashtun areas.[33] As with their predecessors in the mujahedeen, military conscription had made the Taliban increasingly unpopular, particularly as many were dying fighting in the north.[34] The Taliban's inability to bring economic stability despite improvements in physical security had led to growing frustration among the population. Incidences of corruption had become more widespread and there had been a number of armed rebellions throughout their rule, even in those districts that were considered to be the heart of Taliban territory, including Arghandab in the province of Kandahar, and Kajaki in Helmand.[35] Even during the donors mission to investigate the prohibition, the Taliban leadership in the east had to negotiate safe passage for the mission to visit the Mohmand and Pekhar valleys in Achin; an area where the mix of civil disobedience in protest against the ban, the presence of traders and drug processing facilities, and reports of the inflow of weapons raised major concerns for the Taliban given the seniority of some of the diplomats and Taliban's concerns for their security and welfare.[36]

There were also tensions within the Taliban's leadership, which had evolved from a core of Kandahari conservatives in the mid-1990s to include a multiplicity of different groups, including former communists from the Khalq party, who did not necessarily share the same moral and social vision for the country.[37] There were reports of disputes between the 'conservatives' in Kandahar, headed by Mullah Mohammed Omar, and the 'moderates' under the tutelage of Mullah Rabbani who was based in Kabul.[38] The divisions were such that Rashid (2001: 212) saw the potential for the moderates to stage a coup against Mullah Mohammed Omar.

It is important to note that the imposition of the ban changed the nature of the relationship between rural communities the Taliban and those in the rural elite that had played their part in imposing prohibition in these areas. While coercion had been an important element of the bargaining process with rural elites and the local population, it was used only judiciously to encourage compliance. A far more critical element in gaining consent in these more autonomous areas was the potential for patronage and rent from future development assistance. The expectation that development assistance would be forthcoming was high at all levels of society but particularly amongst the rural population and key tribes like the Shinwari who had been instrumental in the imposition of the ban in the eastern region. Ultimately the ban on opium shifted the political settlement that had been reached between the Taliban and much of rural Afghanistan during their rule. If sustained, prohibition had the potential to challenge the political and financial autonomy of the periphery, making them reliant on the patronage of the centre.

In the absence of the capacity to subjugate the population with force–especially those in the mountains and borders where the Afghan state's writ has always been limit–and the necessary development funds to shore up the support of local elites, and at least lessen the impact the ban was having on large swathes of the rural population, there was little prospect of prohibition being pursued for a further year. The fragile deals that were struck in the periphery would have been hard to maintain without some evidence that the rural population's economic prospects would not continue on such a dramatic downward trajectory. It is hard to believe that if development assistance was not delivered the Taliban would not have come under considerable political pressure from key tribal groups to abandon the ban, and that the leadership would not have capitulated, particularly given the availability of weaponry both within Afghanistan and the region, the ongoing conflict, and the Taliban movement's own internal struggles.

Negotiating a second year of a ban under these conditions in the fall of 2001 would have presented a significant challenge for the rural elite as well as the Taliban leadership. Considerable amounts of political capital had been expended by the Taliban leadership, tribal leaders and local elders in the process of implementing prohibition with the expectation that they would see development benefits. The kind of resistance that was seen in the upper parts of Achin during the spring of 2001 could easily have turned to a more widespread rural rebellion that would have challenged the image of sovereignty that the Taliban looked to project both internationally and domestically. In fact, in April 2001 there were already reports that Hajji Qadir was moving weapons across the border into eastern Afghanistan, and the potential for dissent in other parts of the country was extremely high. The Taliban's ban was exacting an economic toll on the population and there were fears this could be exploited by opposition groups both internally and across the borders. As FrancescVendrell noted at the time of the ban, while reflecting on what he saw as the "rebellious mood amongst the rural population', 'The Taliban will not put religious purism ahead of their military ambitions."[39]

Taliban 2.0.

Given the realities of the Taliban's past efforts to prohibit opium, could they pursue such a policy today as others have suggested and their leadership declared in Moscow? For a number of reasons, it seems highly improbable. For one, the Taliban of 2019 does not have the coherence that it had in the 1990s. We should be careful not to read too much into the ceasefire implemented in the Eid of 2018. Mullah Omar is dead, and today's leadership has none of the religious authority or credentials of Amir ul-Mumineen. The movement is also more fractious than it was in the 1990s. Rivalries dominate the leadership and at the local level there is a vast array of different policies and practice that suggests there is a high degree of decentralisation and local autonomy. In the absence of a centralised command and control it is hard to believe that many of the local commanders who have been fighting on the front lines would be willing to abandon opium poppy and the financial independence they have gained through its taxation at the behest of a Taliban leadership in Quetta, Peshawar, or anywhere else. During their previous incarnation it took 6 years, territorial control of 90 percent of the country, and repeated–but ignored–counternarcotics efforts before the Taliban could deliver an effective prohibition in the 2000-01 growing season. And even then, the bargains that were struck left them vulnerable to political opposition and dissent. Today's peace process is not even in its infancy and there are simply too many unknowns involved to garner support from local Taliban commanders for a ban on opium.

Secondly, these same commanders would find themselves facing the ire of local farmers were they to enforce a ban. This has been witnessed many times, not only in 2001 but also during subsequent prohibitions under the Karzai administration, such as in Nangarhar, Helmand and Balkh. In some cases, the aggressive drive to ban opium led to local elites being ousted not only from their positions as community leaders, but from the very valleys where they lived. For example, the role tribal elders played in imposing a ban in Nangarhar between 2007 and 2010 led to just such a move in the upper valleys of Achin. In many instances the push to prohibit opium also led to the local population soliciting the support of armed actors, most notably the Taliban to curtail the government's ability to eradicate the crop.

In fact, for the last decade or more the Taliban has sought to exploit the counternarcotics policies of the Afghan government and western donors, and the perception that crop destruction was at the forefront. They have done so in order to gain the support of farmers by encouraging cultivation with offers to protect the crop. In doing so, the Taliban looked to position themselves as saviours of a rural population that faced the threat of crop destruction; they sought to present themselves as a movement that understood the economic needs of their compatriots in the countryside in stark contrast to an Afghan government portrayed as "puppets" of American counternarcotics policy with no regard for the welfare of the population.

It is hard to see how a Taliban leadership, and in particular local commanders and soldiers who live amongst these farming communities, would retain authority and credibility with a rural population that gave them succour during the conflict, were they to about-turn and announce a ban on opium production. This is also a situation that other armed groups, or those opposing a settlement within the Taliban would look to exploit; and something the Taliban leadership will desperately look to avoid for fear of exposing and exacerbating the divisions within. Daesh might be one of those armed groups. While Daesh have imposed a local ban on opium in places like upper Achin, in Nangarhar between 2014 and 2016, other elements of the Islamic State Khorasan in

Afghanistan have not proven so ideological and could well move to support cultivation to win over recalcitrant commanders and soldiers, as well as farmers who oppose a future poppy ban.

Thirdly, there remains no viable alternative to opium poppy cultivation in many of the areas in which the crop is concentrated, especially in the desert areas of the southwest where up to 2.4 million people are dependent on the crop for their income, shelter, food and water supply. This is the perennial problem: in the absence of opium poppy what are farmers to do? While promises have been made of an uptick in development assistance were there to be peace, those most dependent on opium poppy for their livelihoods have heard these words many times before and have been repeatedly disappointed by the outcomes; a function of funding constraints, corruption and the bulk of assistance going to the rural elite. They have heard declarations from western donors and repeated Afghan governments that large amounts of aid would flow in return for reductions in opium only to see much less than anticipated arrive, and much what of what did flow go to the better endowed areas nearer the provincial centres where farmers are less reliant on opium for their livelihoods, and to wealthier farmers in then more remote areas who also have other assets and revenues to draw upon. This is not an environment where the promises of a "peace dividend" tied to reductions in poppy will yield political support or the hope of a better future from those in the countryside. Hope will not triumph over the hard experience of the past.

There is no doubt that were the Taliban to commit to prohibiting opium poppy, there would be further offers of development support, particularly from the USG, but the reality is this assistance is rarely more than a band aid — short term and single-sector relief aimed at alleviating the political pressures on those who have agreed to ban poppy. The Helmand Food Zone (HFZ) implemented in between 2008 and 2011, was just such an initiative. Providing wheat seed and fertiliser to farmers, it sought to shore up support for the then Governor Gulab Mangal, so he could launch a campaign aimed at deterring planting and eradicating the crop of recalcitrant. The HFZ contributed to dramatic reductions in opium poppy within the canal irrigated areas of central Helmand, but it also impoverished the land-poor, compelling them to look for land in former desert areas, where they turned to cultivation of ever greater quantities of opium poppy. Therefore, on net, the HFZ led to increased production. UNODC can be seen to be pursuing the same kind of short-term single sector development assistance in its Boost Alternative Development Intervention through Licit Livelihoods (BADILL) program, funded by INL. This too ties development assistance directly to reductions in opium poppy-a strategy that has repeatedly proven ineffective in delivering the diversified livelihoods required to produce enduring reductions in opium poppy.[40]

B. Licensing the crop in the absence of a regulatory authority

Legalisation or regulation has been another policy option for those looking to kick the drugs issue in Afghanistan into the long grass; in the advent of the failure of prohibition it is the go-to for those seeking a simple solution.

However, regulation requires an effective government and institutional capacity, something that Afghanistan will be lacking for some years to come, even if there were a political settlement. In many of the areas where opium poppy is currently grown in Afghanistan there is little state presence or capacity to regulate; nor is there the ability to enforce restrictions on cultivation were the crop grown outside the parameters of the law. In the former deserts of south western Afghanistan where opium poppy is at its most concentrated there are no state institutions whatsoever, and in areas such as Bakwa in Farah, even the Taliban's authority is the product of negotiations with the dominant Noorzai tribe. It is quite plausible; however, that many areas of Afghanistan would continue to produce opium illegally even if a future government pursued a policy of regulation, particularly given the low price of opium in the licit market.

The greatest constraint for Afghanistan in developing a regulated opium industry, however, is that of economics; the country does not have a comparative advantage in licit opium production. There are a number of countries that do produce opium legally for export but it is grown under a regulatory authority: where farmers are licensed to cultivate a specific amount; where the crop can only be sold to a recognized state or private entity; and where any refraction lead to punishment including imprisonment. As such, large scale licit cultivation is largely limited to the developed world with the exception of India and Turkey, which have protected status.

In Australia, opium is largely grown on the island of Tasmania, but in 2014 expanded to South Australia[41] and to New South Wales in 2017.[42] In Tasmania farmers cultivated an average of 40 hectares of opium poppy in 2013, with the largest farm growing 480 hectares.[43] Across all three states farmers use improved seeds and combine harvesters, productivity is high and the unit costs of morphine equivalents—the unit of measure for the final product—are the lowest in the world.

In Afghanistan, on the other hand, the opium crop is grown on small farms, typically less than one hectare. It is sown and harvested manually, absorbing as much as 360 person days per hectare, and unit costs are more than 10 times that of Australia.[44] Other nations that grow opium poppy legally, such as Spain, France and Turkey are also more efficient producers than Afghanistan. Even India which is the only country that continues to harvests raw opium - rather than cutting the top 10 centimetres of the plant and processing it to produce what is known as Concentrate of Poppy Straw (CPS)—produces a kilogram of morphine equivalent at a lower price than farmers in Afghanistan.[45]

Furthermore, there is little demand for raw opium in the world of regulated opiates.[46] Large pharmaceutical companies prefer CPS. It makes up the bulk of global supply of opiates, representing 95 per cent of opiate raw material rich in morphine.[47] The extraction of alkaloids from CPS also involves less residual waste than raw opium, and therefore presents less challenges (and costs) for disposal and fewer environmental hazards. CPS is also the preferred method of production: it offers considerable economies of scale compared to the extraction of opium; there are also fewer opportunities for diversion into the illicit market; and the final product has a higher value to weight ratio thereby reducing transport costs and making it to easier to secure.

A shift in production in Afghanistan towards CPS would have a profound effect on the economy. In Australia 22,363 hectares of opium were grown in 2009 and only 1,000 people were employed. In Afghanistan in 2018, an estimated 263,000 hectares of opium poppy were grown, employing as many as 420,800 people FTE. A shift to CPS would require a massive shift to agricultural technology that would not be easy to make and would lead to dramatic unemployment. It would also require expensive capital that the pharmaceutical companies are unlikely to fund given the probability of continued instability in Afghanistan and a supply of CPS from more secure nations that is already surplus to current world demand.[48]

Moreover, changes in US prescription laws in 2013 have had a significant effect on the global demand for legal opiates. Australian farmers have seen a contraction in demand and prices, and the legal opium industry has become much more competitive.[49] Even if it were more stable it is difficult to see how Afghanistan could compete on the world stage with producers like Australia, France or Spain with all the commercial, institutional and infrastructural advantages they have at their disposal.

3. Muddling through with more of the same

There is a risk that the alternative to prohibition and regulation under any future political settlement is more of the same when it comes to counternarcotics: where the drugs issue is boundaried and compartmentalised and the task of addressing the problems associated with illicit drugs is tasked to international and national counternarcotics agencies with few levers and limited capacity.

Yet, we have seen how this works. The SIGAR Lessons Learned report on counternarcotics[50] ably documents past efforts. It illustrates the uncoordinated and inconsistent efforts to tackle the opium trade in Afghanistan; the battles between competing philosophies, strategies, institutional interests and mandates, and how they played out. Where annual targets, such as reducing the level of opium poppy cultivation and eradicating a certain amount of opium drove directives and spending, but undermined the wider effort to achieve stability and security, which in turn led to rising levels of opium production.

Where departments, both within donor nations and the Afghan government, worked at cross purposes: one department or project looking to dissuade opium poppy cultivation while another provided improved irrigation, with no contingency to offset the risks of greater amounts of land being used to grow better yielding opium poppy in future years. And another department looking to target a powerful local actor for arrest due to his involvement in the drugs trade, whilst another sheltered them from harm due to the information they provided on insurgents and a perception that they were key to local stability.

Over the last 18 years we have also seen how reluctant many branches of government were to engage in this most intractable of problems. Development departments and organizations would often only show willingness when levels of cultivation rose and those in Kabul or western capitals decided there was a political imperative to act. Nevertheless, the development response was often lacklustre and poorly considered; more an issue of being seen to do something rather than addressing the causes of cultivation in a meaningful way. In many cases it was business as usual with departments looking to repackage existing expenditure and interventions as counternarcoticsin spite of the fact that some of them may have even contributed to rising levels of production.

The most basic development response-as was seen in 2005 following the imposition of a ban on opium production by Afghan authorities in Nangarhar and parts of the eastern region—was for USAID and DFID to fund the distribution of wheat seed and fertilizer to encourage farmers to shift from opium poppy to wheat cultivation. This was despite an awareness of the inadequacy of such an initiative given the multifunctional role that opium plays in livelihoods, and the risk that the fertiliser would be diverted to poppy cultivation. Despite these reservations the provision of wheat seed and fertiliser was at the heart of the Helmand Food

Zone, counternarcotics initiative that ultimately contributed to increasing provinces capacity to produce more opium than ever before and expanded cultivation into former desert areas far beyond the reach of the state.[51]

Other interventions were also poorly thought through, and were based on an inadequate understanding of the opium economy and its relationships to the rural economy, the insurgency and the wider reconstruction effort. For example, the air strikes against drugs labs launched in November 2017 were intended to deny revenue to the Taliban, based on the claim that 60 per cent of the insurgents revenue was derived from the drugs trade and that 20 per cent of the total value of the trade went to the Taliban in tax.[52]

Even were these assumptions correct - and there is plenty of evidence to suggest they are not[53] — the campaign spent many millions of dollars destroying what were largely inactive labs worth perhaps as much as US$16,000 and which were very easily rebuilt, thereby having little impact on drug trafficking organizations and a negligible effect, if any, on the finances of the Taliban.[54] The airstrikes themselves, however, caused considerable disquiet amongst the rural population and furthered their resentment towards the US military and the Afghan government.[55]

The evidence suggests the biggest challenge associated with the counternarcotics effort in Afghanistan to date has been identifying and agreeing what the problem actually is and how best to manage it. After all, it is not the cultivation of opium poppy that is primary problem; it is more the illegally generated funds, who obtain them and what they are used for. It is problem drug use and the implications that this has for Afghan society as well as further afield that is of concern, not that of whether levels of cultivation contract or expand. It is also the vulnerability that farmers are exposed to when they are reliant on a single crop for more than 80 per cent of their cash income; a crop that can fail due to drought or disease or is subject to falling prices due to over production or a change in consumer preferences. Yet, time and time again the primary strategy has been to target opiate production directly-through coercion farmers not to plant, bombing, eradication and crop substitution—as if eliminating the crop is simple, achievable, and that the benefits of doing so always outweigh the consequences.

4. The way forward

Despite the forced optimism it seems that we are still some way from a meaningful political settlement in Afghanistan; there are still many issues to resolve. One of the issues that might not stand in the way of a deal but could well stand in the way of an enduring peace is what is to become of illegal drugs production and the funds generated.

Currently there are references to the implementation of a widespread ban under a future political deal. However, past experience suggests this would be hard to achieve and would destabilise an already fragile situation. In the absence of viable alternatives - and there continues to be an absence in many parts of Afghanistan—a ban would undermine rural support for a future government and lead to dissent and violent resistance. Even if this did not occur immediately, evidence indicates that there is a strong likelihood of rural resistance in areas where farmers have no viable alternative to opium poppy, including the involvement of armed actors, within two years of a ban being implemented.

Regulation is also not an option. Conditions in rural Afghanistan would need to change dramatically for there to be the kind of institutional capacity and security required for effective regulation. Moreover, Afghanistan cannot produce legal opiates at price points that would be competitive on an international stage. With large farms, mechanisation and highly developed infrastructure and logistics, Australia, Spain and France can produce legal opiates at a fraction of the price compared to Afghanistan.

Yet, ignoring illicit drugs is also not a viable strategy. Illicit drugs generate too much money in Afghanistan and the region, much of which finds its way into the hands of violent actors. As such, illegal drugs and other illicit funds, such as mining, fuel and the transit trade, provide a ready source of funds for transnational organised crime and a variety of actors who have little interest in a future Afghan government that has effective control over its territory. In this context, a level of chaos and instability is good for business and it is clear that it is in the provinces of Afghanistan where drugs are produced, transported and smuggled where the deepest fracture lines in any political settlement will become most apparent and where conflict is most likely.

The production, trade and use of illicit drugs will not be eliminated in Afghanistan, the issue is how best to manage the most deleterious effects. In this regard in the event that a political settlement is reached, the priority would be for a future Afghan government to be in the lead:

- For the government to define the harms caused by illicit drugs as a development priority and compel international, bilateral and national development organizations to do the same
- For the government to make these drug related harms a cross cutting issue for all branches of government to explicitly address in their policies and interventions.
- For a core area of work to be counter threat finance and to monitor and restrict funds flowing to illegal armed groups.
- For a future health strategy to integrate the effects of problem drug use
- For those organisations working in rural development to explicitly target the causes of opium poppy cultivation - recognising how these differ by socio- economic group — and to develop programs that support farmers strengthen and diversify their livelihoods, while not contributing to rising levels of opium poppy cultivation.

The Sun cannot be hidden by two fingers: Illicit Drugs and the Discussions on a Political Settlement in Afghanistan. David Mansfield May 2019, Editing: Usman Shah Zahirzai. The Afghanistan Research and Evaluation Unit (AREU) is an independent research institute based in Kabul that was established in 2002 by the assistance of the international community in Afghanistan. AREU's mission is to inform and influence policy and practice by conducting high-quality, policy-relevant, evidence-based research and actively disseminating the results and promote a culture of research and learning. As the top think tank in Afghanistan and number five in Central Asia according to the Global Go To Think Tank Index Report at the University of Pennsylvania. David Mansfield is a Senior Fellow at the London School of Economics. He has been conducting research on rural livelihoods and poppy cultivation in Afghanistan. He has a PhD in development studies from the School of Oriental and African Studies, London. This publication may be quoted, cited, or reproduced.

Chapter 3

The Myth of 'Afghan Black': A Cultural History of Cannabis Cultivation and Hashish Production in Afghanistan

Fabrizio Foschini and Jelena Bjelica

The cannabis plant has been known to humans since the beginning of time. It is a tall annual plant with a hairy stalk and hand-shaped leaves. The species is dioeciously, meaning both female and male varieties of the plant exist. The male grows taller, from one to three metres, topped with flowers covered in pollen. The shorter, female plant, with its larger, pollen-catching flowers, produces seeds and protects them with a sticky resin. Cannabis grows almost everywhere and can be seen on the waysides not only in Afghanistan, but also in many other countries. It is characterised by a distinctive, pungent smell.

Hashish, called chars in Dari and Pashto, is made from cannabis plant resin and is usually consumed by smoking, although there are some historical records indicating that it was also consumed in drinks mixed with other substances. Afghanistan's chars, also known as 'Afghan Black', are a potent drug produced in Afghanistan. This dispatch traces the story of Afghan Black through historical records and also offers some general information about the history of hashish. The dispatch will first provide a general history of the cannabis plant, then look at hashish through the historical records of the east (where, according to the historians, its use originates), followed by the historical records in the west, where its use spread during both the nineteenth and twentieth century's. This dispatch also looks at the expansion of Afghanistan's hashish production in the 1970s, created by an increase in demand mainly by western travellers, ie hippies, and finally where the country's production stands today.

A short history of the cannabis plant

Russian botanist, Nikolay Ivanovich Vavilov, in his work (published posthumously), The Origin and Geography of Cultivated Plants, points out that although "it is extremely hard to tell when the cultivation of hemp was initiated and what people were instrumental in this," it is obvious, based on the available information, that "hemp is a plant of Asia."[1] Cultivated hemp, the Russian botanist said, originated most probably in the inner-Asiatic centre, an area that comprises north-western India (Kashmir), Pakistan (Punjab and northwest provinces), all of Afghanistan, Tajikistan, Uzbekistan and the western range of Tien-Shan in modern China. Today, both wild and cultivated hemp is present in almost every corner of the world; at least 172 countries across the globe produce their own cannabis primarily to satisfy local demand.

Almost every part of the plant has been used throughout history. The stalks for fibre; the seeds for food and oil; and the flowers, leaves and resin in medical and intoxicating preparations. For example, the United Nation's Bulletin on Narcotics from 1950 (issue number 4 [2], which looks at the history of cannabis, references the Sanskrit medical work known as Sucruta (sixth or seventh century A.D.) that mentions cannabis as a medicine under the name of b'hanga. "This term occurs in the earlier Atharva Veda (2000-1400 B.C.) and in the work of the celebrated grammarian Pannini," the bulletin says. The bulletin also references the Kou-Kin-i-Tong, a Chinese treatise on remedies (dating from the beginning of the Common Era), that mentions the use of a hemp preparation (Ma-Yo) as an anaesthetic in surgical operations.[3] The cultivation and use of hemp for its fibres and medical properties is also well recorded in European and Middle Eastern historical accounts.[4] But even when hemp was first used in Europe, the tribes of eastern and Central Asia had known about cannabis' psychoactive powers and had been using it for many centuries.

Hashish in the East

There is an accepted view among many authors[5] that the use of cannabis for its psychoactive properties, ie as hashish or chars, originated in Central and South Asia. Vavilov, for example, says:

The utilization of hemp for hashish did not even require special creative efforts on behalf of Man. When burning stalks and leaves over a wood fire, the humans could certainly not avoid noticing the stupefying effect of the hemp. The quantity of the narcotics substance increase towards sought, where the utilization of hemp for hashish is concentrated. The 1951 United Nations narcotics bulletin made a similar point: "It has been established beyond dispute," the bulletin said, "that the use of cannabis to induce a special form of intoxication is of Asian origin."

"Europe and the Far East have as yet been but slightly contaminated," it concluded.

The UN narcotics bulletins from the 1950s and most of the 1960s when the UN Commission on Narcotic Drugs, as they said, "has taken great pains in extending the world's knowledge on cannabis from every point of view: medical, scientific, agricultural, etc" are valuable sources of information. The 1950 bulletin, for example, on the history of cannabis, says that hemp owns the single honour of being sung in the Vedas for its intoxicating properties. But according to the same bulletin: "It was probably the peoples of Northern Iran who discovered those properties, for they were already using the leaves (cheng) and the resin (chers) as inebriants and narcotics before the Hindus."

In Islamic societies, the consumption of hashish has usually enjoyed an unclear juridical status, especially when compared to alcohol. Religious leaders and rulers have occasionally tried to disincentivise or even prohibit its consumption, but such a ban never enjoyed wide consensus among scholars of Islamic law (see

Franz Rosenthal, The Herb: Hashish versus Islamic Medieval Society, Leiden, E. J. Brill, 1971).

The famous Hanbali scholar Ibn Taymiyya (1263-1328), a precursor of modern Salafism, justified the absence of any mention of hashish in the Quran and in the Sayings of the Prophet and of the First Caliphs by arguing that the substance had only been imported to Muslim countries at a later stage. According to him, it was the Tartars who came with Genghis Khan's armies who spread its use among the Muslim population of the countries the Mongols were invading, in order to debilitate their capacity to resist conquest. Ibn Taymiyya was writing at a time when many Muslim states and societies were struggling to survive the Mongols' onslaught and therefore he may have been biased in his claim, wishing to attribute all the ills of what he perceived as the decadence of the Islamic World to external causes. However, he may have been partially right at least with regards to the provenance of cannabis in the Muslim World, as being the steppes of Central Asia. It is indeed possible that the lords of the steppes, the Turks and Mongols, had inherited cannabis from their predecessors, the Scythians, which they then brought to the cities of Central Asia and Khorasan (the east of the Iranian Plateau covering parts of Afghanistan), where the people engaged in trade and military relations with the nomads. In other writings, Ibn Taymiyya blames the spread of hashish consumption squarely on the Sufis.

In this respect, even the Egyptian historian Al-Maqrizi (1364-1442) recounts a narrative according to which the first to promote the use of cannabis among Muslims was the Sufi sheikh, Qutbuddin Haydar (d.1221). It is unlikely that the use of cannabis was altogether unknown in eastern Muslim countries at such a late stage. Nevertheless, Haydar's association with an early use of cannabis does seem reasonable, at least in Sufi circles because of the fact that he was based in Khorasan, together with his 'brand' of Sufism. Haydar was the founder of the Malamati (blameworthy) Sufi order; these were mystics who despised mainstream piety and lived on the fringes of society. They were not interested in portraying themselves as respectable and thus were often stigmatised. Cannabis was categorised as a 'low-class' drug and its use associated with people living on the street or not moving in the higher echelons of society.

This was already apparent in the misleading etymology, which gave rise to an enduring misrepresentation or 'black legend'[6] about the Hashishiyya or Assassins, popularised in Europe by Marco Polo and a score of other medieval travellers and chroniclers. 'Hashishiyya' was originally meant as a term of common abuse, directed at political adversaries who rebelled against the constituted powers (with the understood meaning of 'low-life' or 'rabble') to disqualify their status. However, it was recorded by western observers of the time as describing the use of drugs to brainwash the adepts of the Nizari Ismailis (those in possession of Alamut, in modern-day Iran, and several other mountain fortresses across the Middle East and Iranian Plateau) and induce them to commit political murders. Thus, was coined a new word adopted by most European languages. (See Daftary, the Assassin Legends: Myths of the Isma'ilis, London, I.B.Tauris, 1994).

As for the effects of cannabis, while many poets and mystics compared its effects, both beneficial and noxious with those of wine, Al-Maqrizi mentions that the original purpose of some Sufis when using cannabis would have been to 'dry out' their semen in order to reduce their sexual impulses and thus be able to better concentrate on God. The exact same alleged effects of cannabis would sometimes be employed, from a specular point of view, by orthodox religious leaders trying to deter believers from its use.

Meanwhile, it seems certain that cannabis was being used at this time in what is now Afghanistan (the lack of written sources does not indicate a lack of use). The founder of the Mughal dynasty, Babur (1483–1530), a noted party-goer and collector of intoxicating substances, described the use of majoun, an edible confection made with a mixture of honey, dates, oil, spices and hashish (or sometimes opium), in his autobiography, Baburnama.[7]

Later, western travellers to Afghanistan in the nineteenth and twentieth centuries made frequent references to the use of cannabis. Elphinstone's Account of the Kingdom of Caubul from 1809 cites the use of bhang – a drink concoction made with hashish, still common in India and Pakistan (the word presumably deriving from the Sanskrit name for cannabis, 'b'hanga'). Masson, in his Narratives from Various Journeys published in 1842 relays an anecdote involving himself and a group of Afghans who put chits [sic] in the chillum of a Baloch chief who was detaining them to exact a road tax in order to make him fall asleep so they could escape. In Ferrier's 1858 The History of Afghans, he noted that Afghans frequently smoked chillums, although he shies away from mentioning what they put into it. There are also a number of sources from early twentieth century literature which offer very occasional references to hashish consumption habits in Afghanistan. (See Chapter 7 "Drug Use in Afghanistan's History" in Macdonald, D., Drugs in Afghanistan, New York, Pluto Press, 2007).

Hashish in the West

In Europe, hashish consumption spread in the nineteenth century. It arrived with Napoleonic soldiers returning from Egypt, who had discovered hashish during their stay there in the late 18th century. Although Napoleon banned both its use and the establishments that sold it in France, the drug would, half a century later, become a source of inspiration for a number of poets and writers. The best-known example is 'Le Club des Hachichins' ('The Club of Hashish Eaters') in mid-nineteenth century Paris, that held regular meetings at the Hôtel Pimodan on the Seine island of St Louis and included members such as Théophile Gauthier (1811–1872), a French novelist, poet and journalist and famous French poet, Charles Baudelaire (1821–1867).[8]

European poetic glorification of hashish continued during the twentieth century. The famous German-Jewish philosopher, Walter Benjamin, for example, conducted a series of experiments with the drug between 1927 and 1934 in Berlin, Marseilles, and Ibiza, together with a group of friends, including philosopher Ernst Bloch and the writer Jean Selz.[9]

Nonetheless, by the late 1920s, close to 60 countries had prohibited hashish

This was in line with a 1925 revision of the League of Nations' International Opium Convention from 1912, which came into force in 1928 (see here). Afghanistan became a member of the League of Nations only in 1934, and ratified the 1925 International Opium Convention in 1944 (see here). Article 11 of the revised Convention said the contracting parties shall undertake:

To prohibit the export of the resin obtained from Indian hemp and the ordinary preparations of which the resin forms the base (such as hashish, esrar, chiras, djamba) to countries which have prohibited their use, and, in cases where export is permitted, to require the production of a special import certificate issued by the Government of the importing country stating that the importation is approved for the purposes specified in the certificate and that the resin or preparations will not be re-exported.

However, the 1925 Convention, in fact imposed only very limited international control. This was mainly because of the ingrained use of hashish in many countries.

After the Second World War, the 'Beat Generation' of writers in the 1950s revitalised the image of cannabis in their fiction. This trend continued through the 1960s. (See this research on treatment of drug usage in some examples of modern English writing, published in the 1971 UN Narcotics Bulletin). The world's legal regime, however, only became stricter after World War Two. The 1961 United Nation's Single Convention on Narcotic Drugs prohibited the cultivation of cannabis, listing it alongside cocaine and heroin (see here).[10]

In the 1960s, despite this firmer global legal stance, the use of cannabis (as well as various other drugs) became so popular that they received an approval in popular music (see this excellent study published in the UN Narcotics Bulletin in 1969 about praise for drug usage in rock and roll music here). By in the late 1960s and early 1970s, drug use had increased so significantly that the topic often appeared on the agenda of the Commission on Narcotic Drugs (see bulletins from 1970, 1971 and 1972 here). The hippie generation was in full swing. It would be this generation of hippies that brought the west to the east, as opposed to the merchants and small businessmen who had been doing this in reverse for centuries.[11] The first-ever published Lonely Planet travel guide from 1973, entitled Across Asia on the Cheap summarised this encounter of the west and the east with anecdote:

We rolled up to the Afghanistan border at Islam Q'ala [in Herat province] and could find no sign of officialdom. Eventually we found a group of rather stoned looking Americans sitting on the floor in one building. 'Where's everyone?' we asked, and got the obvious answer 'gone for lunch'. 'How long have you been here' we asked –'about six hours'. 'Good grief what have you been doing all that time?' – 'blowing a little dope with customs'. Of course.

On Afghan varieties of the plant

After his explorations in Afghanistan in the mid-1920s, Vavilov concluded that the wild Afghan types of hemp "constitute a morphological link between the wild and cultivated races of hemp" (page 112), meaning that the height of the Afghan cannabis plant, as well as the shape and size of its seeds, represented a link between the wild and cultivated varieties. In 1924, during his travels in the Kunar River valley between Jalalabad in Nangrahar province and Cheghasarai [an old name for Asadabad], the capital of Kunar province, Vavilov discovered a peculiar type of wild hemp with "light-coloured, small seeds, thin membranes, slightly splitting and transparent pericarps." This variety he named Cannabis Indica, f. [forma] afghanica. He also referred to this wild type when he wrote of "belts of 'black hemp' emanating from crops of maize and other cereals," that grow along the Kunar River "from Chekhosarai to Djelalabad [sic] for a distance of 150 to 200 verst [165 to 220 kilometres]" (page 109).

Whether Vavilov unintentionally fathered the name of what would almost half a century later become known as Afghan Black, the common contemporary name for the Afghan hashish is a subject of historical speculation. Nevertheless, Vavilov's observations confirmed that farmers who cultivated hemp often collected seeds from wild hemp types to enrich their fields. It is quite possible that this Afghan-specific wild hemp type gradually became cultivated hemp and thus its main product – hashish or chars – became known as 'Afghan Black'. According to Clarke (1998), this is exactly what happened. He found that the first report of hashish produced from Cannabis Indica, f. [forma] afghanica in northern Afghanistan dates from 1965; asserting an implicit explanation of how Vavilov's 'black hemp' came to be known as 'Afghan Black'.

Cannabis cultivation and hashish production in Afghanistan

Afghanistan has a tradition of chars (resin) manufacture using sieving techniques probably dating back to the nineteenth century. Cultivation of cannabis and trade in chars represented a major economic asset for some areas of Afghanistan (Balkh, Khyber and surrounding areas) at the end of the nineteenth and beginning of the twentieth century.

Clarke (1988), for example, says that "hashish from Bukhara in Russian Turkestan [present-day Uzbekistan] was considered by Indian users of the early 1800s to be the highest quality available." The majority of Bukhara hashish was shipped south through Mazar-e Sharif to Kabul in Afghanistan and on to Peshawar in present-day Pakistan. The trade between Russian Turkestan and present-day Pakistan, through Afghanistan, continued through the mid 1860s when Russia extended its territory and influence into Turkestan and changed traditional patterns of hashish production. It is unclear whether Russia officially forbade the production of hashish in Turkestan, but hashish production became less common (Clarke, 1998). In the late 1800s, hashish production shifted from Bukhara (in Uzbekistan) to Yarkand (today's China). Nevertheless, Afghanistan continued to be an important trade route for the hashish produced in Chinese Turkistan, too.

In fact, until 1934 when the Chinese government issued instructions in a circular to the provinces and municipalities for the suppression of Indian hemp (see this UN Narcotics Bulletin from 1953), Afghans were the main traders between British India (especially the Punjab) and Chinese Turkestan, which was a main producer of chars in the region between the mid 1860s and the

1930s. The route passed from Yarkand and Kashgar through Hunza or through Wakhan. After the Chinese government ban, Afghans gradually started producing their own chars in export quantities.

However, according to the Indian government's annual reports from 1942 and 1944, mentioned in this 1953 UN Narcotics Bulletin this chars was "heavily adulterated" with tobacco, catechu (an extract from acacia trees) and honey, or it was "garda chars (chars of an inferior quality)." The Indian government's 1945 report said:

Garda chars. This inferior quality of chars is prepared by various artificial means from the hemp plant growing wild in mountainous regions... Cases of smuggling [it] into the North West Frontier Province and Baluchistan from Gardez in Afghanistan were quite common during the year.

As consumption in British India dwindled towards the late 1940s, so the story of Afghan chars production disappeared from historical records.

Cannabis cultivation and hashish production from the 1970s until today

The global legal regime changed after the Second World War and although Afghanistan signed a new convention, the UN Single Convention of Narcotic Drugs in March 1961 and ratified it March 1963, there are very few historical records about cultivation levels in the country in the 1960s. Even after the Single Convention of Narcotic Drugs entered into force in December 1964, Afghanistan reporting to the UN continued to be irregular and erratic.

Nevertheless, according to other sources, during the 1970s production and export of Afghan chars expanded beyond traditional markets. The European Monitoring Centre for Drugs and Drug Addiction study on cannabis production and markets in Europe found that the production of cannabis resin in Afghanistan, as in Nepal and Pakistan, began to change in this decade:

From a cottage industry geared to supplying local and neighbouring long-standing 'traditional' markets, it became a commercial enterprise orientated towards large-scale exportation, especially to

Europe and North America. As a result, Afghanistan, along with Pakistan and Lebanon, became a major supplier of cannabis resin to Europe for a period of about ten years before the large-scale arrival of Moroccan resin in the early 1980s and the concomitant expansion of European consumer markets.

In 1973, Afghanistan's King Zahir Shah outlawed cannabis production, following it up with a genuine commitment to eradication – backed by 47 million USD in funding from the United States government. However, a US cable from the same year detailing the involvement of King Zahir's personal valet in an attempt to smuggle 40 kilograms of hashish oil to the US is an illustration of how difficult it was for Afghanistan to start its anti-drug trafficking operations.

Afghanistan's general cultivation and production levels in the 1970s are matter of guesswork, as the country only occasionally reported to the UN. Cables published by Wikileaks offer some statistical overview of the estimated production which, they say, varied between 150 to 400 metric tonnes between about 1975 and 1979. For example, a US cable on narcotics from November 1977 reported that the year's production may fall short of the 1976 production estimated at 200 to 400 metric tonnes. The report said that preliminary data showed that in 1977 Paktia province produced 12 metric tonnes; Logar 15 tonnes; Ghazni three tonnes; Samangan 1.5 tonnes; Balkh two tonnes; Jawzjan three tonnes; Faryab 4.5 tonnes and; Badghis 5.5 tonnes. In 1979, the US estimated that the year's production was at the same level as production in 1976.

There is almost no data about cultivation and production levels in the 1980s. According to Macdonald, the Soviet invasion of Afghanistan meant that areas under cannabis cultivation shifted each year to avoid the ongoing war (Macdonald, pp 193). It also meant that many fields that had been abandoned because most of the local population had become refugees in Pakistan were now available for growing cannabis. Thus, for example, in parts of Logar land was rented from absent owners by sharecroppers from Sayyed Karam district in Paktia; they greatly expanded cannabis cultivation, expanding it to cover more than 50 per cent of all the agricultural lands of Azra district and up to 80 per cent of those of the Dubandi Valley of Khoshi district. The European Monitoring Centre for Drugs and Drug Addiction study on the supply of hashish to Europe also quoted Howard Marks, a published English drug trafficker, who:

> ... mentioned how, "the dope supplies in [...] Afghanistan had almost dried up when the Russians took their tanks to Kabul in 1980" and how the millions of refugees that ended up in Pakistan's North West Frontier Province helped develop the production of what became known in the West as "border hash" (Marks, 1998: 249- 250).

The Russian soldiers themselves constituted a prime recipient for Afghanistan's hashish production: in one of the lanes of Kabul's KhairKhana neighbourhood, aptly re-named Sarak-e Russ-ha (Russians' Street), they would engage in petty trade with locals and one of the most sought-after items to barter Red Army supplies for, was chars. The Taleban regime in the mid-1990s focused on stopping cannabis cultivation and introduced draconian sanctions on cultivators (Macdonald, pp 25, 193). It is difficult to assess how successful these measures were, as there is no data on cannabis cultivation or production levels for the 1990s. The UNODC first reported on cannabis cultivation well after the fall of the Taleban regime in Afghanistan, in 2005, when it estimated that around 30,000 hectares were under cannabis cultivation in 22 out of the 32 provinces in the country.

Since 2001, three counter-narcotics laws have been adopted in Afghanistan (see this AAN's analysis); each of them banned cannabis cultivation and prescribed penalties for it. The first, adopted in 2005, was drafted with the support of the UK, the then-lead donor nation on counter-narcotics. The second law was adopted in 2010 and aimed to address levels of both opium and cannabis cultivation. The most recent revision of the law began in 2015 to address a gap in criminal provisions related to synthetic drugs, the production and consumption of which had become more widespread in the country and was passed by the Parliament in 201. It again criminalised cannabis cultivation and hashish production, trafficking and consumption.

The first detailed estimates of cannabis harvests and hashish production in Afghanistan were carried out in 2009 by UNODC. It reported that between 10,000 and 24,000 hectares of cannabis were grown in Afghanistan every year and estimated that between 1,500 and 3,500 metric tonnes of hashish were produced a year. UNODC also said that in the late 2000s and early 2010s, hashish production declined in Morocco and resumed in both Afghanistan and Lebanon; it reported that Afghanistan was the biggest hashish producer in the world. Nevertheless, this statement has been questioned by some authors and organisations. For example, the European Monitoring Centre for Drugs and Drug Addiction study on the supply of hashish to Europe offers an in-depth analysis of UNODC data and statements. "Moroccan hashish," concluded its 2011 study, "remained the most consumed resin [on European markets]."

In 2012, UNDOC somewhat changed its methodology and reported that there were 12,000 hectares of mono-cropped commercial cannabis crops that year with a potential production of 1,300 metric tonnes of hashish. The 2012 cannabis survey was the last such survey carried out in Afghanistan. There has been no systematic data on cannabis cultivation or hashish production in Afghanistan since 2012.

Although cannabis is an indigenous plant to Afghanistan and its region, it was not until the late nineteenth/early twentieth century that Afghanistan started producing chars for export mainly to markets in then-British India. Although consumption there dwindled in the late 1940s, the production and export of Afghan chars saw a 'renaissance' in the 1970s as its reach expanded beyond traditional markets to Europe. This expansion of the Afghan export market coincided with a general popularisation of hashish in modern culture and popular music, globally – with hippies as a hallmark of it. The hippies were also the bridge between relatively new western cultural narratives on hashish emanating from nineteenth and twentieth century poetry, literature and philosophy and the ancient ones of the east.

The name 'Afghan Black' may have originated with Russian botanist Vavilov, who, in 1924 named Afghan cannabis the 'black hemp' because it grew 'blackly' among crops of maize and other cereals. Whether or not it did, it was the hippies who popularised the 'brand' of 'Afghan Black'. Among Afghans, the use of their own product has increased significantly during the last 40 years of conflict, as will be explored in the second dispatch in this series, which looks at the cultural history of consumption of 'Afghan Black' in Afghanistan. It is a rich, contradictory, sometimes poetic and sometimes bitter tale.

Hashish or chars is a fairly common substance in Afghanistan. Its use, without ever attaining the levels of mass consumption that characterise other lightly-intoxicating substances in other war-torn countries, like the chewing of qat in Yemen or Somalia, for example, has remained relatively widespread. This does not mean that it is condoned by society: hashish-users, known as charsi, are stigmatised in popular discourse as lazy or even unhinged. However, the use of hashish in Afghanistan has also acquired an element of communal ritual, allowing sometimes for a different depiction of hashish-smokers to emerge, one more acceptable to dominant Afghan values and traditions. In this dispatch, AAN's Obaid Ali, Fabrizio Foschini and Jelena Bjelica look at the cultural history of hashish in Afghanistan.This is the second dispatch in a two-part series on the cultural history of hashish in Afghanistan. The first dispatch, which looks at the cultivation and production of hashish, is available here.

Although opiates have understandably dominated the discourse around drug use in Afghanistan (read AAN analysis here and here) over the past decades, hashish has long been a mainstay of recreational drugs throughout the country. In fact, its use has traditionally been more widespread than that of opium (which was once widely consumed, often as a form of self-medication in places such as Badakhshan or Herat). Nowadays, the number of hashish smokers has increased to over a million users and has spread among the young and educated class in urban areas.

Afghans' familiarity with hashish is also quite apparent from its references in Afghan folklore. There are, however, different perceptions of hashish-smokers in society. Arguably, an ordinary Afghan could smoke an occasional spliff in order to relax and still keep his social status untainted more easily than if he consumed alcohol or opiates (the social stigma for women consuming any drugs, including alcohol, would be far higher). Even so, regular smokers get the rather nasty label of charsi. The social stigma attached to smoking hash seems to stem less from the illegality of the substance, than from the real or imagined effects it provokes. Hashish smokers have a reputation for being rascals and criminals.

Use of hashish in Afghanistan from the 1970s until today

The use of hashish in Afghanistan from the 1970s to the mid 2000s is not well-documented. Sources from the 1970s, such as the US 1974 cables (here and here) offer rare insights into local habits. However, these documents mainly portray an official narrative, ie the Afghan government blaming local consumption on "the bad example of youthful western tourists." In another cable, also from 1974, the Afghan government informed its American counterpart there had been no indications of significant 'abuse' of the drug by Afghans themselves. In this 1975 cable the US reported that "GOA [the Government of Afghanistan] does not, however believe there to be an urban drug abuse problem with exception of foreigner transients." The cable said that, "Widespread traditional use of hashish is either overlooked, ignored or not seen as constituting a problem." The post-1978 coup State Department's annual narcotics report on Afghanistan said that between "150 and 250 metric tons of hashish per year is derived from locally cultivated cannabis," while the "statistics on drug abuse within Afghanistan are virtually non-existent."

In the 1980s, during the anti-Soviet jihad, the use of cannabis spread. Former United Nations Office on Drugs and Crime (UNODC) drug advisor in Afghanistan David Macdonald in his book Drugs in Afghanistan writes that "many mujahideen fighters were paid or rewarded for their fighting with hashish, which they often consumed before going to the battle." Macdonald was told this by Mullah Akhundzada, the then-head of the Taleban High Commission for Drug Control, at a meeting held in 1999. Hashish consumption has long since been connected to the primary actors of this conflict. The use of chars by some notorious Kandahari commanders and their militiamen was associated with the loss of all moral order and breakdown of social rules that characterised the Civil War of 1992-94 there and in many other parts of the country. Even more recently, the age-old connection between the use of hashish and fighting has not been denied. Policemen (both ANP and ALP) in particular have been known to consume hashish, especially when left stranded to man isolated and remote security outposts. The Afghanistan Ministry of Interior (MoI) conducted nationwide urinary drug screening of Afghanistan National Police (ANP) in 2009 and 2010, which found that of the 9,034 ANP who tested positive for drug use, 80.5% (7,269) screened for tetrahydrocannabinol (THC), a psychoactive constituent of cannabis. (1) The 40 years of continuous wars in Afghanistan undeniably contributed to an increase in drug use, not only of hashish but of others too (see this AAN dispatch on drug use in Afghanistan here).

During the Taleban regime, hashish was perceived as a 'traditional Afghan vice', as its use was widespread and an old habit among parts of the population. The Taleban imposed "draconian sanctions against both producers and users" (Macdonald, pp 25). In 1997, the Taleban issued a statement, which said that the use of hashish and heroin was not permitted in Islam (Macdonald, pp 80). These measures, however, were not particularly enforced. In 2003, a UNODC assessment on problem drug users in Kabul city, Macdonald reported, found that almost 24,000 people were regular hashish users, as reported by doctors, mullahs, shopkeepers and other key informants. But this number, according to him, was incorrect and probably an underestimate due to a lack of data and limitations of the UNODC assessment.

The latest Afghan drug use survey carried out in 2015 by the United States Bureau of International Narcotics and Law Enforcement Affairs (INL) found that approximately 900,000 to 1.1 million Afghans use cannabis. The survey also found that cannabis is the second most prevalent drug used in urban centres in the country, with the highest rates of cannabis use in Herat (4.0 per cent of the population) and Kabul (3.9 per cent). Cannabis, the INL survey found, is used by 2.4 per cent of the adult population, with men being the predominant users. Evidence of cannabis among women and children was negligible, the survey found. Smoking charsis almost entirely a male pastime, then. Before looking at how hashish is viewed in Afghanistan, it is worth stressing that its use is not an entirely 'happy' phenomenon, a point Macdonald makes (p26):

Western sensibilities and perception of cannabis often neglect the fact that the hashish produced in Afghanistan is often more powerful than much of the hashish available in Europe, and daily consumption rates among Afghan users significantly higher than their western counterparts. Reports suggest that hashish use in such an impoverished country as Afghanistan contributes to severe financial problems for the family, leads to arguments and fights among family members over money spent on drugs and exacerbates endemic health problems such as bronchitis, pneumonia, tuberculosis and other respiratory complaints.

Hashish to suit different tastes and budgets

Afghan hashish is found on sale in different varieties, which largely refer to where it was produced and also define its quality and price. Balkh and Panjshir provinces are famous for their high-quality chars, known as shirak. Their hashish, compared to that in other parts of the country, is also more expensive. Northern Balkh province has for some decades been home to the most famous type of Afghan hashish: the so-called 'Afghan Black' of international renown largely coincides with the hashish produced in this area. Over the course of the last few years, however, Shirak-e Panjshir has become the most sought-after and expensive product on the Afghan market, with seven grams fetching a price of 250 Afghanis (around 3,5 USD). Shirak-e Panjshir has a peculiar green hue and a very strong smell and easily melts in the cigarette or chillum. Among those who smoke it, Balkh now ranks second in the chars'varieties in Afghanistan. Shirak-e Mazar is the most famous type of hashish originating from this province: it is of a dark brown colour and has a pungent smell. Compared to Shirak-e Panjshir, its effects are less strong and therefore it is comparatively cheaper (7g for 200 Afs). Kandahar and Logar[2] provinces provide products of a relatively lower quality that rank in third place. Both provinces produce chars of a black-colour, which is found in the market for the relatively cheap price of 150 Afghanis for seven grams. The 'best price' product available to consumers without much money to spend is that coming from Nangrahar province: it sells at 100 Afghanis for seven grams and is also the lowest quality chars on the Afghan market.

Besides commercial production, habitual charsis sometimes produce home-made chars for their own consumption. In Kabul, for instance, there are a number of mini-production factories that only produce small amounts of chars. Basically, hemp is cultivated in the house courtyard, usually in a corner of the garden that remains out of sight of potential guests or neighbours. Once the bush grows enough and its blossoms have dried, it is cut off and dried. This process takes at least six months. Once it is dry, then the dried blossom is removed, and it goes through a filtering process in order to collect the particles and pieces of dried blossom. The collected parts are then slowly warmed up over a fire and mixed together for around ten minutes. The preparation turns into an oily substance and is pressed together into a piece of chars.

Hashish in Afghan popular culture

Hashish is an established topic in popular Afghan culture, being the subject of many jokes and songs.[3] The most famous hit about hashish is probably the Pashto classic folk song "Adam Khana Charsi", performed by many singers throughout the years (here in a rendition by Naghma). Written in the tradition of landai women's poetry (read also here), the lyrics lambast Adam Khan's lack of virility, enjoining him to remove his bed from the nuptial chamber to the courtyard as his wife is not interested only in sleeping, as he seems to be. From the title of the song to the mimicry usually enacted by singers who perform it (see also this video), the figure of Adam Khan is a stereotype of the chronic hashish-smoker, apathetic and lethargic.

In fact, one of the effects most frequently associated with the use of hashish in Afghan popular belief in the reduction of the sexual impulse and thus of the inability of a man to fulfil a husband's obligations thereby securing his progeny. As these are issues of some importance in the eyes of the Afghans, the inculcation of this notion by society at large can well represent an attempt to discourage the use of hashish through psychological propaganda. Interestingly, the same fears had already been raised by medieval Islamic scholars in order to deter believers from indulging in hashish smoking (although some ascetics actually sought a reduction of their sexual urge through smoking, in order to better concentrate on spiritual matters).

Compounding the apathy it induces, hashish is also said to provoke fits of rage and madness, making charsis extremely aggressive at times. The term charsi can thus be used in Afghanistan to refer to anybody who behaves over the top, arguing, bragging or boasting to the point of appearing out of his mind. This is partly due to the long-term impact of cannabis: cannabinoids lodge in the fatty deposits of the brain and remain there for weeks, unlike alcohol or many other drugs, which the body excretes rapidly through urine. The effects of the drug are therefore longer-term and can appear to affect a person's character or personality. This can give regular hashish smokers a recognisable appearance and attitude, which has given rise to a stereotype applied to other people as well, as a way of slighting them. Overall, Afghans view hashish-smokers as generally being socially useless. However, there seem to be niches of popular discourse in which the charsis are not just criminals or despicable characters but a peculiar class of people, noted for their generosity and with their own sociability. In some parts of the country, this tradition seems to still be alive.

In the chillumkhana of Baba Qu

Ways of smoking chars in Afghanistan indicate a rural-urban divide, slowly bridging towards a standardisation of practices by young people countrywide. While urban hash smokers generally prefer a to empty a cigarette and fill it with hashish and tobacco (with youngsters developing creative ways of smoking bongs, such as piercing holes in an apple to inhale the smoke through it) – the rural, and, arguably traditional, way of consuming hashish still practiced by the elderly is through an earthen pipe or chillum. This can sometimes take the form of a collective act, one more sociable and ritualised than sharing a joint among friends, as will be seen in the most famous of all Afghan chillum-smokers, Baba Qu-ye Mastan.

Baba Qu, a figure who lived in the first half of the twentieth century and whose historical persona borders on the mythical, still inspires a form of mystical devotion. He is buried in the ancient town of Balkh of the namesake province, and is still remembered across northern Afghanistan as a generous and chivalrous man, who would always provide lavish hospitality of food and chars to anyone in need. Even today, when local charsis light their cigarettes or chillum filled with chars, they first praise Baba Qu:

> Baba Qu-ye Mastan
>
> Your grave is a flower garden
>
> Be it summer or winter

When charsis being smoked collectively and the cigarette or chillum passes from one person to another, smokers repeat this invocation:

Pass on; pass on to the brave youngsters, death to those who hate.

(The word parah describes the act of passing a cigarette or chillum filled with chars from one person to another).

After Baba Qu's death, his fellow charsis built what is known as the chillumkhana (chillum-house) or saqikhana next to his grave.[4]This is a small building consisting of a main hall, very dark and with a low ceiling, furnished with stone-made benches lining the inner walls. There are several chillums available in the room and a caretaker in charge of filling and lighting them. The rules of the chillumkhana are clear: whoever gets inside has to smoke and failing to do so would be disrespectful. Visitors are welcome to contribute with offers of money or chars – provided they have a good batch, for in the chillumkhana only top-quality Shirak-e Mazar is used. If they do not wish or cannot afford to contribute, this is no problem: they get to smoke for free, but most importantly they have to smoke and pay a tribute to Baba Qu. At any rate, inside the chillumkhana the air is saturated with the fumes of burning hemp: all the windows and doors are kept shut and there is no fresh air circulating, augmenting the effects on the smokers. This way of smoking is called shishaband or darwazaband (closed-window/door).

Seeking solace in Kandahar

Baba Qu-e Mastan was by no means an isolated instance. A senior teacher in Kabul recalled how in the time of Zaher Shah, when he had been posted to a school in Spin Boldak, he would go on days off together with his colleagues to the place of Zabar Ali Padsha in Khadanay, roughly halfway between Spin Boldak and Kandahar city. Zabar Ali was an elderly man who had never married and had a big guesthouse with many servants devoted only to providing guests with chillums filled with the best-quality hashish. He was apparently well-off, or received sumptuous donations from the more affluent guests, because he would attend to his guests' needs for whole evenings, not only offering them a smoke, but even having lambs slaughtered and cooked to feed them when, later in the night, they would go hungry. After some years of such visits, having become well acquainted with Zabar Ali, the teacher was astonished to see the old man, by now over ninety years old, performing a series of gymnastic exercises that would have put to shame a circus acrobat. Zabar Ali attributed his body strength to his still being a virgin, something he confessed to his friend, the teacher, and to his steadfast use of only the best quality hashish.

A more recent character familiar to many Kandaharis – Mrech Agha – has taken the place of Zabar Ali Padsha. In his guesthouse outside Kandahar city, until quite recently, Mr Chili Pepper, as his name translates, would host whoever wanted to enjoy a joint, assisted by a small army of servants and volunteers. Mrech Agha assiduously held his darbar (court),[5] utterly indifferent to the fierce battles being fought between first, the mujahedin, then between the Taleban and government forces, until his death in 2014. Mrech Agha was for a long time a local celebrity. Taxi drivers in Kandahar would sport placards with poetry praising his goodness, something along the lines of: "This person is good, that one is also good, but I salute Mrech Agha!" (A video of a Pashto song praising Mrech Agha here.)

After his death, a tense standoff took place at his home. His eldest son, feeling he could not step into his father's large shoes, summoned all the assistants and announced he was dismissing them, as he would have to discontinue his late father's habit of providing hospitality to half of Kandahar's charsis because of the costs it entailed. Mrech Agha, however had two wives, the son being born from the first one. Reportedly, at the critical moment, the other, younger wife, summoned him and enjoined him not to dismiss the house-servants, "not to destroy Mrech Agha's langar (refectory)": she herself would provide whatever economic means was required in order to continue her late husband's enterprise. Thus, she showed the same resolve as Malalai on the battlefield of Maiwand, even if the cause was not quite so noble.

The role played by figures such as Baba Qu, Zabar Ali and Mrech Agha sit somewhere between that of a private entertainer – with all the ideas of individual hospitality that that entails – and that of an institution which offers a service to the public at large. The idea of making a langar is obviously connected to the practice of providing food for everybody attending a religious ceremony or festival, common to Islamic communities across Central and South Asia, and often, but not exclusively, connected to Sufi brotherhoods. More significant than showing a connection in terminology between this type of hosts and the sphere of Sufi mysticism is the fact that Mrech Agha's assistants came to call themselves his muridan, which translates closely into 'disciples' and is a term used quite exclusively for the followers of a Sufi tariqa or 'brotherhood'. It is also possible to listen to a tarana (in the context of southern Afghanistan, a mostly vocal song often dealing with religious topics) sung by the muridan of Mrech Agha.

Baba Qu himself had reportedly been the disciple of a famous Sufi leader in Balkh. Also, marginality and eccentricity in Afghanistan are seldom allowed to totally develop as such, as a sort of counter-culture in open opposition to the established social order. Thus, these 'social charsis' have developed their own sub-culture and gatherings in the shadow of some holy shrines. Notable individuals among them were connected to these or followed established patterns of networking and symbolic codes in order to achieve some degree of public recognition.

But what is the purpose of such a social institution, then? The comparison to Sufi spirituality can again be useful. The latter, as described by scholars of Afghan history such as Robert Edwards or Nile Green (6), has often been enjoyed by Afghan men in order to transcend boundaries of kinship and fulfil the universal human need for avenues of social and spiritual engagement, detached from the strife and tensions of everyday life. At another level – and for different kinds of souls – this peculiar type of hashish-smoking gathering may have served the same primary purpose.

Other invocations uttered routinely by Afghan smokers point to this therapeutic aspect of the use of cannabis:

Nushnush, dehkegham-et faramush

Smoke, smoke, come on so that you may forget your sorrow

Or the more caustic:

Nushnush, dushmanha-et kus-forush

Smoke, smoke, your enemies are just pimps

By allowing Afghan men to fraternise beyond divisions of class, ethnicity or tribe, characters like Mrech Agha may have played an important role in allowing Afghans not to lose their humanity amid the havoc of a lifelong conflict.

Conclusion

In the West, for hash users at least, Afghan chars have acquired something of the status of a legend: 'Afghan Black' has a reputation as a potent psychoactive drug, as seen in the first dispatch in this mini-series. Afghan experiences and views of hashish use are quite different. Most respectable Afghans continue to consider charsis a useless and marginal category of people. Nonetheless, the great number of Afghan hashish smokers may show, instead, the growing strains affecting many strata of beleaguered Afghan society. From soldiers to students, many seek solace in a puff of smoke. That they are almost all men shows something about who can access such solace and points to costs paid by wives and children if limited household income is 'misspent' by husbands and fathers. Even so, it can also be recognised that the charsi subculture also has its legends and rituals, and that these connect to the great Afghan values of generosity and hospitality, and to music, poetry and Sufism.

Courtesy: The Afghanistan Analysts Network (AAN) is an independent non-profit policy research organisation. It aims to bring together the knowledge, experience and drive of a large number of experts to better inform policy and to increase the understanding of Afghan realities. It is driven by engagement and curiosity and is committed to producing analysis on Afghanistan and its region, which is independent, of high quality and research-based. Our aim is to be bi-taraf but not bi-tafawut – impartial, but not indifferent. Since its establishment in 2009 AAN's publications have informed and influenced the work of policymakers, journalists, academics and development workers working on Afghanistan. AAN's analysts are regularly asked to speak at conferences and briefings around the world, and frequently appear as commentators in the media. Unless specifically stated otherwise, all material on this site was created, authored and/or prepared by AAN. AAN's material is licensed under

Chapter 4

Money Laundering, Terrorist Financing, and Hawala's Damage to the Afghan Economy

Michael Kelvington

Killing terrorists is not all about kinetic strikes, area clearances, and pinpoint raids. Terrorist organizations must be pressured in every aspect of their organization's lifeblood. Attacking their coffers, often referred to as "counter-threat financing," or CTF, is a key aspect of hurting terrorists from growing future capabilities and preventing future high profile attacks. A key method terrorist organizations manage to accomplish their financial business is by laundering money through many different venues and exploiting local "cash crops," a term used loosely in a place like Afghanistan, where it could mean poppy and marijuana, or marble mines, timber, and lapis stones. However, while terrorist organizations benefit from money laundering, the more serious aspect of this issue continues to be its epidemic hindering of the economic growth and sustainability of the government of Afghanistan; and the hawala system is the primary liability.

Money laundering, including the financing of terrorism, along with drug trade, criminal activity, and corruption, is devastating Afghanistan's already weak economy. The 2015 GDP for the country of Afghanistan was only $19.33 billion.[1] With an economy suffering from a deficit in balance of trade of -$7.1 billion and current account of over -$4.8 billion[2], the last thing their economy needs is a rampant money laundering epidemic where illicit and often untraceable "dirty money" freely flows, further frustrating the economic instability of Afghanistan.[3] A Ministry of Finance report indicated "only 35 percent of the financial flows within the country are legal."[4]

The main culprit is the hawala system, "an important informal institution . . . handling both financial transfers and currency exchange."[5] If the U.S. wants to help Afghanistan stabilize its economy and attack terrorists' financial lifeblood, it must work with its government to develop an action plan to implement "a fully functioning banking system . . . sensitive to the needs of an emerging licit economy."[6] Providing full visibility of money transfers would allow the government to manage money demand, interest rates, levy taxes and duties, and provide long-term stability for the Afghan economy and legitimacy to its government, all the while cutting off a key element of the CTF efforts against the Taliban, ISIS-K, and Al-Qaeda.

Money laundering is a widespread problem plaguing even well-functioning, developed countries. To portray how much of issue money laundering is globally, the International Monetary Fund in 2008 estimated the annual amount of "dirty money" laundered worldwide was "about $1.8 trillion,"[7] or the equivalent of 10 percent of U.S. GDP. The cycle of money laundering happens in many forms, but occurs through a basic three-stage process including placement, layering, and integration.[8] The first stage, placement, is where terrorists and criminals move the cash from its original form and attempt to process it in such a way that it can then be "blended" into other forms of currency (ex. drug money, black tar opium, lumber, precious stones). In doing so, they separate the original source of income from the criminal act committed to acquire the asset.[9]

The second, and most complicated, step of the money laundering cycle is layering. During this stage, the illegal actor disguises the trail of the source of illicit income to prevent any domestic or international legal or law enforcement body to pursue the assets, freeze funds, or make arrests affiliated with the "black money."[10] During this phase, the illegal money is "washed" to move it from the black to the "white," or clean, side of the economy by passing through the layered "gray zone." The illegal actors can then bypass any legal monitoring and governments' ability to enforce customs or taxes on the import/export, charge exchange fees, and track the influx of money moving in and out of its economy. This not only complicates the counterterrorist and law enforcement's ability to enforce the law against the illegal activity, but also destabilizes economies, especially already weak ones such as Afghanistan.

The third stage, integration, completes the cycle by "making the money available to the criminal, once again, with its occupational and geographic origins hidden from view."[11] The money can then be appropriated for both legal and illegal activity by criminals, terrorists, smugglers, and corrupt officials alike. The easiest method to accomplish money laundering in countries with weak and sparse banking institutions in the Muslim world is the hawala system.

The Arabic word hawala means "change or transform and those who provide the services are known as hawaladars. In the 1990s, the Taliban regime replaced the formal banking system with the hawala market.[12] Today, the hawala system in Afghanistan is a covert means to move terrorist funds, however, it also serves as the "most effective, reliable, and sometime sole method for moving funds across the country,"[13] because most rural Afghans do not have access to the central banking, specifically outside Kabul. An international anti-money-laundering organization known as the Financial Action Task Force estimates "more than half of all transactions in Afghanistan involve hawala brokers."[14] Not all hawala transactions are for illicit activity, but based on the volume, its lack of centralized oversight, and limited monitoring, it is difficult for the economy of Afghanistan to properly maintain sound monetary policy.

Despite 18 years of international involvement, vast amounts of cash flow cannot be regulated by the government, or even taxed in most cases.[15] In 2015, estimates place Afghanistan's illicit economy activity at $1 billion, which includes "drug trafficking, smuggling, unregulated trade, and fraud in procurement contracts [that] are encumbering the country's economic development and funding the terrorist groups that undermine its stability."[16] The opium economy in Afghanistan is worth approximately "$1.5 billion, or around seven percent of the country's GDP."[17] While there are many other factors afflicting the Afghanistan government and economy including security issues, corruption, smuggling, opium as a cash crop, and unaccommodating neighbouring nation-states, the hawala system must be addressed if the Afghanistan government and the U.S.-led NATO efforts will ever see its economy stabilize and its resident terrorist organizations financially chocked out.

Due to the destructive effects the hawala system has on the Afghanistan economy, the government and advisors from the international community should consider adopting multiple policy changes for Afghanistan reconstruction efforts. First, integrating and eventually replacing the hawala system with a centralized banking system will assist the Afghan government with stabilizing a volatile economy. Over the years since September 11, 2001, the Afghan government "continues efforts to increase revenues by improving revenue administration and enforcement and broadening the tax base . . . essential for achieving fiscal sustainability, delivering priority development expenditures and a reduction in aid dependency."[18] This cannot be accomplished when the country relies upon an informal system that largely still exists outside the government's control. It also adds a level of accountability and transparency to the Afghan government, still plagued by accusations of corruption, real and perceived.

If the U.S. does not assist the Afghan government in preventing the hawala system to exist, largely unchecked, "money laundering can erode the integrity of a nation's financial institutions. Due to the high integration of capital markets, money laundering can also adversely affect currencies and interest rates."[19] One of the biggest constraints to private sector development continues to be high interest rates, currently set at 15%, largely due to high inflation and risk premiums. The high interest rates "could jeopardize the growth of the nascent financial sustainability of the private sector."[20] To promote growth, the U.S. must assist the Afghans in converting the informal hawala system into a part of the legitimate banking system of the state. In addition to the adverse effects money laundering can have on Afghanistan's currency, it "can increase the threat of monetary instability due to the misallocation of resources from artificial distortions in asset and commodity prices."[21] In the long run, shifting Afghans away from the hawala system will take time and effort, but is necessary for economic stability.

Second, addressing the hawala system will help stabilize the economy by isolating and obstructing terrorist financing and corrupt government officials. This action will legitimize their economy while also reducing the funding available for insurgent and terrorist activities continuing to erode the security of the country. These illegal activities ultimately reduce the production possibility frontier of the country and limits foreign direct investment because of the high level of risk involved for investors and those interested in private sector growth and development. This reform would have a cross-cutting effect that would not only benefit the Afghan economy but also our counterterrorism and counternarcotics efforts with our partners in the country and region.

Third, corruption, which remains rampant in the Afghan government, must be more severely addressed. Based on the findings in the 2016 Special Inspector General for Afghanistan Reconstruction report on the Afghanistan High Office of Oversight, an institution created in the summer of 2008 to "combat corrupt practices within the government" remains largely inept and ineffective in holding corrupt officials accountable for illegal actions.[22] Eliminating the hawala system would be a productive measure in reducing corruption and CTF by taking away a key input into the corruption deeply nested in the Afghanistan government, which ranked a horrific 11 out of 100 on the 2015 Corruption Perceptions Index reported by Transparency International.[23] Abolishing the hawala system would obstruct corrupt officials from participating in illegal activity and force them to move assets above the table rather than below it.

Fourth, money laundering leads to a significant loss in tax revenue. This "indirectly harms honest taxpayers . . . [and] makes government tax collection more difficult. This loss of revenue generally means higher tax rates than would normally be the case if the untaxed proceeds of crime were legitimate."[24] The country suffers from a GDP per capita income of $624 per year (only 5% of the world's average), a 40% unemployment rate, a 20% corporate and personal income rate, and a 10% sales tax.[25] It is no wonder many Afghans are frustrated, and potentially radicalized, against a highly corrupt and inept government taking a large percentage of their measly income while many in the higher, more connected class enjoy under the table deals with hardly any oversight or accountability.

Overall, the Afghan government's inability to properly address the hawala system as an informal means of cash flow "may result in inexplicable changes in money demand and increased volatility of international capital flows, interest, and exchange rates. The unpredictable nature of money laundering, coupled with the attendant loss of policy control, may make sound economic policy difficult to achieve."[26] Pragmatically and culturally, eliminating the hawala system will be a long, expensive, and emotional endeavour.

However, it is a lynchpin to stabilizing the Afghanistan economy, reducing terror and criminal influence on its population, preventing corruption in the government and eroding its legitimacy, and promoting growth. Reformation of their banking system, including the hawala transactions, could eventually lead to economic independence without the reliance on external donors to keep its economy and government afloat. It is a long-term venture well worth its eventual return on investment, both for their domestic economic situation and our own national security interests.

Small Wars Journal facilitates the exchange of information among practitioners, thought leaders, and students of Small Wars, in order to advance knowledge and capabilities in the field. We hope this, in turn, advances the practice and effectiveness of those forces prosecuting Small Wars in the interest of self-determination, freedom, and prosperity for the population in the area of operations. Small war journal, 2005-2018, Small Wars Journal is published by Small Wars Foundation-a 501(c)(3) non-profit corporation. Original content is published under a Creative Commons License per our Terms of Use. Major Mike Kelvington grew up in Akron, Ohio. He is an Infantry officer in the U.S. Army with eleven deployments to Iraq and Afghanistan, including with the 75th Ranger Regiment.

Chapter 5

War on Drugs for Peace in Afghanistan: Lessons from South America

By SADF

Trafficking of opiates as a means to finance armed conflicts in Afghanistan dates back to the Jihadists' fight against the Soviet invasion in the 1980s. This policy brief is based on finding a way to eliminate the repercussions of this drug economy both in Afghanistan and in the drug destination countries in the so-called 'West'. The paper uses the similarly situated conflict between the FARC rebel group and the Colombian government as an inspiration for approaches to peace in Afghanistan. It argues, based on an analysis of the development of illicit crop cultivation in both Afghanistan and Colombia that Afghan farmers are most likely to be encouraged to cultivate food crops instead of opium poppy, the base plant for opium and heroin, when the profit margins of opium remain consistently low. The paper further asserts that a comprehensive rural reform as well as a voluntary crop substitution scheme, as stipulated by the 2016 FARC peace agreement with the Colombian government, is feasible to be implemented also in Afghanistan.

Moreover, the policy brief puts a focus on how the West, as a major market for Afghan heroin, can help the situation in the country. Using the 2013 cannabis legalisation regulations in Uruguay and other cutting-edge approaches to drug use, the paper encourages

Western nations to experiment with national measures aimed at reducing the adverse effects of drug consumption while at the same time reducing demand in black-market narcotics. It is suggested that implementing such legislation would help drain profits from transnational drug syndicates and sustainably decrease the profit margins of illicit crops, such as opium poppy.

Introduction

Dating back long before the current armed conflict, Islamist insurgents in Afghanistan have been relying heavily on funds extracted from opiate trafficking. In view of this deeply rooted practice, the first part of this paper will analyse the interdependencies between armed struggle and opium cultivation as well as drug trafficking in Afghanistan over the past four decades – from the Jihadist resistance against the Soviet invasion, through the 1990s civil war to the Taliban insurgency of the present. This policy brief follows the opinion of those who consider that peace in Afghanistan also requires an end to the drug trafficking network which finances the current conflict. To explore approaches to this objective, we regard the South American reality – although obviously different in many features, nonetheless, with some interesting points of contact – as an apt source of inspiration for the policy to be followed in Afghanistan.

Therefore, the second part of this paper aims to analyse how far lessons from the peace agreement between the Colombian government and the FARC rebels from November 2016 has the potential to be applied to the current conflict in Afghanistan. It will focus on the sections of the Colombian peace deal regarding illicit crops and drug trafficking networks. There will be also an analysis of possible drawbacks of the Colombian peace deal, considering the lingering resistance of the ELN rebel group and the shift of drug trafficking to the pure private sector. The third focus will be cast on what impact a strictly regulated legalisation of narcotic and psychotropic substances in Western countries could have on the peace process in Afghanistan, based on experiences from the legalisation of cannabis in Uruguay in 2013.

Hence, the policy brief will first enquire whether the existing Afghan peace process can be enhanced through a Colombian-inspired approach of a comprehensive rural reform and substitution of illicit crops. On the other hand, it will also analyse the responsibility which may rest with the Western world as regards peace in Afghanistan; it will be determined whether countries in the West would be well-advised – following the Uruguayan model of strictly regulated cannabis legalisation – to make marijuana and other currently illicit substances legally available and whether this measure is likely to drain the tremendous profit margins of drug traffickers.

Backgrounds: Drug and the War in Afghanistan

Pakistan, US and the Jihadists

According to Maass (2011, p.6) and Peters (2009, p.7), despite the fact that in the Golden Crescent region of Pakistan, Afghanistan and Iran – so called for the high profitability of the regional opium poppy cultivation – the opium poppy flower has been grown for centuries, only the Jihadists' fight against the Soviet invasion of Afghanistan in the 1980s laid the foundation for today's flourishing narcotics economy. The decrease of opium production in Southeast Asia, Iran and Turkey during the second half of the 1970s created a rise in prices for opiates on the world market and thus fertile conditions for opium poppy cultivation in Afghanistan (Maass, 2011, p.6).

International funds funnelled through the Pakistani secret service (Inter-Services Intelligence (ISI)) – in particular from the United States (US) and the Gulf States – for the Jihadist resistance against the Soviet Union were being distributed unevenly among the spectrum of rebel groups; Islamist commanders finding themselves on the short end of this deal took to protecting and levying charges on opiate shipments crossing their areas of control so as to sustain their fighting infrastructure (Peters, 2009, p.7; Burns, 1989). Some rebel commanders also grew opium poppy on their own land holdings, realising that profits would be 100 times higher than any other crop grown under the harsh Afghan climate such as cotton or wheat (Bonner, 1986, Para 19). Both insurgents and regular farmers benefitted from generous both Iranian and Pakistani buyers as well as from inherently easy storage and transport of raw opium; another oft-cited reason among opium farmers in favour of drug cultivation was that its profits allowed them to stay on their land instead of having to seek refuge from the armed conflict abroad (Bonner, 1986, pares 24, 32-33).

By turning a blind eye to the dramatically growing opiate production, refining and cross-border trafficking, the US helped to midwife a global opiate trafficking network (McCoy, 2018; Peters, 2009, p.9). During this period of Islamist insurgency, opium poppy, grown for the most part in Southern and Eastern Afghanistan, was shipped to both Iran and Pakistan for processing in heroin laboratories; from here the drugs were trafficked to Europe and America (Maass, 2011, p.7; Peters 2008, p.8).

Civil War

After the Jihadist insurgency and Soviet occupation of the 1980s, large swathes of land were left with their irrigation infrastructure, orchards and arable land all in ruins, thus robbing the returning refugees of most legal means to make a living (Felbab-Brown, 2009, p.11). As opium poppy cultivation requires less water in the hot summer months and is more labour-intensive during harvesting season than other crops, it was the ideal choice with which to revive Afghanistan's war-ravaged agricultural sector -- while at the same time providing employment for a large number of returnees (Maass, 2011, p.9). During the ensuing civil war of the early 1990s, local warlords – former Islamist rebels and local military commanders alike – struggled against each other in local, decentralised fights for power. They took advantage of the virtual absence of governmental control and of the well-functioning drug economy which had sprung up all over the country by levying taxes on the drug industry (Maass, 2011, p.9). Powerful Islamist leaders, who had amassed local influence due to good relations with the Pakistani ISI during the Soviet occupation, founded heroin laboratories on the Afghan side of the Afghan-Pakistan border region in order to imbibe an even larger share of the drug trafficking profits (Peters, 2009, p.8).

The ousting of the Communist government in 1992 furthermore resulted in the end of foreign military aid which had been flowing continuously from the US through Pakistan to the anti-Communist rebel groups. This development placed additional financial pressure on actors throughout the whole rebel spectrum. As a result, both warlords and farmers professionalised more and more the production chain of opiates which laid a resilient foundation for an export-oriented drug industry, thus moving increasingly further away from the traditional subsistence agriculture (Maass, 2011, p.8). It is to be kept in mind, however, that Afghan farmers opt to plant opium poppy not only out of ambitious pursuit of personal profit but often only for purely basic subsistence needs. According to observers, in order to survive the bitter Afghan winter months both farmers and sharecroppers must borrow money from drug lords - which they are then bound to pay back with future crops. Only with the higher profit margins of an opium poppy crop are these producers sure to pay back the loan. These dynamics have a distinct potential towards vicious cycles (Maas, 2011, p.15; Blanchard, 2009, pp.25-26; Siddique & Salih, 2007).

Additionally, the actors involved in the armed conflict drew on smuggling consumer goods, mostly from Dubai, to Pakistan as another source of revenue; most notably, the Taliban extracted a considerable part of their funds in this manner (Maass, 2011, p.9; Peters, 2009, p.13; Rubin, 2000, p.1795). As a result of the Afghanistan Transit-Trade Agreement of 1965, goods shipped to Pakistani ports were free to transit to landlocked Afghanistan without being subject to Pakistani customs. Under the so-called 'U-Turn Scheme', the insurgents would cheaply purchase consumer goods in Dubai, have them shipped to Karachi, then truck them to the tribal areas just behind the border with Pakistan and finally smuggle the merchandise (together with Afghan-produced drugs) back across the border so as to be sold at special smuggler markets within Pakistan -- without ever paying duties (Peters, 2009, p.13).

The Taliban Rule

After most of the country fell to the Taliban in 1996, the drug industry became a legalised part of the national economy. The Taliban levied a 10% agricultural tax and a 20% alms tax on the production and trading of opium (Maass, 2011, p.10). Although the Taliban themselves eventually handed down a strict ban on opium cultivation (not on drug trafficking, however) in 2000, their regime also benefited considerably from opium taxes, generating US$9 million in 1996-1997 with an estimated peak of US$45 million in 1999 alone (Maass, 2011, p.10; Rubin, 2000, p.1796). These figures, together with the fact that the international community began pressuring the Taliban, as de facto leaders of Afghanistan, after the record-breaking harvest of 1999, to curb the seemingly endless supply of Afghan opiates, lead many analysts to believe that the ban was merely rooted in the objective of counteracting falling prices for opiates on the international market (Mancini & Sati, 2017; Maass, 2011, pp.11-12) or in the Taliban's desire for international recognition as legitimate power-holders in Afghanistan (Blanchard, 2009, p.23; Peters, 2009, p.14). Nonetheless, this prohibition yielded astounding effects on the production of opiates in Afghanistan for 2001; in the parts of the country controlled by the Taliban, opium poppy cultivation had virtually disappeared (Blanchard, pp.23-24; Peters, 2009, p.14).

In the two provinces in the north of the country, Badakhshan and Samangan, which were mostly controlled by a diverse group of Taliban adversaries -- who had joined together in the loosely associated 'Northern Alliance' and were nominally led by 1992-1996 Afghan President Burhanuddin Rabbani -- opium poppy cultivation kept flourishing during the entire period of Taliban rule (Maass, 2011, p.11; Goodhand, 2009, pp.12-13).

Post 2001 Afghanistan and Taliban insurgency

After the coalition of Western nations, supported by the Northern Alliance, forced the Taliban to release power-which led the Islamists to regroup in the south and east of the country -- the Taliban stuck to imposing the 10% agriculture tax on poppy cultivation within their sphere of influence. In exchange they offered protection from forced crop eradication and government raids on heroin labs (Maass, 2011, p.15; Peters, 2009, p.18). This approach generated abundant assets to recruit fighters and acquire arms (McCoy, 2018). Due to this effective strategy, moreover, the number of opiate-producing Afghan provinces increased from seven of 34 in 2008 (Maass, 2011, p.15) and to 24 in 2017 (UNODC & MCN, 2018, p.13). On the other hand, the geopolitical situation at the time also failed to work in favour of the new Afghan elites. Their attempts at eradicating the already deeply rooted drug cultivation and trafficking networks were marred, on the one hand, by rising opium prices on the world market which followed the ban on poppy cultivation by the Taliban and, on the other, by new foreign subsidies to local commanders in the name of the war against terror -- which eventually ended up in opium poppy fields (Goodhand, 2008, pp.208-209).

Former well-known drug lords publicly disassociated themselves from the opium economy and successfully made their way into national politics -- eventually into parliament (Maass, 2011, p.14). Reportedly, involvement in opium poppy cultivation and drug trafficking involved every administrative level of President Karzai's cabinet, from the lowest local officials to the highest central ones (Mansfield, 2018, p.336; Maass, 2011, p.18; Blanchard, 2009, p.28; Kreutzmann, 2007, p.616). Meanwhile, the capacity to produce high-quality crystal heroin in laboratories located along the border with Iran and Pakistan increased to a level at which by 2008 70% of Afghan opium was refined across an estimated 50 labs on Afghan soil (employing up to 60 persons each; Maass, 2011, p.13; Peters, 2009, p.21; Siddique & Salih, 2007, Para 11). According to McCoy (2018, Para 37), the number of drug refineries in Afghanistan had increased to 500 by 2018. The United Nations Office on Drugs and Crime (UNODC) and the Afghan Ministry of Counter Narcotics (MCN), however, estimated – based on data from 2014 to 2016 – which the share of processed heroin in Afghanistan's opiate exports could at most lay at 55% (UNODC & MCN, 2018, p.44).

A major post-Taliban attempt to counteract this development was yet another ban on opium poppy cultivation by the governor of Helmand, which lasted from 2008 to 2011, together with a crop substitution scheme for Helmand province called the Helmand Food Zone (HFZ). This project had a three-pronged approach. Farmers received wheat seeds and fertiliser subsidised by the US and UK governments while being deterred from planting opium poppy through information campaigns; eventually existing poppy crops were eradicated (Mansfield, 2018, p.336). Opium poppy being an annual plant, producers can decide each year anew where and how much opium they want to cultivate, depending on the overall price structure of agricultural commodities; this has led to a high flexibility of the agricultural sector in Afghanistan (Maass, 2011, p.13).

Therefore, the decrease in opium poppy cultivation following the HFZ ban may also be attributed to a rise in prices for wheat, both locally and globally, and to a dramatic downturn in opium prices (Mansfield, 2018, p.337; Maass, 2011, p.14). Between 2008 and 2011 it seemed that this advantageous price structure, in combination with an emergence of work opportunities in the legal economy and an increased presence of armed forces, had led to a sustainable decrease in opium production (Mansfield, 2018, pp.337-338). Mansfield (2018, pp.344-346) concludes, however, that the cultivation of less labour-intensive crops such as wheat built up pressure on landless opium labourers to find work elsewhere. Due to this readily available workforce and along with affordable deep-well technology becoming available for farming previously barren land as well as the Taliban protection of opium production on these lands, farmers were able to expand the total area of arable land suitable for planting opium poppy out of the reach of government control. Thereby opium production was kept at stable levels throughout the HFZ ban and easily picked up momentum to reach new record highs by 2017.

Opiate trafficking

Before the opium leaves Afghanistan, it is usually directly sold by the farmers to Afghan traders who go on to sell their merchandise at local or regional bazars so as to be either directly trafficked abroad or first processed into heroin in Afghanistan (Maass, 2011, p.20; Kreutzmann, 2007, p.618). Sometimes buyers from neighbouring countries will also make the journey so as to purchase opiates directly in Afghanistan (Sulaiman, 2018). All individuals involved in this industry pay protection fees to whoever is wielding higher state power in the respective case (Maass, 2011, p.20). While raw opium is virtually entirely consumed or processed within the Golden Crescent region (for the most part in Iran), opium in its refined form (as heroin) is being proliferated globally (UNODC, 2018, p.15).

Observing the amount of confiscated contraband, the three busiest opiate trafficking routes out of Afghanistan lead to and through Iran and then through Turkey towards Europe (Balkan Route), to and through Pakistan and then across the sea towards other parts of the world (Southern Route) and through Tajikistan towards Central Asia and Russia (Northern Route) (Kreutzmann, 2007, p.618). The Iranian corridor, according to the latest figures from 2016, can be considered as attracting five times more trafficking in opiates than second-placed Pakistan, while the Central Asian route comes in a distant third (UNODC, 2018, pp.15-16).

The UNODC (2018, p.16), based on data collected between 2012 and 2016, cites that an estimated 86% of heroin consumed in Western Europe originated in Afghanistan. The American market, on the other hand, according to United States Drug Enforcement Administration (DEA) data from 2015, has been dominated at almost 100% by heroin brought into the country from Mexico or South America (DEA, 2017, 1). However, since 2005, US authorities have apprehended several mid- to high-profile both Afghan and Pakistani heroin smugglers (Blanchard, 2009, p.31), the latest case being the 2018 indictment of the Pakistani narcotics kingpin Shahbaz Khan for conspiring to make shipments of up to 10 tons of heroin to New York City (United States Department of Justice, 2018). Source: UNODC. 2016

Iran

Iran accounts for the overwhelming majority of Afghan opium and heroin seizures. An estimated 80% of heroin which finds its way to Western and Central Europe keeps being shipped through that country (UNODC, 2018, p.16). According to SADF (Casaca&

Wolf, 2017, pp.5-8). DEA sources (Warrick, 2012, pares 9-10) as well as local Afghan politicians and political and military analysts (Sulaiman, 2018), point to the fact that the Iranian Revolutionary Guard Corps (IRGC) control the smuggling of opiates throughout the Iranian territory. Any trafficker who wishes to sell their contraband in Iran or use the so-called 'Balkan Route' in order to reach customers in Europe will be allowed to enter the country with their illicit merchandise as long as they have resilient ties with the Iranian border authorities (Sulaiman, 2018, pares 16-17; US Department of the Treasury, 2012, Para 3). Working closely with the Lebanese Islamist group Hezbollah, the Iranian regime keeps expanding their terror financing network, which includes strong ties with the Afghan Taliban and various narco-terrorists in South America (Sulaiman, 2018, Para 19; Majidyar, 2017, Para 4; US Department of the Treasury, 2012, paras 2-3; Warrick, 2012, paras 9-10).

At the same time, a combination of extremely low consumer prices for both opium and heroin, virtual despair (especially among the younger generation) and the Iranian Regime's subversive policy not to dissuade their youth from abusing narcotic substances has over the past two decades guaranteed Iran a place among the countries with the highest per capita number of opiate addicts (Vick, 2005) Official 2018 figures from Iran's Drug Control Organisation suggest that the number of regular drug users actually more than doubled over a period of six years -- from 1.3m in 2011 to 2.8m users in 2017 in a country with a population of 80m (Rudaw, 2018, Para 4).

Pakistan

The Southern Route through Pakistan links the drug lords from both Afghanistan and Pakistan by air or sea to the consumer markets of the Middle East, India, Southeast Asia, and Africa and even to Europe and North America (UNODC, 2018, p.17). UN research furthermore indicates that of the Afghan heroin trafficked to Pakistan roughly one third continues its route to Iran or through the Balkan Route to Europe (UNODC, 2018, p.17; UNODC, 2009, p.48). As soon as the production of opiates picked up momentum in Afghanistan in the 1980s, raw opium was being clandestinely shipped to Pakistan by means of trucks which had previously brought American military supplies to the Islamist rebel groups fighting the Soviet invasion (McCoy, 2018, paras 6-9; Maass, 2011, p.7). Today, with their connections to crime syndicates in Karachi, along the shores of Baluchistan, in the Pakistani tribal areas as well as to banks in Dubai, the Taliban and other profiteers of the Afghan drug industry encounter no major obstacles while trafficking their contraband to customers around the globe -- and receiving payments electronically (Ahmed, 2015; Green, 2012; Maass, 2011, pp.25-26).

This money laundering scheme heavily relies on the traditional Afghan hawala system of informal money transfer, wherein money is moved through several brokers to banks -- mostly in Dubai -- which undertake the necessary electronic transactions (Maass, 2011, p.25). This system also provides the illicit Afghan economy with cash. Hawala bureaus in Pakistan obtain large amounts of US dollars which they then smuggle into Afghanistan. Here the dollars are converted into Afghan currency and serve as cash payments for any kind of services provided by the Taliban or other non-state actors; sometimes they are paid out through hawala middlemen as wages or to settle other liabilities (Maas, 2011, p.26). Pakistan has also become a significant final destination for both Afghan heroin and opium; whereas almost no drugs being consumed in the late 1970s, numbers rose to an estimated 44 tons of heroin being injected or smoked in 2014, thus turning Pakistan into the country with the worldwide highest per capita use of heroin (McCoy, 2018, Para 7; Browne, 2014, paras 5; Quigley, 2014, Para 5).

Tajikistan

Due to its proximity to the opium-rich provinces of North-Eastern Afghanistan and good relations between the Tajik tribes on either side of the border, an ideal framework for drug trafficking was in place when the collapse of the Soviet Union and the 1990s Afghan and Tajik civil wars and state breakdowns plunged the region into turmoil (Goodhand, 2009, pp.11-12; Paoli, Rabkov, Greenfield & Reuter, 2007, p.953). Numerous criminal groups took advantage of the scarcely controlled borders and corrupt law enforcement officials so as to establish well-connected drug trafficking networks operating with the consent of state actors throughout the following two decades (De Danieli, 2014, p.1237; Paoli et al., 2007, pp.955-958).

However, the importance of the Northern Route, as judged according to confiscated opiate shipments, appears to have diminished in recent years. In 2007, 18% of opiates produced in Afghanistan were estimated to have taken the route through Tajikistan (Goodhand, 2009, p.12); according to data from 2016, this figure can be considered to have dropped by three quarters, which is being attributed to the declining market for opiates in Russia – where synthetic drugs appear to have overtaken heroin in demand (UNODC, 2018, pp.17, 20). At the same time, the Central Asian corridor has been facing competition from a branch of the Balkan Route which leads from Iran through Azerbaijan and the Northern Caucasus towards Russia and Eastern Europe. There, Chechen rebels are suspected to use their connections to Islamist groups and – considering that the heroin has passed through Iran – to the Iranian Regime and the IRGC so as to reap profits from heroin trafficking and distribution (cf. Blanchard 2009, p.33).

Drug and the Afghan Peace process: Lesson from Colombia

In order to get a new perspective on the drug cultivation and trafficking component of the long-lasting conflict in Afghanistan, this paper turns to the experiences of the Colombian government in their fight against a cocaine-financed insurgency. After over 50 years of guerrilla warfare, the Revolutionary Armed Forces of Colombia (FARC) signed a peace agreement with their government so as 'to end the armed conflict and build a stable and lasting peace' which entered into force on 24 November 2016. Beside regulations on the end of hostilities between the two parties and matters concerning political participation and post-conflict justice, this peace treaty contains intricate stipulations on a comprehensive rural reform, including a substitution programme for illicit crops. This section of the policy brief is, hence, dedicated to assessing the practical suitability and potential impact of the measures negotiated by the two Colombian former conflict parties on the drug-economy-driven conflict in Afghanistan. Due to their intrinsic connection to the vicious cycle of drug cultivation and trafficking, the analytical focus will be placed on the comprehensive rural reform and the illicit crop substitution programme.

History of Colombian insurgency

The historically rigid political landscape in Colombia, consisting of only two political parties -- Conservative and Liberal -- routinely condemned all opposition outside this two-party system as a threat to national security. Leftist movements and right-wing paramilitary groups founded in the 1960s and 1970s both felt a strong pressure to go underground, arming and militarising themselves in the process (LeGrand, Van Isschot&Riaño-Alcalá, 2017, p.261). These groups, such as the leftist FARC, eventually established themselves in remote areas with low governmental control and unclear land ownership, where the local populations–so as to escape poverty–were already taking advantage of coca cultivation and both producing and selling cocaine (Avila Ceron, De los Rios-Carmenado& Martín Fernández, 2018, p.204; Norman, 2017, 640-641). During the following two decades, these outlawed groups began to cooperate with drug cartels in order to seek a strategic advantage over other armed groups and maximise the benefits from their illegal activities by using the cartels' global networks so as to traffic their cocaine towards more distant consumer markets (Avila Ceron et al., 2018, p.204; Norman, 2017, p.642).

In 1997, 'Plan Colombia' was inaugurated; it was a bilateral US-Colombian effort supposed to strengthen Colombian combat forces so as to fight drug trafficking and armed groups while at the same time applying a 'social support strategy' for those affected by the conflict (Avila Ceron et al., 2018, p.204). Although military operations successfully disrupted communications and cut off the coca trafficking routes of specific FARC subgroups (Felbab-Brown, 2009, p.15), Plan Colombia eventually failed in its basic objective to consolidate territorial security on a nation-wide scale (Avila

Ceron et al., 2018, p.205). Moreover, its focus on coca eradication by spraying glyphosate (a highly toxic herbicide, the aerial use of which was outlawed in 2015 by the Santos government) from helicopters or planes on illicit crops resulted in a higher fragmentation of areas with coca production, as cultivation shifted to previously coca-free regions (The Economist, 2018b, Para 13; Mancini & Sati, 2017, p.14).

The conservative Uribe government's decisive course of action against the FARC and other armed leftist groups as well as against coca farmers in the early 2000s, nonetheless, appears to have persuaded the FARC to begin peace negotiations. These started with the succeeding and more left-leaning Santos government in 2012 (Shenk & Kugelman, 2017, paras 10-11). On 24 November 2016, the negotiations culminated in the ground-breaking peace agreement between the Colombian government and the FARC rebels so as to end the armed conflict and build a stable and lasting peace. After the peace accord was ratified by the Colombian Congress and, in a second attempt, endorsed by a deeply divided Colombian public through a referendum, the equally polarised legislature embarked on the daunting task to create the legal framework demanded by the treaty.

Despite attempts by the conservative opposition at delaying legislation until after the 2018 presidential elections, the legal foundations necessary to implement the peace agreement were laid in 2017 and 2018. The elections were won by Iván Duque, an ardent proponent of former president Uribe's unyielding coca extermination policy. This kindled fears not so much about the FARC returning to guerrilla warfare but about persisting coca cultivation -- as well as the criminal activities, deforestation and food insecurity it entails (The Economist, 2018a, Para 7; The Economist, 2018b, paras 5, 10; Mancini & Sati, 2017, p.15). Small-scale coca growers, as the most vulnerable link in this drug production chain, may quickly find themselves at the mercy of drug gangs or paramilitary forces pressuring them into continuing to grow coca (The Economist, 2018b, paras 6, 10). Indeed, new conflict dynamics between FARC dissidents who reject the peace deal, right-wing paramilitaries and drug trafficking thugs have already arisen in many of the rural areas previously under FARC control (The Economist, 2018b, Para 5; Daniels, 2018, Para 14).

Comprehensive rural reforms

As unclear land rights and a historically inequitable land distribution were featuring highly on the FARC's ideological agenda (LeGrand, Van Isschot&Riaño-Alcalá, 2017, p.271), section 1.1. Of the 2016 peace agreement deals with measures aimed at legal certainty vis-à-vis land rights. Another focus of the comprehensive rural reform consists in a policy framework for rural development schemes, which are outlined under sections 1.2. and 1.3. of the treaty. These are aimed at substantially improving the living conditions for the rural population all over Colombia and oblige policy makers to implement action plans which are supposed to take especially into consideration the participation of local communities in order to adequately address the particular needs and assets of each region.

In Afghanistan, land is divided according to age-old customary rules between villages and tribes; even in the case of reclaiming desert land for cultivation there exist clear tribal customs and traditional land rights which determine who will be allowed to capture which land (Mansfield, 2018, pp.338, 342-343). Therefore, the question of equitable land distribution cannot be considered as pressing an issue as in the case of the Colombian coca farmers. Rural development schemes, on the other hand, may hold valuable insights for leading the way out of the crippling dependency of Afghan peasant farmers on drug lords which was created by the drug economy and for encouraging cultivators to move away from opium poppy.

Rural development programme

Implementing one of the FARC's oldest demands (Norman, 2017, p.640), sections 1.2. and 1.3. of the peace agreement oblige the Colombian legislature to enact rural development programmes which set the framework for measures meant to improve the livelihoods of the peasant and more generally rural populations. As pointed out in sections 1.3. and 1.3.4., their underlying aim is to eradicate extreme poverty and progressively implement the human right to food over a 15-year period. Twelve specifically national plans for comprehensive rural reform, which address topics ranging from the improvement of road infrastructure to marketing of local produce, are supposed to lay down the precise measures to be implemented for achieving these goals.

Section 1.2.4

Of the agreement stipulates the contributions from communities affected by the individual national plans as the most crucial part of the comprehensive rural reform. In order to facilitate citizen participation, 'forums' made up of community representatives will have to be set up at every administrative level wherein decisions will be taken on the implementation of the development programmes. This process of public participation furthermore stresses the role of women in building a sustainable future for a prosperous countryside.

Section 1.3

Underlines the need for distinct measures to be put into action in order to ensure equal opportunities between men and women, and throughout all national development plans special consideration is given for the support of women in their communities as well as for the participation of women and their organisations in rural development.

Section 1.3.1 of the peace agreement regards the responsibilities agreed to by the government concerning the road, irrigation, electricity and connectivity infrastructures in the form of four national plans to be implemented. The agreement emphasises the rendering of technical assistance, the promotion of appropriate practices in cooperation with community representatives and the raising of awareness for measures to alleviate the impact of climate change. Section 1.3.2. contains measures to be taken regarding health, rural education, and housing and drinking water infrastructures in another three national plans. It also focuses on individually adapted measures for specific communities according to their needs and, furthermore, stresses the needs of women and girls, the goal of providing free education up to the secondary school level. It puts forward the idea of a linkup between adolescent education and agricultural training.

According to section 1.3.3., five additional national plans aimed at stimulating agricultural production and a shift towards a 'cooperative economy' must be set up. These include different tools such as the establishment of government-sponsored agricultural associations and networks of differently sized food producers, processors, traders and exporters. The four latter plans are arranged around the first plan (section 1.3.3.1.), which encourages rural solidarity and the introduction of a 'cooperative economy' as a baseline for rural development. The state is supposed to provide both small and medium-sized agricultural entrepreneurs with the necessary finances and skills to create cooperatives and other community based organisations in order to enhance their agricultural skill set as well as their access to means of production, vocational training, credit, marketing opportunities, etc.

The second through fourth plans regard a system of comprehensive technical assistance- This includes IT and marketing training as well as promotion of most suitable seed material, as free-of-charge public services (section 1.3.3.2.); a system of simplified access to agricultural credit and non-reimbursable seed funding for start-up cultivators as well as subsidies for harvest insurance and encouragement of further individual risk management (section 1.3.3.3.); and a marketing system that allows farmers to sell their produce through less middlemen (thus, at higher prices to a wider public) state co-financing of food storage facilities, a system of regional price information for producers as well as advertising campaigns to boost demand of nationally produced agricultural products (section 1.3.3.4.). The fifth plan (section 1.3.3.5.) deals with the realisation of worker rights. It aims to eradicate child labour, open all labour market opportunities to women, and introduce a labour inspection system as well as effective protection against the economic risks of old age, pregnancy and child rearing.

Rural communities in Afghanistan would undoubtedly benefit greatly from measures such as those stipulated in the Colombian rural development programmes. As Mancini and Sati (2017, p.52) state, a comprehensive stimulus programme for the rural economy could offer a resilient counterbalance to the dependence of the rural population on an illicit drug economy. In order to achieve such ambitious goals, a strong presence of state institutions in every region of the country as well as the cooperation between local communities and state representatives would be necessary (Mancini & Sati, 2017, p.48).

In 2003, the Afghan government brought into being the National Solidarity Programme (NSP). This programme was supposed to support rural development projects on a nation-wide scale until 2016. Under this scheme, the Ministry of Rural Rehabilitation and Development directs a grass-roots process in which a facilitating partner – usually another state institution or a non-governmental organisation (NGO) – cooperates with a Community Development Council (CDC) in order to plan and implement development project (The World Bank, 2017, p.6; UNITAR, 2011). As CDC members are directly elected by and through the members of affected communities specifically for the purpose of analysing the needs of the village in question as well as planning every step of the project in cooperation with the facilitating partner and bringing the specific project to completion, this forum fulfils the basic requirements for a participation mechanism according to section 1.2.4. of the FARC peace agreement. Furthermore, well over a third of CDC members nation-wide are women (The World Bank, 2017, pp.12, 13). However, women's participation in the governance process still lags behind their more eminent role in project selection. It is suggested that a better involvement of women could be achieved through a better adapted facilitation by NGOs or government institutions (UNITAR, 2011, p.3).

Although--following the government's own final project outcome assessment--96% of the communities involved in the NSP considered their local CDC as an institution that genuinely represents their community (The World Bank, 2017, pp.13-14), according to a survey done by the Asia Foundation (2018, p. 98) in 2017 (which polled a representative number of Afghans from all 34 provinces) only 58% of respondents indicated to have confidence in CDCs to fulfil the expectations of the locals they represented.

On the other hand, the same survey showed that confidence in NGOs, parliament and provincial councils was significantly lower, at well under 50% (The Asia Foundation, 2018, pp.97-98). If CDCs could attain a lasting, omnipresent and generally respected status as point of contact between local rural communities and state institutions within the Afghan institutional landscape, they might also boost the chronically low trust of rural Afghans in institutions outside their immediate surroundings.

Despite the completion of promising projects such as irrigation, road and electricity infrastructure as well as education projects specifically directed at women and girls ('Third Eye Photojournalism Centre', 2013), the presence of the Afghan state remains weak. The security situation is the more volatile the further away provinces are from the capital, giving reason to doubt a sustainable nation-wide implementation of functioning CDCs (Mancini & Sati, 2017, p.42). Furthermore, any development scheme will be confronted with one of the world's worst perceived levels of corruption; according to the Transparency International corruption perception index for 2017, Afghanistan is placed 177th out of 180 surveyed countries (Transparency International, 2018). Conforming to data collected by the Asia Foundation (2018, p.99), 87.3% of Afghans were describing corruption as a major problem for Afghanistan. The World Bank (2017, p.12), on the other hand, considers this persistent corruption in all aspects of life as an important reason to continue to strengthen CDCs as institutions of trust between the rural population and public authorities.

As regards rural development programmes as those negotiated by the FARC and the Colombian government, analogous implementation in Afghanistan would be facing considerable obstacles. While the institutional setting for such programmes does exist in Afghanistan, the current security situation as well as rampant corruption and lingering distrust of state institutions make a comprehensive and equitable implementation of development projects very much dependent on an institutional stabilisation process in the Afghan countryside.

Illicit crop substitution programme

As an integral part of the comprehensive rural reform, section 4.1.1. of the FARC peace agreement provides the scaffolding for a substitution programme for illicit crops. This substitution scheme is most notably based on consultation and dialogue with the affected communities, underlining the voluntariness of the decision-making processes by those farmers directly affected by the programme.

Section 4. of the FARC peace agreement reiterates poverty, the weak presence of state institutions and the existence of drug trafficking organisations as main causes for the illicit drug problem in Colombia. Therefore, it prescribes as an essential priority the participation of rural communities at every step of the programme's implementation process. Furthermore, it demands more effective, efficient and transparent social care and security institutions. The parties of the peace agreement also stipulated that criminal organisations involved in the trafficking of drugs must be fought and eventually be eliminated from Colombian society. In order to achieve these goals and attain a comprehensive substitution of illicit crops, both a national programme and municipal comprehensive plans (adapted to the assets and needs of the individual communities) will have to be enacted in pursuance of section 4.1.3.

The physical protection of rural communities by state forces from any coercion or threat has been enshrined in section 4.1.3.1. as the indispensable baseline for the implementation of any crop substitution measures. Farmers must be safe from pressure by criminal gangs or whatever kind of militias aiming to abuse them so as to maximise their drug profits. Section 4.1.3.2. provides the rule that all crop substitution must be conducted in unison with the affected communities and according to agreements between community and state representatives. Only if coca growers, for reasons unconnected to unforeseeable circumstances, resist substitution, or if no agreement was reached with a specific community, did the government retain the right to eradicate the illicit crops by force. No agreement was however reached on the technique for forced crop eradication. The government was not willing to relinquish the last resort option of aerial spraying of coca plantations with glyphosate while the FARC insisted on manual eradication under all circumstances. According to section 4.1.3.5., both community assemblies – which will identify the respective community's needs, opportunities and priorities – and municipal committees – tasked with the formulation of the comprehensive illicit crop substitution plan – will be established. Maintaining the bottom-up and voluntary notions in the programme, all community assemblies in each municipality will send delegates to the municipal committee, and all decisions will be taken with 'the maximum consensus possible'.

Section 4.1.3.6. lays down the necessary components to be included in the municipal plans for the substitution of illicit crops. These comprise short-term food and technical assistance to compensate the income loss of coca farmers, sharecroppers and harvesters as well as long-term productive projects supposed to be conducted in coordination with plans regarding comprehensive rural reform. Using positive outcomes from employment generation projects under the comprehensive rural reform, harvesters' loss of employment is supposed to be offset. A special focus is also put on achieving food security, in particularly as regards children and the elderly. In order to strengthen output of licit agricultural products, the plans will have to include considerations on soil adaptation and recovery as well as on other environmental factors faced by the individual communities. Remote areas, moreover, must receive special attention; special measures pertaining to illicit crop substitution and directed at year-round accessibility to those outlying regions and at food and employment security according to local needs and assets must be implemented. Communication with the affected communities is being additionally pointed out by section 4.1.5. as an essential means to motivate farmers so as to actively work towards switching to legal crops and supporting each other through both the municipal and communal comprehensive crop substitution plans.

Article 7 of the Afghan Constitution[1] expressly obliges the Afghan state to counteract narcotics cultivation, production and smuggling. In 2015, the Ministry of Counter Narcotics decreed the 'Afghan National Drug Action Plan 2015-2019'[2], which aims at sustainably decreasing the cultivation of opium poppy as well as the production and trafficking of opiates. The action plan also emphasises national reduction in demand of illicit drugs and improvement of treatment facilities for users. In order to realise a reduction of opium poppy cultivation, the action plan is designed to pursue a balanced approach between stimulating sustainable alternative development and agriculture, on the one hand, and crop eradication, on the other. The plan appropriately recognises the immense profit margin – compared to licit crops – as one main driver of the vicious cycle of drug trafficking and addiction.

In a concerted effort by different national ministries and in consultation with local farmers and their associations, the government is supposed to offer assistance in cultivating alternative licit and locally suitable fruit and vegetables as well as in accessing arable land and water resources through repurposing of government owned land as farmland. The action plan also obliges the government to encourage farmers to join their forces through associations so as to more effectively promote their own interests and facilitate access to both credit and markets for their produce as well as advance the use of improved seed and livestock varieties. Road and electricity infrastructure development in rural areas is identified as another factor able to decrease the dependency of remote areas on poppy cultivation by making conventional agriculture more competitive and linking agricultural producers more effectively to the food processing and marketing chain.

As regards crop eradication the action plan argues that forced eradication can encourage farmers to switch to legal agricultural activities by creating uncertainty about the expected profit margin. The plan further asserts that increased security, economic opportunities and the fight against corruption are essential for forced eradication to bear the fruit of licit agricultural development. Another objective of the action plan is the continued fight against syndicates of drug production and trafficking and to effectively prosecute narcotics kingpins in coordination with foreign partners. According to the action plan, further measures, such as asset forfeitures, need to be directed against money laundering. Cooperation with foreign partners, both regionally and globally, rounds off the plan's section on measures against drug proliferation; border controls are supposed to be strengthened in cooperation with neighbouring countries and agreements with drug transit and destination countries on controlled narcotics shipments are to be established or reaffirmed.

The measures to be taken in the context of alternative rural development under the Afghan drug action plan can be considered as widely consistent with the measures laid down in section 4. of the FARC peace agreement. Instead of limiting local consultation to farmers associations alone, and as whole communities will be affected by development projects to be implemented under the action plan, the Afghan government could extend public participation to the consultation of CDCs. Underlined by section 4.1.1. of the FARC peace agreement as an 'essential priority', the decision-making process on how to switch from illicit crops to a legal agriculture should, therefore, be owned by communities as a whole. The consultation of CDCs would also ensure a more comprehensive inclusion of members of a community who are indirectly affected by crop substitution schemes.

The argumentation on which the approach to poppy eradication is based in the Afghan drug action plan also deserves a closer analysis. By simply alleging that creating uncertainty about planting decisions for farmers would suffice to push the weakest link in the drug production chain away from participating in the drug economy, the decision makers underrate the pressure both peasant farmers and sharecroppers are exposed to from local drug lords. If they are not per se forced to cultivate opium poppy, they at least opt for this line of action so as to quickly repay the loans they took out from their drug lord in order to survive the winter months. Opium poppy, being an annual plant, additionally increases farmers' flexibility and makes them still less susceptible to changes in eradication policy. Therefore, unless the life-or-death dependency of small farmers on the drug economy is severed, all forced drug eradication campaigns will only be followed by the replanting of opium poppy – under the protection of powerful drug trafficking networks themselves under the aegis of the Taliban or other local anti-government elements.

Recognising this element of duress, which very much resembles the situation of Colombia's small coca farmers, the Afghan government needs to adjust their opium poppy eradication policy and put a heavier focus on voluntary crop substitution as well as protection of small-scale farmers and their immediate communities. A more equitable approach is suggested by sections 4.1.3.1. and 4.1.3.2. of the FARC peace agreement: instead of focusing on combating mismanagement in the eradication effort and reducing economic development and security efforts to accompanying measures to the eradication campaigns, the Afghan government should make the concern for rural security and sustainable economic development in cooperation with the affected communities the overarching element of their anti-drug policy.

Challenges for peace in Colombia and Afghanistan

As promising and desirable as the above plans for rural development and voluntary illicit crop substitution may seem, in Colombia they are encountering significant obstacles. Also, if implemented in Afghanistan they may face formidable challenges. In Colombia, the armed leftist group National Liberation Army (ELN) has recently declared its unwillingness to accept conditions for re-entering peace negotiations initiated by former President Santos (The Associated Press, 2018). A complete breakdown of their peace talks would mean an increased danger for small farmers to fall prey to ELN pressure to keep cultivating coca. In addition, a dichotomous development can be observed in the reaction of drug cartels and other criminal organisations to the dismantlement of the FARC, which created a power vacuum in some drug producing and trafficking regions.

On the one hand, it has proven difficult for government forces to fill this void, mostly due to unyielding violent competition between drug trafficking organisations and the ELN -- who all use the same guerrilla tactics as employed previously by the FARC (The Economist, 2018b, Para 5; Asmann & Yagoub, 2018,

Para 12; Forero, 2018). On the other hand, both drug cartels and traffickers are also changing the tactics of their day-to-day operations. Instead of running their businesses from fortified lavish countryside manors, they now camouflage themselves with a convoluted façade of legitimate enterprises in plain sight of the authorities (McDermott, 2018, Para 5). Instead of protecting their interests with a personal militia, they are making it difficult for anti-narcotics agents to determine where licit investments end and drug related ventures begin (ibid.).

This change in tactics, additionally, keeps enabling the illicit cultivation of coca and requires measures to counter drug trafficking organisations beyond the FARC peace agreement. According to the Colombian farmers union, many coca farmers are also disappointed with the implementation of the voluntary crop substitution schemes. They state that no realistic policy proposals have been made that would spare them significant profit losses when changing cultivation to licit crops (Kazmi, 2017). Indeed, until early 2018 – therefore long before the FARC peace accord sceptic Iván Duque became president–small farmers have been stalled on receiving the promised government subsidies in either cash or seeds, while forced eradication of coca plantations through herbicides went to full swing almost immediately – including against coca plantations earmarked for voluntary substitution (The Economist, 2018b, paras 1-2, 12). Furthermore, the government has not even yet begun implementing the stipulated road infrastructure projects in remote areas, which greatly exacerbates the challenges for state institutions aiming to reach the communities most in need of alternatives to coca cultivation (The Economist, 2018b, Para 4).

As affirmed by the NGO Fundación para la Paz, this government approach to implementing the peace agreement is being perceived by many among the supposed beneficiaries of the rural development programme as unjust, leading to increased distrust in state institutions in areas which have been, so far, at least indifferent in their attitudes towards the government (The Economist, 2018b, para 15). Therefore, even though more than the targeted area of coca plantations was eradicated by force in 2017, the UNODC estimates that up to 30% of destroyed coca bushes will be replanted (The Economist, 2018b, paras 16-17).

In Afghanistan, the Taliban insurgency has been gaining momentum and peace itself is still a far cry away (Osman, 2018; Walsh, 2018). Considering that the combined US-Colombian military efforts aimed at defeating the FARC rebels in the wake of 'Plan Colombia' during the early 2000s have been credited by scholars for weakening the FARC rebels enough to agree to peace negotiations (Shenk & Kugelman, 2017, paras 13-14; Ríos, 2015), the current position of strength the Taliban find themselves in may very well pose an additional challenge for peace talks to resume in Afghanistan. At the same time, both US officials and Taliban commanders alike are quoted stating that they expect their intensified military offensives to motivate the other side so as to return to the negotiating table (Osman, 2018, paras 8, 13). Therefore, it would appear that peace is not completely out of reach for war-torn Afghanistan, on condition that an eventual peace process takes into account the needs of those most affected by the violence – according to a plan for comprehensive rural reform and voluntary crop substitution which directly engages with the affected communities.

How the West can help: Strictly regulated drug legislation

Both the FARC peace accord, in section 4.2., and the Afghan drug action plan, under chapter V., identify drug consumption and addiction as major obstacles for combating the cultivation of illicit crops. As national legal instruments, they naturally only address measures to be taken in Colombia and Afghanistan respectively. However, this paper is aiming to open the issue of drug abuse up to the global level, particularly as concerns Western nations where a very large share of the drugs leaving Afghanistan and Colombia is being consumed. SADF would hence like to emphasise both the responsibilities and the opportunities for legislative action in drug destination countries. In this context, the drug policy approach of Uruguay, which led to a highly regulated legalisation of cannabis in 2013, shall be analysed as to its suitability to counteract illicit drug cultivation and production in Afghanistan.

Goals of the drug legislation

Already in 2011, the Global Commission on Drug Policy (GCDP, 2011, p.2) – a globally represented board of high-profile personalities working on a paradigm shift in drug policy towards health and safety – noted that the forty-year old "war on drugs" waged by the United States and the United Nations had not shown any sustainable results. Eliminated sources of drugs and drug trafficking were replaced immediately, while the weakest links in the production chain, namely the cultivators and users, kept suffering from both exploitation and stigmatisation (GCDP, ibid.). The GCDP (ibid.), further, encouraged national policy makers to introduce innovative measures on the regulated legalisation of drugs, specifically to 'undermine the power of organized crime and safeguard the health and security of their citizens'. Withstanding US pressure (von Hoffmann, 2016, p.30), the Organization of American States (OAS, 2012), subsequently, issued a report analysing scenarios on how to deal with the drug problem in the Americas between 2013 and 2025. In this report (p.52), 'the disruption of the profits of organized crime' is named as one significant mid-term goal. These seminal developments in new concepts for drug legislation frameworks, of which the Uruguayan approach is one example, deserve therefore a closer analysis as to their potential impact on the illicit drug production and trafficking situation in Afghanistan.

Cannabis legislation in Uruguay: The Way forward?

In the wake of marijuana legalisation in different countries within the Americas -- such as Uruguay -- an article in The Economist (2016) pointed out that, although there was no going back to staunch prohibition of this substance, policy makers needed to thoroughly deliberate within which boundaries they wanted to allow its use. Questions regarding where to set the limit for per capita consumption, how high to tax, what potency of base-drug to allow and whom to grant licenses for cultivation and marketing needed to be determined with all feasible medical and economic expertise (The Economist, 2016, paras 5-8). The spectrum of regulation, logically, spans from total prohibition to a free market model where the supply of the drug is left to profit-maximising companies whose decisions are guided by demand alone. In between those two extremes there are many different options on how to dissuade drug abuse while still drying up the black market.

In Uruguay the initiative to allow the purchase of marijuana for non-medical consumption under strict regulation was spearheaded by the governing party and the ruling administration under President José Mujica in 2012 and signed into law in December 2013 (Hudak, Ramsey & Walsh, 2018, pp.1, 2). On the supply side of the issue, Uruguayan legislators opted for a mixed approach. On the one hand, they legalised home growing and communal cultivation of a limited amount of cannabis plants in state-authorised 'cannabis social clubs'. Furthermore, two commercial entities were licensed to exclusively supply pharmacies where any adult Uruguayan resident can purchase a certain amount of the drug per week (Hudak et al., 2018, p.3; Kilmer &LiccardoPacula, 2017, pp.1129-1130). A state-institution was created and placed under the authority of the Ministry of Public Health so as to register both cannabis cultivators and users, oversee adherence to existing legislation and act as liaison between other state bodies involved in different aspects of the cannabis legalisation scheme (Hudak et al., 2018, p.4). The plants' potency is to be capped at a level that is just potent enough to compete with existing illicit options while the retail price is state-regulated as well (Cerdá& Kilmer, 2017, p. 119).

Cerdá and Kilmer (2017, p.119) argue that, according to surveys from 2016, it is very likely that habitual drug users will opt for one of the legalised options for supply of marijuana. This attitude of the drug using public would make for a smooth transition to a state-controlled drug supply system, which would, in turn, quickly render the black market unprofitable for drug traffickers. According to von Hoffmann (2016, p.31), moreover, the Uruguayan example of cannabis legalisation may very well serve as a role model for other jurisdictions to draft their own drug legalisation laws. The Economist (2016, paras 3, 10) also argues that legalisation under strict and country specific regulations is the only way to deal with, especially, marijuana consumption.

Application to opiates

While those kinds of regulations can be considered well-balanced for the case of marijuana, the same kind of legalisation effort vis-à-vis opiates such as heroin must be regarded as highly questionable due to their extreme level of addictiveness and high number of deadly overdose victims. Albeit an end of heroin and opium prohibition must remain out of the question, legislative measures aiming to alleviate the suffering of opiate addicts while at the same time fighting the global drug trafficking networks wreaking havoc also in rural Afghanistan are being put on the table. Hall (2018, p.1218), for example, suggests the supplement of a strict ban on both heroin and opium through legislation which decriminalises the use of opiates, thus encouraging users to seek a way out of addiction which could be provided through enhancing treatment facilities, needle and syringe programmes as well as sentencing low-level opiate-addicted dealers to treatment rather than prison. Moreover, the OAS (2012, pp.55-56) argues to consider drug addiction a disease and therefore commend national as well as local and community-based undertakings to strengthen community resilience to drug abuse through training programmes for members of drug afflicted communities on how to reduce harm caused by this sort of environment to users and non-users. The OAS report (2012, p.56) puts forward the aim of providing free-of-charge drug treatment facilities and offering sports or cultural activities, especially for youths, as alternatives to drug abuse.

Even though the above described harm reduction measures combined with a continuing ban on the legal purchase of opiate products may take several years, or even a decade or more, to produce sustainable regional or national results, this approach will also eventually lead to a decrease in demand of substances such as heroin in destination countries (OAS, 2012, pp.56-57).

Lesson for Afghanistan and the West

The above analysis has shown that opium poppy cultivation and heroin production in Afghanistan not only share an intricate connection with global drug trafficking networks, creating an environment not unlike that surrounding the FARC insurgency in Colombia, but also can benefit from progressive attitudes of legislatures in drug destination countries, many of them located in the so-called 'West'.

The peace deal reached between the FARC rebels and the Colombian government, despite its uncertain future within Colombia, holds several lessons for Afghan policy makers. With the Afghan National Solidarity Programme (NSP) and National Drug Action Plan (NDAP), many of those lessons have been already implemented into national policies. Both policies are, however, limited in their temporal scope; the NSP expired in 2016 and the NDAP has been designed for the period between 2015 and 2019. The similarity of these measures to those demanded by the FARC peace agreement, and the particular success of the NSP, should encourage Afghan officials to renew the policies and reallocate resources to national programmes which will strengthen a balanced counter-narcotics approach -- and continue rural reforms in cooperation with already existing locally owned Community Development Councils.

Regarding opium poppy cultivation policies, a shift from the current NDAP approach favouring forced eradication towards a more sustainable policy which is built around direct cooperation with opium poppy growing communities (which would create greater trust in state-institutions) is the main lesson to be taken away from sections 4.1.1., 4.1.3.1. and 4.1.3.2. of the FARC peace agreement. Forced eradication should be limited to cases where illicit crop cultivators persistently refuse to go along with the community decisions to avail themselves of a crop substitution programme or where farmers fail to comply with the communal agreement to switch crops, as provided for under section 4.1.3.2. of the FARC peace agreement.

Rural development programmes, as conducted under the NSP until 2016, already proved that the Afghan government is committed to increasing cooperation with grass root level community representatives in order to create mutual trust and better living conditions in rural Afghanistan. In keeping with this approach, the

Community Development Councils model should be applied in all regions of the country where the government can guarantee both the safety and security of the respective communities at all times. In order to increase trust in state institutions, it is indispensable that state institutions be reliably accessible for all Afghans. In order to enhance the participation of women in the activities of Community Development Councils beyond project selection and into project management should be considered as a further lesson from the omnipresent references to gender equality in the FARC peace agreement and, in particular, from its section 1.3. -- which calls for specific measures to be implemented so as to materialise equal opportunities for both men and women to free themselves from poverty.

The policy makers of Western countries, furthermore, have it within their power to enact legislation which could aid in the counter narcotics efforts in Afghanistan. Learning from the example of cannabis legalisation in Uruguay and other progressive policy proposals being put forward -- notably by the OAS and GCDP -- legislators in drug destination countries should move away from strict prohibition regimes and towards basing their policy approaches around harm reduction measures. For cannabis, this should mean a strictly regulated and state-controlled legalisation of the substance analogous to the Uruguayan model. In the case of heroin, more efforts should be made to overcome the stigma of drug use, according to OAS and GCDP recommendations. Both these measures would have a positive impact on the enduring fight against drug trafficking out of Afghanistan by steadily drying up the profits of the criminal networks through which the Taliban and other insurgents finance most of their infrastructure. Therefore, these measures, implemented hand in hand with a comprehensive rural reform, promise much potential to drain the drug swamp in Afghanistan and foster peace in the country.

Recommendation

In order to prevent drug production and traffic to fuel terrorism and war, SADF puts forward the following recommendations.

To the United Nations drug policy, as supported by the UNODC:

1. Consider alternatives to the strictly prohibitionist and punitive approach to drug use;

2. Encourage member states to enact legislation which is designed to deal with drug use focusing on harm reduction to users. The Uruguayan experience of strictly regulated cannabis regulation could be taken as a yardstick and expanded both geographically and regarding substances, taking into account OAS and Global Commission on Drug Policy proposals.

To the European institutions and the international community:

1. Support the Afghan government in its continued fight against opium poppy cultivation and heroin production and trafficking by assisting it in the implementation process of its rural development and crop substitution programmes;

2. Continue to prosecute narcotics kingpins and counteract narcotics trafficking on a global scale;

To the Afghan authorities:

1. Continue and improve the national programmes for rural development and counternarcotics action;

2. Focus counter-narcotics efforts on voluntary crop substitution and treat forced eradication as a measure of last resort for cultivators who persistently refuse to go along with the decisions taken by their communities;

3. Enhance efforts to create mutual trust between the rural population and state institutions. This could best be achieved by enhancing Community Development Councils to be present in all regions of the country where the authorities are able to ensure the safety and security of all participants and by expanding the Councils' material scope beyond the National Solidarity Programme and towards other community development related activities such as crop substitution programmes;

4. Enact measures to encourage rural women to become more involved in matters of development project management.

Courtesy: I am highly indebted for the South Asia Democratic Forum for the permission of reproduction of this paper. Policy brief No-8, 31 October 2018

Notes to Chapters

Chapter 1: At any Price we will take the Mines: the Islamic State, the Taliban, and Afghanistan's White Talc Mountains

1 Details on the background of ISKP and their competition with the Taliban are set out later in the main text.

2 'Who are the Taliban?', BBC News, May 26, 2016 http:// www.bbc.com/news/world-south-asia-11451718

3 Other estimates using different methodology (and estimates from the Taliban themselves) are in the same general area. Bill Roggio and Alexandra Gutowski, 'LWJ Map Assessment: Taliban controls or contests 45% of Afghan districts', Long War Journal, September 26, 2017 https://www.longwarjournal.org/ archives/2017/09/lwj-map-assessment-taliban-controls-or-contests-45-of-afghan-districts.php

4 See main text for details of the continued Taliban presence in areas such as Khogyani and Sherzad districts. Mujib Masha, 'Afghan ISIS Branch Makes Inroads in Battle Against Taliban', New York Times, October 13, 2017 https://www.nytimes.com/2015/10/14/world/asia/afghan-isis-branch-makes-inroads-in-battle-against-taliban.html; Caitlin Forrest, 'Afghanistan Partial Threat Assessment: November 22, 2016', Institute for the Study of War, November 23, 2016 www.understandingwar.org/backgrounder/afghanistan-partial-threat-assessment-november-22-2016; 'IS, Taliban fight for key towns in Nangarhar', Dawn, November 29, 2017 https:// www.dawn.com/news/1373507

5 Vera Bergengruen, 'Here's what the 'Mother of All Bombs' did for US fight in Afghanistan', Task and Purpose, April 29, 2017 http://taskandpurpose.com/ moab-fight-afghanistan/

6 Borhan Osman, 'The Battle for Mamand: ISKP under strain, but not yet defeated', Afghanistan Analysts Network, May 23, 2017 https://www.afghanistan-analysts. org/the-battle-for-mamand-iskp-under-strain-but-notyet-defeated/; Jessica Purkiss and Abigail Fielding-

Smith, 'Islamic State in Afghanistan: Is US assault working?', The Bureau of Investigative Journalism, July 28, 2017 https://www.thebureauinvestigates.com/stories/2017-07-28/islamic-state-in-afghanistan-us-military

7 See for example Borhan Osman, 'The Islamic State in 'Khorasan': How it began and where it stands now in Nangarhar', Afghanistan Analysts Network, July 27, 2016 https://www.afghanistan-analysts.org/the-islamic-state-in-khorasan-how-it-began-and-where-it-stands-now-in-nangarhar/

8 Harleen Gambhir, 'ISIS in Afghanistan', Institute for the Study of War, December 3, 2015 http://www.understandingwar.org/sites/default/files/ISIS%20in%20 Afghanistan_2.pdf

9 Lizzie Dearden, 'Isis vs Islamic State vs Isil vs Daesh: What do the different names mean – and why does it matter?', The Independent, September 23, 2014 http:// www.independent.co.uk/news/world/middle-east/ isis-vs-islamic-state-vs-isil-vs-daesh-what-do-the-different-names-mean-9750629.html

10 The most comprehensive list of names was from the IMMAP Oasis software, which includes some geographic features but is mainly made up of settlement names.

11 Almost all our sources expressed prices in terms of Pakistani rupees.

12 'XE Currency Charts: USD to PKR,' XE.com http://www. xe.com/currencycharts/?from=USD&to=PKR&view=5Y

13 'XE Currency Charts: USD to AFN,' XE.com http://www.xe.com/currency charts/?from=USD&to=AFN&view=5Y

14 While two of our sources mentioned tourmaline or a mineral that could be tourmaline, they did not present it as a major focus for extraction, and other sources did not mention its presence. See 'The Threat on the Ground', below.

15 'The Mineral Talc', Minerals.net, http://www.minerals. net/mineral/talc.aspx

16 'Talc', Etymology Online http://www.etymonline.com/ index.php?term=talc

17 'Talc: the softest mineral', Geology.com http://geology. com/minerals/talc.shtml

18 'Global Talc and Pyrophyllite Market Exhibits Slow Demand Growth', Ceramic Industry, December 1, 2014 https://www.ceramicindustry.

com/articles/94359-global-talc-and-pyrophyllite-market-exhibits-slow-demand-growth

19 Ian Wilson, 'Global Talc Markets'

20 Mark Cocker, 'Summary for the Mineral Information Package for the Ghunday-Achin Magnesite and Talc Area of Interest', in Stephen G. Peters, Trude V.V. King, Thomas J. Mack, and Michael P. Chornack, 'Summaries of Important Areas for Mineral Investment and Production Opportunities of Nonfuel Minerals in Afghanistan', United States Geological Survey, 2011, p 1423 https:// pubs.usgs.gov/of/2011/1204/pdf/20A.pdf

21 'Minerals in Afghanistan: The Achin Magnesite Deposit', Ministry of Mines and Petroleum http://mom.gov.af/ Content/files/The%20Achin%20Magnesite%20Deposit.pdf

22 'Chromite', Geology.com http://geology.com/minerals/ chromite.shtml

23 'Mineral Commodity Summaries: Chromium', United States Geological Survey, January 2018, pp 46-47 https://minerals.usgs.gov/minerals/pubs/commodity/ chromium/mcs-2018-chrom.pdf

24 GolnarMonetvalli, 'Afghanistan sees great white hope in marble sector', Reuters, April 21, 2010 https://www. reuters.com/article/us-afghanistan-marble-idUSTRE63K00C20100421; 'Marbles of Afghanistan', Ministry of Mines and Petroleum of the Islamic Republic of Afghanistan, January 2014 http://www.mom.gov.af/ Content/files/MoMP_MARBLE_Midas_Jan_2014_NEW. pdf

25 Sune Engel Rasmussen, 'Afghan government money reaching Taliban through marble trade', The Guardian, June 3, 2016 https://www.theguardian. com/global-development/2016/jun/03/afghan-government-money-taliban-marble-trade; 'Letter dated 9 June 2014 from the Chair of the Security Council Committee established pursuant to resolution 1988 (2011) addressed to the President of the Security Council', United Nations Security Council, June 10, 2014, pp 19-20 http://www.securitycouncilreport. org/atf/cf/%7B65BFCF9B-6D27-4E9C-8CD3-CF6E4FF96FF9%7D/s_2014_402.pdf

26 The movement headed by Abu Bakr al-Baghdadi generally refers to itself as the Islamic State, though other terms are often used. They include ISIS (the Islamic State in Iraq and Al-Shams, roughly corresponding the area known as the Levant), ISIL (the Islamic State in Iraq and the Levant), and Daesh (from the Arabic acronym for Islamic State – the term preferred by many observers who wish to

avoid legitimising the movement, as it has negative connotations in Arabic). The movement's claim to represent a new Islamic Caliphate is abhorrent to many within Islam.

27 'Mapping the emergence of the Islamic State in Afghanistan', Long War Journal, March 5, 2015 https://www. longwarjournal.org/archives/2015/03/mapping-theemergence-of-the-islamic-state-in-afghanistan.php

28 Historic Khorasan includes parts of Iran, Afghanistan and Turkmenistan, and some definitions of the term include Pakistan. Adam Taylor, 'The strange story behind the 'Khorasan' group's name', Washington Post, September 25, 2014 https://www.washingtonpost.com/news/worldviews/wp/2014/09/25/the-strangestory-behind-the-khorasan-groups-name/?utm_term=.6ac9453709a7; Seth Jones, James Dobbins, Daniel Byman, Christopher Chivvis, Ben Connable, Jeffrey Martini, Eric Robinson, and Nathan Chandler, 'Rolling back the Islamic State, RAND Corporation, 2017 p 153 https://www.rand.org/content/dam/rand/ pubs/research_reports/RR1900/RR1912/RAND_RR1912.pdf

29 Karen Leigh, Jason French and Jovi Juan, 'Islamic State and its affiliates', Wall Street Journal, 2017 http:// graphics.wsj.com/islamic-state-and-its-affiliates/

30 Some Islamic texts indicate that the army of true believers will gather in Khorasan before the apocalypse. Harleen Gambhir, 'ISIS in Afghanistan', p 2

31 Harleen Gambhir, 'ISIS in Afghanistan', p 2

32 It was not until September 2015 that ISKP began attacking Afghan government and international targets. Harleen Gambhir, 'ISIS in Afghanistan', p 3; Bill Roggio, 'Afghanistan's terrorist resurgence: Al Qaeda, ISIS, and beyond', Long War Journal, April 27, 2017 https://www. longwarjournal.org/archives/2017/04/afghanistans-terrorist-resurgence-al-qaeda-isis-and-beyond.php

33 Harleen Gambhir, 'ISIS in Afghanistan', p 4; Lauren McNally, Alex Amiral, Marvin Weinbaum, and Antoun Issa, 'The Islamic State in Afghanistan: Examining its Threat to Stability', p 3

34 The Institute for the Study of War refers to commanders pledging allegiance from Kunar, Nangarhar, and Logar – presumably meaning defectors from the Taleban rather than TTP. As the United States Institute for Peace notes, ISKP appointed recruiters in nine other provinces beyond these core provinces. Four of these (Kunduz, Sa-

mangan, Sar-e Pol, and Faryab) are in northern Afghanistan: "perhaps a telling allocation of resources, and an indication that [ISKP]'s strategy is to recruit outside of traditional Taliban areas of influence and move northward from their current base along the Afghanistan-Pakistan (Af-Pak) border through northern Afghanistan into Central Asia." Casey Garret Johnson, 'The rise and stall of the Islamic State in Afghanistan', United States Institute for Peace, November 2016, p 3 https://www.usip.org/ publications/2016/11/rise-and-stall-islamic-state-afghanistan; Harleen Gambhir, 'ISIS in Afghanistan', p 4; Lauren McNally, Alex Amiral, Marvin Weinbaum, and Antoun Issa, 'The Islamic State in Afghanistan: Examining its Threat to Stability', Middle East Institute, May 2016, p 3 https://www.mei.edu/ sites/default/files/ publications/PF12_McNallyAmiral_ISISAfghan_web. pdf; Casey Garret Johnson, 'The rise and stall of the Islamic State in Afghanistan', United States Institute for Peace, November 2016, p 3

35 Other individual commanders had pledged loyalty or support to the Islamic State before July 2015, but statement in July 2015 from the IMU's spiritual leader Usman Ghazi was a formal commitment on behalf of the whole organisation. Edward Lemon, 'IMU pledges allegiance to Islamic State', Eurasianet, August 1, 2015 http://www.eurasianet.org/node/74471

36 Borhan Osman, 'Descent into chaos: Why did Nangarhar turn into an IS hub?', Afghanistan Analysts Network, September 27, 2016 https://www.afghanistan-analysts.org/descent-into-chaos-why-did-nangarhar-turn-into-an-is-hub/

37 A Russian estimate of 10,000 fighters overall is contested, while an American figure of 600 is likely out of date, even if it was not over-optimistic to begin with. Noor Zahid, 'A Look at Islamic State's Operations in Afghanistan', Voice of America, April 29, 2017 https:// www.voanews.com/a/a-look-at-is-operation-in-afghanistan/3831169.html; Lauren McNally, Alex Amiral, Marvin Weinbaum, and Antoun Issa, 'The Islamic State in Afghanistan: Examining its Threat to Stability', p 6; Casey Garret Johnson, 'The rise and stall of the Islamic State in Afghanistan', United States Institute for Peace, November 2016, p 2 https://www.usip.org/ publications/2016/11/rise-and-stall-islamic-state-afghanistan; 'Letter dated 9 May 2017 from the Chair of the Security Council Committee established pursuant to resolution 1988 (2011) addressed to the President of the Security Council', United Nations, May 25, 2017, p 12 http://www.un.org/en/

ga/search/view_doc. asp?symbol=S/2017/409; GulabuddinGhubar, 'Army Chief Rejects Russia's Figures On Daesh Fighters', ToloNews, December 25, 2017 http://www.tolonews.com/ afghanistan/army-chief-rejects-russia%E2%80%99sfigures-daesh-fighters; Ayaz Gul, 'US Military Rejects Russian Claims About Number of IS Fighters in Afghanistan', Voice of America, February 24, 2018 https:// www.voanews.com/a/us-military-rejects-russia-numbers-of-islamic-state-fighters-in-afghanistan/4268999. html; Noor Zahid, 'A Look at Islamic State's Operations in Afghanistan', Voice of America, April 29, 2017 https:// www.voanews.com/a/a-look-at-is-operation-in-afghanistan/3831169.html

38 Harleen Gambhir, 'ISIS in Afghanistan', p 4; Casey Garret Johnson, 'The rise and stall of the Islamic State in Afghanistan', United States Institute for Peace, November 2016, pp 1-3 https://www.usip.org/publications/2016/11/rise-and-stall-islamic-state-afghanistan

39 The NATO estimate is that 70% of ISKP fighters originated from the TTP; the Afghan government estimate is that 80% of ISKP fighters are Pakistani. 'IS in Afghanistan: How successful has the group been?', BBC ; 'The rise and stall of the Islamic State in Afghanistan', United States Institute for Peace, November 2016, p 2 https://www.usip.org/publications/2016/11/ rise-and-stall-islamic-state-afghanistan.

40 Borhan Osman, 'Descent into chaos: Why did Nangarhar turn into an IS hub?', Afghanistan Analysts Network, September 27, 2016 https://www.afghanistan-analysts.org/descent-into-chaos-why-did-nangarhar-turn-into-an-is-hub/

41 Global Witness interview with Graeme Smith, UNAMA political officer, February 2018; Christian Bleuer, 'Chechens in Afghanistan 1: A Battlefield Myth That Will Not Die', Afghanistan Analysts Network, June 27, 2016 https://www.afghanistan-analysts.org/chechens-in-afghanistan-1-a-battlefield-myth-that-willnot-die/; 'French fighters appear with Islamic State in Afghanistan', Agence France Presse, December 17, 2017 https://www.thelocal.fr/20171210/french-fighters-appear-with-islamic-state-in-afghanistan

42 Within the ISIS structure, beneath the senior leadership is a Diwan [ministry] for the "Administration of Distant Wilayat" [provinces], under which ISKP would be organized. How ISIS Describes its Government Structure', Stanford University http://interactive. achariricenter.org/wp-content/uploads/2016/07/ Structure-of-ISISFinal-1. pdf; 'IS in Afghanistan: How successful has the group been?', BBC,

February 27, 2017 http://www.bbc.com/news/world-asia-39031000; Sune Engel Rasmussen and Zahra Nader, 'Iran Covertly Recruits Afghan Shias to Fight in Syria,' The Guardian, June 30, 2016, https://www.theguardian.com/ world/2016/jun/30/iran-covertly-recruits-afghan-soldiers-to-fightin-syria

43 The July 2016 attack on a Shia rally in Kabul was claimed to be in retaliation for Afghan Shias who have gone to fight in Syria on behalf of the Assad government. The number of Afghans recruited from Afghanistan and Iran to fight for ISIS is Iraq and Syria is estimated to be anywhere from a few thousand to 20,000. 'IS in Afghanistan: How successful has the group been?', BBC, February 27, 2017 http://www.bbc. com/news/world-asia-39031000; Sune Engel Rasmussen and Zahra Nader, 'Iran Covertly Recruits Afghan Shias to Fight in Syria,' The Guardian, June 30, 2016, https://www.theguardian.com/world/2016/jun/30/ iran-covertly-recruits-afghan-soldiers-to-fight-in-syria

44 'Is Daesh really in Afghanistan?', TRT World, November 10, 2016 https://www.trtworld.com/magazine/ is-daesh-really-in-afghanistan--3692; Martin Sahak and Girish Gupta, 'Islamic State seizes new Afghan foothold after luring Taliban defectors', Reuters, December 1, 2017 https://uk.reuters.com/article/uk-afghanistan-islamic-state/islamic-state-seizes-new-afghan-foothold-after-luring-taliban-defectors-idUKKBN1DV3G3

45 Global Witness interview with Caitlin Forrest, March 2017

46 The ISIS statement accepting ISKP's allegiance in January 2015 also claimed ISKP had already submitted an overall military strategy to them. The spokesman was reportedly Abu Muhammad al-Adnani. Harleen Gambhir, 'ISIS in Afghanistan', p 4; Global Witness interview with an Islamic State commander, 2015

47 'Letter dated 9 May 2017 from the Chair of the Security Council Committee established pursuant to resolution 1988 (2011) addressed to the President of the Security Council', United Nations, May 25, 2017, p 12 http:// www.un.org/cn/ga/scarch/vicw_doc.asp?symbol=S/2017/409

48 Caitlin Forrest, an analyst with the Institute for the Study of War, also reported that two groups are in contact, even if only by SMS. Brian Dodwell and Don Rassler, 'A View from the CT Foxhole: General John W. Nicholson', Combating Terrorism Center at West Point, February 22, 2017 https://ctc.usma.edu/posts/a-viewfrom-the-ct-

foxhole-general-john-w-nicholson-commander-resolute-support-and-u-s-forces-afghanistan; Global Witness interview with Caitlin Forrest, Institute for the Study of War, Foundation for Defense of Democracies, March 21, 2017

49 Unlike the significant capture and reporting of Al Qaeda and ISIS documents over the decades as well as other analysis of their financial resourcing, no such documents has been publicly reported in the media or from other experts for ISKP that we are aware of. 'The Islamic State in Afghanistan', Middle East Institute, p 3; Harleen Gambhir, 'ISIS in Afghanistan', p 6

50 'Letter dated 11 January 2017 from the Chair of the Security Council Committee pursuant to resolutions 1267 (1999), 1989 (2011) and 2253 (2015) concerning Islamic State in Iraq and the Levant (Da'esh), Al-Qaida and associated individuals, groups, undertakings and entities addressed to the President of the Security Council', United Nations, January 13, 2017 http://www.securitycouncilreport.org/atf/cf/%7B65BFCF9B-6D27-4E9C-8CD3-CF6E4FF96FF9%7D/s_2017_35.pdf

51 'Letter dated 9 May 2017 from the Chair of the Security Council Committee', United Nations

52 Caitlin Forrest says there is evidence that ISIS sends funds to ISKP forces in Zabul Province in Afghanistan, perhaps due to pre-existing relationships with the Islamic Movement of Uzbekistan (IMU) factions there that defected from Al Qaeda to ISKP. But it is unknown whether that applies to all ISKP groups, especially the core groups in Nangarhar. General Nicholson for his part also stated that some funds come from ISIS, claiming that ISKP "have had some financial difficulties, but there's still money getting through." Global Witness interview with Caitlin Forrest; Dodwell and Rassler, 'A View from the CT Foxhole'; 'Letter dated 9 May 2017 from the Chair of the Security Council Committee', United Nations

53 ISKP operates an FM radio station as well as internet propaganda and Facebook and Twitter accounts. 'IS in Afghanistan: How successful has the group been?', BBC; Thomas Joscelyn, 'US: 'Major' Islamic State media 'hub' destroyed in Nangarhar, Afghanistan', Long War Journal, June 17, 2017 https://www.longwarjournal. org/archives/2017/06/us-major-islamic-state-media-hub-destroyed-in-nangarhar-afghanistan.php

54 Harleen Gambhir, 'ISIS in Afghanistan', p 6

55 In early 2017 General Nicholson claimed that ISKP fighters are paid almost twice as much as their Taliban rivals. This was supported by our sources from Nangarhar and Logar. In Logar one Global Witness source alleged a salary of 70,000 Afghanis – more than $1,000 – was being paid to ISKP fighters, although the figure is worth treating with some scepticism given the implications for the funding of the group: it is possible this was just an initial sum that would fall away quickly after recruitment. In Nangarhar, a Global Witness source reported in 2016 that ISKP had "a lot of money – they give $600 a month salary for a soldier." This same figure was cited in a May 2017 UN report, although the salaries reportedly gradually fell back to parity with the Taliban after recruitment – and one ISKP commander reportedly estimated that his expenses per soldier were a much lower average of between $145 and $290 a month. Dodwell and Rassler, 'A View from the CT Foxhole'. Global Witness interview, mid-2016; Global Witness interview with Source T, late 2016; 'Letter dated 9 May 2017 from the Chair of the Security Council Committee established pursuant to resolution 1988 (2011) addressed to the President of the Security Council', United Nations, May 25, 2017, p 12 http://www.un.org/en/ga/search/view_doc. asp?symbol=S/2017/409; Franz Marty, 'Speaking to an Afghan Disciple of the Caliphate', The Diplomat, July 28, 2016 https://thediplomat.com/2016/07/speakingto-an-afghan-disciple-of-the-caliphate/

56 There are unconfirmed reports that some groups may in fact profit from the drugs trade. ISKP has officially banned poppy cultivation and drug sales, very publicly burned narcotics fields, and kidnapped some poppy farmers, and yet at least turning a blind eye to the drug trade may be a necessity. If this activity does take place, it does not seem to have been either condemned or condoned by the IS leadership overall. IS Senior Leadership and the IS franchise in Libya both reportedly engage in various forms of narcotics use and smuggling, so similar activities from ISKP would be plausible. Harleen Gambhir, 'ISIS in Afghanistan', p 6; Zarifi, 'Daesh Seizes 8 Nangarhar Farmers for Poppy Cultivation'; Osman, 'The Islamic State in "Khorasan"'; Allen et al., 'The Big Spin'; 'Turkey Seizes 11m Amphetamine Pills Used to Fuel Isis Fighters in Combat'.

57 Zakat is an Islamic tax raised on wealth, while Ushr is a form of Zakat charged on goods produced from land, including output from mines. It is charged at 5% (or 10% for the produce of unirrigated land). 'Zakat', Islamic Voice, December 1998 http://www.islamicvoice.com/ december.98/zakat.htm#MIN

58 One victim in Shinwar district of Nangarhar reportedly said that ISKP took "whatever they liked—goods in stores, our homes, our livestock, even our firewood." Another source noted, "They held people for ransom. They began to ask everyone, even teachers, for payments. They would say: 'We are mujahids, it is our right.'" An informed source from Nangarhar also said that ISKP would "take money from a person who was a little richer, they will beat him to the edge of death and detain them" – although another reported in contrast that "unlike the Taliban, [ISKP] do not take food and things from the people." Ali M. Latifi and Mohsin Khan Mohmand, 'When Islamic State Showed up in a Corner of Afghanistan, "Nothing Was Safe, Not Even the Cows"', Los Angeles Times, June 3, 2016 http:// www. latimes.com/world/asia/la-fg-afghanistan-daesh-advsnap-story.html; Ali M. Latifi and Mohsin Khan Mohmand, 'When Islamic State Showed up in a Corner of Afghanistan, "Nothing Was Safe, Not Even the Cows"'; Global Witness interview with an informed source from Nangarhar, late 2016; Global Witness interview with an informed source, mid-2016

59 Global Witness interview with Matt DuPée, April 2017

60 See US News and World Report article for a list of attacks up to the end of 2017. ISKP's claimed operations include an attack on a military hospital in March 2017 which killed at least 38, although an AAN analyst expressed some doubt that ISKP rather than the Taliban actually carried it out. More recent attacks claimed by ISKP have included an April 2018 suicide bombing against civilians waiting to register to vote which killed at least 52. Interview with Kate Clark, November 2017; 'IS in Afghanistan: How successful has the group been?', BBC; Global Witness interview with Matt DuPée, April 2017; Sayed Salahuddin, 'At least 52 Afghans killed in Kabul by suicide bomber, health ministry says', Washington Post, April 22, 2018 https://www. washingtonpost.com/world/at-least-31afghans-killed-in-kabul-by-suicide-bomber-officialsays/2018/04/22/30174d76-4615-11e8-9072-f6d4bc32f223_story.html?utm_term=.26b9a91f500e; 'A Look at Islamic State Attacks in Afghanistan', Associated Press/U.S. News and World Report https://www. usnews.com/news/world/articles/2017-12-28/a-lookat-islamic-state-attacks-in-afghanistan; Hasib Danish Alikozai and Mohammad Habibzada, 'Afghan General: Haqqani Network, Not IS, Behind Spike in Violence', Voice of America, January 13, 2018 https://www.voanews.com/a/afghan-general-haqqani-network-islamic-state/4206961.html ; Borhan Osman, 'A Black Week in Kabul (2): Who are the most likely perpe-

trators?', Afghanistan Analysts Network, June 7, 2017 https:// www.afghanistan-analysts.org/a-black-week-in-kabul-2-who-are-the-most-likely-perpetrators; Harleen Gambhir, 'ISIS in Afghanistan', p 4; Lauren McNally, Alex Amiral, Marvin Weinbaum, and Antoun Issa, 'The Islamic State in Afghanistan: Examining its Threat to Stability', 2016, pp 3-4; Michael Safi, 'Isis militants disguised as doctors kill 38 in Kabul hospital attack', The Guardian, March 8, 2017 https:// www.theguardian. com/world/2017/mar/08/gunmen-dressed-as-doctors-attack-military-hospital-in-kabul

61 Notorious reported incidents include the alleged beheading of women and children and the execution of village elders using explosives. An attack on the offices of the humanitarian NGO Save the Children in Jalalabad may or may not have been deliberately targeted at them. Global Witness interview with NGO security advisor in Kabul, February 2018; 'Death Toll Rises to 6 In Save The Children Attack In Jalalabad', Tolo News, January 25, 2018 http:// www.tolonews.com/afghanistan/death-toll-rises-6-save-children-attack-jalalabad; Heather Barr, 'From the Taliban Frying Pan to the Islamic State Fire', Human Rights Watch, September 28, 2016 https://www.hrw.org/news/2016/09/28/ taliban-frying-pan-islamic-state-fire; Mujib Mashal and Taimoor Shah, 'Afghan Fighters Loyal to ISIS Beheaded 7 Hostages, Officials Say', New York Times, November 9, 2015 https://www.nytimes.com/2015/11/10/world/ asia/ afghan-fighters-loyal-to-isis-beheaded-7-hostages-officials-say.html?_r=0; Lauren McNally, Alex Amiral, Marvin Weinbaum, and Antoun Issa, 'The Islamic State in Afghanistan: Examining its Threat to Stability', p 7; Shereena Qazi, 'Afghans protest 'beheadings of ethnic Hazara by ISIL', Al Jazeera, November 11, 2015 http:// www.aljazeera.com/news/2015/11/afghans-protest-killings-hazara-isil-151110135854342.html;

62 Lauren McNally, Alex Amiral, Marvin Weinbaum, and Antoun Issa, 'The Islamic State in Afghanistan: Examining its Threat to Stability', p 8; Heather Barr, 'From the Taliban Frying Pan to the Islamic State Fire'; Mirren Gidda, 'Why ISIS is failing to build a caliphate in Afghanistan', Newsweek, March 25, 2017 http://www. newsweek.com/ afghanistan-isis-taliban-caliphate-kabul-bombing-574198; 'ISIS in Afghanistan', p 4; Lauren McNally, Alex Amiral, Marvin Weinbaum, and Antoun Issa, 'The Islamic State in Afghanistan: Examining its Threat to Stability', Middle East Institute, May 2016, pp 7-8 https:// www.mei.edu/sites/default/files/publications/PF12_McNallyAmiral_ISISAfghan_web.pdf

63 ISKP claimed responsibility for a July 2016 bomb attack on a Hazara demonstration which killed at least 80 people, and for a December 2017 attack on a Shia cultural centre which killed at least 40. A March 2018 attack on a Hazara mosque killed at least 10. The Taliban have also targeted Hazaras in the past, but they have not made sectarian part of their official platform in the struggle against the current Afghan government. 'Hazaras and Afghan insurgent groups', Land Info, October 3, 2016 https://landinfo.no/asset/3483/1/3483_1.pdf ; Borhan Osman 'With an Active Cell in Kabul, ISKP Tries to Bring Sectarianism to the Afghan War', Afghanistan Analysts Network, October 19, 2016 https://www.afghanistan-analysts.org/with-an-active-cell-in-kabul-iskp-tries-to bring-sectarianism-to-the-afghan-war/; Sune Engel Rasmussen, 'Isis claims responsibility for Kabul bomb attack on Hazara protesters', The Observer, July 24, 2016 https://www.theguardian.com/world/2016/jul/23/ hazara-minority-targeted-by-suicide-bombs-at-kabul-protest; Fahim Abed, Fatima Faizi and Mujib Mashal, 'Islamic State Claims Deadly Blast at Afghan Shiite Center', New York Times, December 28, 2017 https:// www.nytimes.com/2017/12/28/world/asia/afghanistan-suicide-attack.html; Emma Graham-Harrison and Haroon Janjua, 'Scores killed in Isis bombing of Kabul news agency and Shia centre', The Guardian, December 28, 2017 https://www.theguardian.com/world/2017/dec/28/blast-afghan-news-agency-kabul-kills-dozens; Andrew Kramer. 'Hazaras Protest After an ISIS Attack Kills 10 in Kabul, New York Times, March 9, 2018 https://www.nytimes.com/2018/03/09/world/asia/suicide-attack-kabul-hazaras.html

64 By the end of 2015 the Taliban had liquidated ISKP-affiliated forces in Zabul and Logar, and a significant group led by former Taliban commanders in Farah. A combination of Taliban, government and international pressure also effectively eliminated the ISKP presence in Helmand. Borhan Osman, 'The Islamic State in 'Khorasan'

65 Dodwell and Rassler, 'A View from the CT Foxhole'

66 Borhan Osman, 'The Battle for Mamand: ISKP under strain, but not yet defeated'; Borhan Osman, 'Another ISKP leader "dead": Where is the group headed after losing so many amirs?', Afghanistan Analysts Network, July 23, 2017 https://www.afghanistan-analysts.org/another-iskp-leader-dead-where-is-the-group-headed-after-losing-so-many-amirs/

67 Borhan Osman, 'Another ISKP leader "dead": Where is the group headed after losing so many amirs?'

68 Jeff Seldin, 'Afghan Officials: Islamic State Fighters Finding Sanctuary in Afghanistan', Voice of America November 18, 2017 https://www.voanews.com/a/ afghan-officials-islamic-state-finds-sanctuary-in-afghanistan/4122270.html; AnimeshRoul, 'Islamic State Gains Ground in Afghanistan as Its Caliphate Crumbles Elsewhere', Jamestown Foundation, January 26, 2018 https://jamestown.org/program/islamic-state-gains-ground-afghanistan-caliphate-crumbles-elsewhere/

69 The danger of ISKP organising attacks in the US should perhaps be treated with a certain caution as it appears to be based on a single statement made to an undercover FBI officer by a Canadian plotter, who said he "was in contact with an ISIS affiliate about obtaining official sanction of the planned attacks by the Khorasan Province, a branch of ISIS active in Pakistan." It is less clear how far ISKP's leadership is taking any active steps to organise such attacks themselves. Jennifer Cafarella, 'ISIS Plotting Attacks from Afghanistan', Institute for the Study of War, November 17, 2017 http://www. understandingwar.org/backgrounder/isis-plotting-attacks-afghanistan; 'Charges Unsealed Against Three Men for Plotting to Carry out Terrorist Attacks in New York City for ISIS in the Summer of 2016', United States Department of Justice, October 6, 2017 https://www.justice.gov/opa/pr/charges-unsealed-against-three-menplotting-carry-out-terrorist-attacks-new-york-city-isis

70 Sarah Almukhtar, 'How Much of Afghanistan Is Under Taliban Control After 16 Years of War With the U.S.?', New York times, August 23, 2017 https://www.nytimes. com/interactive/2017/08/23/world/asia/afghanistan-us-taliban-isis-control.html

71 The ISKP incursion into Jawzjan can be traced at least as far back as 2015, given that in late 2016 the Taliban reportedly launched an unsuccessful offensive against a local commander, QariHekmat, who had defected to ISKP the previous year. However, the tempo of their activities there seems to have increased since mid-2017. See lower in the main text for a discussion of ISKP links to mining in all the areas mentioned, and the resources involved. '34 provinces mines info', Pajhwok Afghan News, March 1, 2015 http://mines.pajhwok.com/ article-categories/34-provinces-mines-info; Obaid Ali, 'QariHekmat's Island: A Daesh enclave in Jawzjan?', Afghanistan Analysts Network, November 11, 2017 https://www.afghanistan-analysts.org/qari-hekmatsisland-a-daesh-enclave-in-jawzjan/; Jeff Seldin, 'Afghan Officials: Islamic State Fighters Finding Sanctuary

in Afghanistan', Voice of America November 18, 2017 https://www.voanews.com/a/afghan-officials-islamic-state-finds-sanctuary-in-afghanistan/4122270.html; Khalid Zerai, 'Illegal logging, mining help bankroll militants in Kunar Province', Salaam Times, October 18, 2017 http://afghanistan.asia-news.com/en_GB/articles/cnmi_st/features/2017/10/18/feature-01; MatinSahak, 'Islamic State seizes new Afghan foothold after luring Taliban defectors', Reuters, December 1, 2017 https://www.reuters.com/article/us-afghanistan-is lamic-state/islamic-state-seizes-new-afghan-foothold-after-luring-taliban-defectors-idUSKBN1DV3G5

72 See below in the main text for a discussion of the ISKP presence and mineral resources in these provinces.

73 Borhan Usman, 'The Islamic State in 'Khorasan': How it began and where it stands now in Nangarhar'

74 The fighting included ISKP fighters capturing and beheading ten Taliban commanders in June 2015. Lauren McNally, Alex Amiral, Marvin Weinbaum, and Antoun Issa, 'The Islamic State in Afghanistan: Examining its Threat to Stability', p 5; Borhan Usman, 'The Islamic State in 'Khorasan': How it began and where it stands now in Nangarhar'

75 The Taliban themselves acknowledged I March 2017 that "DehBala, Kot, Spin Ghar, Achin and Naziyan districts are 25% under Mujahideen control, 30% enemy and 45% under miscellaneous bandits". By "bandits" they presumably meant ISKP. AAN also noted that a significant ISKP presence also remained in the small district of Nazian. DehBala is also known as Haska Mina. 'HaskaMeyna District', Wikipedia, https://en.wikipedia.org/ wiki/Haska_Meyna_District; 'Afghanistan: The security situation in Nangarhar province', Landinfo, October 13, 2016 pp 11-14 https://landinfo.no/asset/3493/1/3493_1.pdf; Borhan Usman, 'The Islamic State in 'Khorasan': How it began and where it stands now in Nangarhar'; 'Percent of Country under the control of Mujahideen of Islamic Emirate', Voice of Jihad, March 26, 2017 https:// alemarah-english.com/?p=12443

76 See interview testimony below; Borhan Osman, 'The Battle for Mamand: ISKP under strain, but not yet defeated', Afghanistan Analysts Network, May 23, 2017 https://www.afghanistan-analysts.org/the-battle-formamand-iskp-under-strain-but-not-yet-defeated/; Jessica Purkiss and Abigail Fielding-Smith, 'Islamic State in Afghanistan: Is US assault working?', The Bureau of Investigative Journalism, July 28,

2017 https:// www.thebureauinvestigates.com/stories/2017-07-28/ islamic-state-in-afghanistan-us-military

77 There were seven US servicemen killed in Nangarhar in 2017. Chad Garland, 'Nangarhar is the deadliest Afghan province for US forces in the past year', Stars and Stripes, January 8, 2018 https://www.stripes.com/ news/nangarhar-is-the-deadliest-afghan-province-forus-forces-in-the-past-year-1.505390

78 Borhan Osman, 'The Battle for Mamand: ISKP under strain, but not yet defeated,' Ayaz Gul, 'IS Says It Has Captured E. Afghan District From Taliban', Voice of America, May 1, 2017 https://www.voanews.com/a/islamic-state-claims-to-have-captured-district-from-rival-taliban-in-afghanistan/3833364.html;

79 That concern is shared by some diplomats. 'Saba: Daesh Seeking to Exploit Mines for Funding', Tolo News, June 8, 2015 http://www.tolonews.com/ business/saba-daesh-seeking-exploit-mines-funding; Global Witness interview with a senior official in a Western embassy, 2015

80 'Afghanistan: The security situation in Nangarhar province', Landinfo, October 13, 2016 pp 11-14 https:// landinfo.no/asset/3493/1/3493_1.pdf; Yousuf Zarifi, '11 Daesh fighters eliminated in Nangarhar drone raid', Pajhwok Afghan News, September 6, 2017 https:// www.pajhwok.com/en/2017/09/06/11-daesh-fighters-eliminated-nangarhar-drone-raid; Yousuf Zarifi, 'Daesh restricted to limited areas in Nangarhar', Pajwhok Afghan News, November 19, 2017 http://www.file.pajhwok.com/en/2017/11/19/daesh-restricted-limited-areas-nangarhar; 'Dozens Killed In Daesh, Taliban Clash in Afghanistan's Nangarhar', Tasnim News, October 16, 2017 https://www.tasnimnews.com/en/ news/2017/10/16/1547299/dozens-killed-in-daesh-taliban-clash-in-afghanistan-s-nangarhar; 'IS, Taliban fight for key towns in Nangarhar', Dawn, November 29, 2017 https://www.dawn.com/news/1373507; Borhan Osman, 'The Islamic State in 'Khorasan'

81 Sune Engel Rasmussen, 'Devastation and a war that rages on: visiting the valley hit by the Moab attack', The Guardian, April 17, 2017 https://www.theguardian. com/world/2017/apr/17/moab-bomb-site-afghanistan

82 In late 2016 the source said that after ISKP captured two Taliban outposts and killed a prominent commander, the source said, "a lot of the Taliban became scared and fled the area." One of the Talebs who was reportedly killed was called Maulavi Abdul Salam, assas-

sinated in the village of Khune Kalai. The source later reported that around April 2017 ISKP had taken over several more villages which had been in the hands of their rivals. Global Witness interview, late 2016; Global Witness interview, mid-2017

83 The source mentioned ISKP taking over mines in locations called Ruidod, Sherzad, Safed Koh, but they could not be identified on the map. Safed Koh is the Dari translation of Spinghar – the White Mountain – which can refer to the whole of the range on the Pakistan border with southern Nangarhar. Sherzad may have been a reference to the district of that name. In addition, there are two locations in Achin called Nargesai, one around 34.0732 North / 70.5556 East, and one at 34.0535 N / 70.6893 E. However, the first of these is in the area of the other mines mentioned by the sources, and fits the testimony. The satellite imagery does not appear to show any mines in the immediate vicinity of the second Nargesai. A village called Sangorai is marked on the best available maps (based on declassified Soviet military maps), but it appears to consist of a few houses a few hundred yards from the larger hamlet of Chaperai, and in fact on more modern satellite imagery no houses are visible in that specific location. It is of course still possible that the name has been applied to a larger mining area distinct from the village.

84 The source referred to the mineral as emerald, but also as 'like emerald.' They said it was found at Ai Tang, Nargesai, and Sangorai, but searches including on Mindat.org did not reveal any history of emeralds in Nangarhar (the Badel emerald mine which is sometimes listed appears to be in Kunar province). Tourmaline however can have a green colour and be easily be mistaken for emerald. See further mentions of emeralds in the main text for more details. Global Witness interviews, late 2016 and mid-2017

85 Global Witness interview, mid-2016

86 The source gave a rough date of early 2015 for the takeover of the mines by ISKP, which is about six months before the movement openly emerged to challenge the Taliban (although they were present in the area before this). But their recollection on dates in general was somewhat vague, as is often the case for sources of this nature. Global Witness interview, mid-2016

87 Global Witness interview, mid-2016

88 The source earlier said that in total nine different mines were in the hands of ISKP, but it was somewhat unclear if this referred to the

number of mines he had more detailed information on, or the total number of mines across the wider local region. Global Witness interview, mid-2016' Global Witness interview, late 2016

89 An elder originally from Achin mentioned a 'blue stone' he called lapis being extracted in Ai Tang. Global Witness interview with an elder originally from Achin district, mid-2017

90 Based on data from the iMMAP OASIS software and satellite photos, locations of the places which were linked to three of the mining areas, Nargesai, Lagharjo, and Shne Kanda, are shown on our map, but the mines themselves were not necessarily immediately proximate to the villages in question. The source described these three mines as producing white marble. The location of Yanak, which he said also produced chromite, was unclear from the testimony. Global Witness interview, late 2016; Global Witness interview, mid-2016

91 Global Witness interview, mid-2016

92 Borhan Osman, 'The Battle for Mamand: ISKP under strain, but not yet defeated'

93 Global Witness interview, mid-2017

94 Yousuf Zarifi, 'Daesh rebels continue to get equipment: Achin residents', Pajhwok Afghan News, November 25, 2017 https://www.pajhwok.com/en/2017/11/25/ daesh-rebels-continue-get-equipment-achin-residents

95 Ayaz Gul, 'IS Says It Has Captured E. Afghan District From Taliban'; Thomas Joscelyn, 'Taliban and Islamic State clash in eastern Afghanistan', Long War Journal, May 1, 2017 https://www.longwarjournal.org/archives/2017/05/taliban-and-islamic-state-clash-in-eastern-afghanistan.php

96 The government claimed to have evicted Daesh from Tora Bora by the end of June. Borhan Osman, 'Another ISKP leader "dead": Where is the group headed after losing so many amirs?', Afghanistan Analysts Network, July 23, 2017 https://www.afghanistan-analysts. org/another-iskp-leader-dead-where-is-the-groupheaded-after-losing-so-many-amirs/ ; Rod Nordland and Fahim Abed, 'ISIS Captures Tora Bora, Once Bin Laden's Afghan Fortress', New York Times, June 14, 2017 https://www.nytimes.com/2017/06/14/world/ asia/isis-captures-tora-bora-afghanistan.html; ZiarYaad, 'Tora Bora Completely Cleared of Daesh: MoD', Tolo News, June 25, 2017 http://www.tolonews.com/afghanistan/tora-bora-completely-cleared-daesh-mod

97 The quote was from Source W. Global Witness interview with Source W, early 2018; Global Witness interview with Source X, early 2018.

98 Global Witness interview with Source W, early 2018; Global Witness interview with Source X, early 2018

99 Ahmed Sultan, 'Few clues on casualties at site of huge U.S. bomb in Afghanistan', Reuters, April 23, 2017 https://uk.reuters.com/article/uk-afghanistan-usa-bomb/few-clues-on-casualties-at-siteof-huge-u-s-bomb-in-afghanistan-idUKKBN17P0I6; Borhan Osman, 'The Battle for Mamand: ISKP under strain, but not yet defeated'; Global Witness interview with Source Z, early 2018; 'After the Dust Settles — Making Sense of the Non-sense', ALCIS, May 3, 2017 https:// stories.alcis.org/after-the-dust-settles-making-senseof-the-non-sense-c97da619a20f

100 ISKP still seem to be very much present in the area. Global Witness interview, mid-2017; Yousuf Zarifi, '7 Daesh rebels killed in Nangarhar airstrikes', Pajhwok Afghan News, March 16, 2018 https://www.pajhwok. com/en/2018/03/16/7-daesh-rebels-killed-nangarhar-airstrikes; 'Internecine rifts: 15 Daesh insurgents decapitated', Pajhwok Afghan News, November 23, 2017 https://www.pajhwok.com/en/2017/11/23/internecine-rifts-15-daesh-insurgents-decapitated

101 Global Witness interview, mid-2017. The source spoke of people mining 'aluminium', which seems fanciful – but could be plausible if it refers to people recovering scrap metal from the remains of the bomb itself.

102 One source claimed 'aluminium' was being mined at the site. That is profoundly improbably – but it is possible that locals were salvaging metal fragments left from bombing. Global Witness interview, mid-2017

103 Global Witness interview, late 2016.

104 Global Witness interview, mid-2017

105 Global Witness interview, late 2016

106 Global Witness interview, September 2016

107 Global Witness interview, late 2016

108 Global Witness interview, mid-2016

109 Global Witness interview, late 2016

110 Global Witness interview with an Afghan civil society researcher, February 2018

111 Global Witness interview, late 2016

112 We were not able to confirm the identity of this source, and there was some grounds for slight caution that he was in fact with ISKP, but other elements of the interview appeared credible. Global Witness interview with a purported ISKP official, mid-2017

113 Global Witness interview, late 2016

114 Global Witness interview, mid-2016; Global Witness interview, mid-2016.

115 Global Witness interview, late 2016.

116 The source also directly called the stones 'emeralds'. While mineral identifications by non-experts are often unreliable, the source's description of small green gemstones found in white rock is compatible with reports of emeralds in other mines. Some sources also mention emeralds found in white talc stone. However, searches including on Mindat.org did not reveal any clear history of emeralds in Nangarhar. The ancient Badel emerald mine is described variously as located in Nangarhar, Parwan and (most commonly) Kunar provinces: references which include a map have it in Kunar. Tourmaline can have a green colour, which could easily be mistaken for emerald. Global Witness interview, late 2016; 'The gemstone tourmaline', Minerals.net, http://www.minerals.net/gemstone/tourmaline_gemstone.aspx ; 'Beryl (Var: Emerald) Sold', The Arkenstone http://www.irocks.com/minerals/specimen/12467; Mindat search, November 8, 2017 https:// www.mindat.org/minlocsearch.php?frm_id=mls&cform_is_valid=1&cf_mls_ page=1&minname=emerald&region=afghanistan&sort=&submit_mls=Search; Selina Denman, 'Emeralds: The journey of a gem ', The National, May 1, 2014 https://www.thenational.ae/ lifestyle/emeralds-the-journey-of-a-gem-1.242915; 'Emerald on matrix', Mineral auctions https://www. mineralauctions.com/auctions/inventory-liquidation-auction-end-june-11-45/emerald-on-matrix-6920. html; 'Beryl var. Emerald on Talc from Badel Mine, Nangarhar, Afghanistan', Online Mineral Museum, http://www.johnbetts-fineminerals.com/jhbnyc/ mineralmuseum/picshow.php?id=49366; 'The Mineral Beryl', Minerals.net http://www.minerals.net/mineral/ beryl.aspx; 'Badel Mine (Budel Mine), Narang District, Konar Province (Kunar Province; Konarh Province; Konarha Province; Nuristan), Afghanistan,' Mindat. org, https://www.mindat.org/loc-30624.html; 'Beryl from Badel Mine (Budel Mine), Narang District, Konar Province (Kunar Province; Konarh Province; Konarha Province; Nuristan), Afghanistan', Mindat.org

https:// www.mindat.org/locentry-988391.html; G.J. Orris and J.D. Bliss, 'Mines and Mineral Occurrences of Afghanistan ', United States Geological Survey, 2002 https:// pubs.usgs.gov/of/2002/0110/pdf/of02-110.pdf; Global Witness interview, late 2016

117 Global Witness interview, mid-2016

118 Matt DuPée, an author and Afghan expert with the US Department of Defence, also reported that he "heard as well that [ISKP] is extracting directly." Global Witness interview with Matt DuPée, November 9, 2017

119 Global Witness interview, mid-2016.

120 Global Witness interview, late 2016

121 Global Witness interview, mid-2016

122 Global Witness interview, mid-2016

123 This counts the four sources who we directly interviewed and the sources who informed Matt DuPée and Borhan Usman.

124 DuPée reported that: "It looks like the activity has begun again, the taxation scheme [on minerals] is in place. The Afghan government in December 2016 was tracking more Taliban involvement in terms of taxation on talc – [but] by February 2017 we see data points on the Islamic State making money from talc. That time period from November 2016 to February 2017 – I think if we looked at the dynamics of what is happening, we would see both groups making a lot of money from both the exploitation and shipping of talc." DuPée's sources included locals, but he was unable to be more specific. Global Witness interviews with Matt DuPée, November 2017 and January 2018 In November 2017

125 Global Witness interview with Borhan Usman, late 2017

126 William Byrd and JavedNoorani, 'Industrial-Scale Looting of Afghanistan's Mineral Resources', United States Institute for Peace, June 2017, p 8 https://www. usip.org/sites/default/files/2017-05/sr404-industrial-scale-looting-of-afghanistan-s-mineral-resources.pdf

127 ZiarYad, 'Daesh, Taliban Plundering Mines, Destroying Forests In Nangarhar', Tolo News, April 3, 2017 http:// www.tolonews.com/afghanistan/provincial/daesh-taliban-plundering-mines-destroying-forests-nangarhar

128 Global Witness interview with ISKP official, mid-2017

129 As we were unable to confirm the identities of the sources, there is some slight possibility that they were the same individual. The quote is from Marty's paraphrase of the conversation. Marty also reported that "the commander told me back in May 2016 that they did not have any financial problems at that time and did not need to do other work than fighting," which might be relevant to explaining why ISKP would not be interested in the potentially lucrative mines. Global Witness email correspondence with Franz Marty, January 20, 2018

130 Global Witness email correspondence with Franz Marty, January 19, 2018

131 Global Witness interview with a leading talc trader from Nangarhar province, mid-2017

132 Global Witness interview with local source from Shadal, mid-2017

133 Mansfield added that there were some reports in early 2018 that more locals were again being allowed into the mining areas. "My understanding is that things are back on line." Global Witness interview with Daniel Mansfield, January 18, 2018

134 Global Witness interview with a senior Afghan police official, February 2018

135 Global Witness interview, late 2016

136 Global Witness interview, mid-2017

137 Global Witness interview, mid-2017

138 Global Witness interview, mid-2016; Global Witness interview, late 2016. In late 2016 the source said that it was locals who did the work at the mines he knew of, and that "only the drivers are from outside." In the same interview however, the source said that: "the workers are 25% locals and 75% foreigners. Most of the locals escaped (…) some of those who left are in favour of them – the rest are foreigners." Global Witness interview, mid-2016; Global Witness interview, late 2016

139 The source spoke of foreigners who "would come and observe" the mining who were not labourers – but also that the extraction was done by both locals and foreigners. There is a small chance that this implies some uncertainty in their testimony over the presence of foreign labourers at all, but the most plausible explanation appears to be that they were highlighting that the visitors were not labourers. Global Witness interview, mid-2016.

140 None of our sources indicated such a route existed, and none was visible in the available satellite imagery. Borhan Osman, 'The Battle for Mamand: ISKP under strain, but not yet defeated', Afghanistan Analysts Network, May 23, 2017 https://www.afghanistan-analysts.org/the-battle-for-mamand-iskp-under-strain-butnot-yet-defeated/; 'Why Daesh chose Achin district as its base in Afghanistan', Pajhwok Afghan News, May 9, 2016 https://www.pajhwok.com/en/2016/05/09/whydaesh-chose-achin-district-its-base-afghanistan

141 Global Witness interview with a leading talc trader, mid-2017

142 Global Witness interview with a former senior police officer from Nangarhar, early 2018

143 The source referred to buying the minerals for Rs50,000 ($476) and sold it in the Korkhano area of Peshawar for Rs90,000-Rs130,000 ($857-$1,238), but there was some confusion whether it was per ton or for the whole load. There is also a possibility they carried talc. Global Witness interview with Source K, early 2018

144 Global Witness interview, late 2016 145 Global Witness interview, late 2016

146 A number of additional images in the missing time period do exist – mostly at lower resolution – but they were not among those Global Witness was able to access. One image from April 2015 was accessible, but was unusable because of 100% cloud cover.

147 Immediately before publication, we were able to view one 50cm image from March 2016. It contained some ambiguous indications that might be interpreted as vehicles around at least one mine, but could equally have been vegetation or rock formations: resolution and quality were too poor to draw any conclusions.

148 One image from relatively close to the Momand valley (about 5km east of the valley mouth) shows several vehicles, but at a location which suggests they might belong to the Afghan Local Police, a government militia force. Three images from April 14, April 29, and May 4 2017 show the vehicles (and possibly people) at a location about 5km east of the mouth of the Momand valley. An image from September 17, 2017 shows the letters ALP scoured on the landscape at that location near a new structure that first appears (possibly in incomplete form) in an image of July 23, 2017.

149 Global Witness exchanges with SARMAP, April 2018

150 Borhan Osman, 'The Battle for Mamand: ISKP under strain, but not yet defeated', Afghanistan Analysts Network, May 23, 2017 https://www.afghanistan-analysts. org/the-battle-for-mamand-iskp-under-strain-but-notyet-defeated/; Jessica Purkiss and Abigail Fielding-Smith, 'Islamic State in Afghanistan: Is US assault working?', The Bureau of Investigative Journalism, July 28, 2017 https://www.thebureauinvestigates.com/stories/2017-07-28/islamic-state-in-afghanistan-us-military

151 Global Witness interview, mid-2017.

152 This is based on a total of 24,112 tons of extraction a year (10,800 tons of talc, 4,992 tons of chromite, and 8,320 tons of marble), carried in trucks with an average capacity of 6 tons. That suggests an average of 11 trucks per day. See Annex B

153 Multiple sources claim extraction was ongoing when the Islamic State took over in mid-2015 (see below). See Annex E for the satellite image mentioned in the text

154 Global Witness interview, mid-2017. Other sources also referred to some extraction happening by hand, although trucks were still used for transport. One local source from Shadal said at the time the Taliban still controlled the Momand valley, he was aware of a mine where "the excavator worked for an hour and made a hole in mountain, after clearing you could see the talc, then put it in plastic bags and carry it by donkeys from the mountain and load it in the trucks to take to Shadal bazaar, and sell it [there]. Global Witness interview with a local source from Shadal, mid-2017

155 Global Witness interview, mid-2017 Another source from Logar said that ISKP 'do a lot of extraction at night' but it was unclear what his own source for this information was. Global Witness interview with Source U, mid-2016

156 The stockpiles were of varying sizes but all much smaller than those at Shadal, and there was no clear sign of them being active in the 2016 or 2017 imagery

157 Global Witness interview with a local source from Shadal, mid-2017

158 The first source gave a date of about March 2017 for this, when the satellite imagery suggests January, but this seems within the range of a plausible rough recollection from a source interviewed some months later. Another source from Shadal, interviewed by the journalist Franz Marty, also confirmed that the people who owned the mined material had reached an agreement with Daesh to allow it

to leave the area. Global Witness interview with a local source from Shadal, mid-2017; Global Witness interview with a tribal elder originally from Achin district, mid-2017; Global Witness email correspondence with Franz Marty, January 19, 2018

159 Osman's source put the Taliban's take at Rs25,000 ($238). Global Witness email correspondence with Borhan Osman, November 2017

160 Global Witness interview with David Mansfield, January 2018. One image from relatively close to the Momand valley (about 5km east of the valley mouth) shows several vehicles, but at a location which suggests they might belong to the Afghan Local Police, a government militia force. Three images from April 14, April 29, and May 4 2017 show the vehicles (and possibly people) at a location about 5km east of the mouth of the Momand valley. An image from September 17, 2017 shows the letters ALP scoured on the landscape at that location near a new structure that first appears (possibly in incomplete form) in an image of July 23, 2017.

161 Global Witness interview with Matt DuPée, November 2017

162 Global Witness interview with Islamic State commander, 2015

163 On the Islamic State in Iraq and Syria, see box below, but also: Sam Jones, Guy Chazan, and Erika Solomon, 'Black gold fuels the 'caliphate' war machine', Financial Times, October 15, 2015; Brian Perkins, 'Islamic State Eying Afghanistan's Natural Resources', The Diplomat, June 28, 2015 http://thediplomat.com/2015/06/islamic-state-eying-afghanistans-natural-resources/

164 The source specifically mentioned the infiltration had been from the Momand valley. They dated this infiltration to late 2015, while other sources indicate that the Taliban had fled Achin and Kot by the middle of 2015. However, this may reflect local variations and very back and forth nature of the conflict, the distinction between the initial take-over of the Momand valley and later expansion to other districts, and the Taliban launched an attempt to retake the district in July. Global Witness interview, mid-2017; Borhan Osman, 'The Islamic State in 'Khorasan' Global Witness interview, late 2016

165 Global Witness interview, late 2016

166 Local sources confirm ISKP's presence and clashes between them and the Taliban. One reported evidence of 'Chechen and Uzbek' families travelling through the district to Tora Bora, and said Arabs were also in the district; possible evidence of an ISKP presence. An-

other source described fighting between the local ISKP commander in his village and Taliban supporters. Global Witness interviews with two credible sources, late 2017.

167 Ayaz Gul, 'Suicide Bomber Kills Six Afghan Civilians', Voice of America, December 3, 2017 https://www. voanews.com/a/suicide-bomber-kills-6-afghan-civilians/4147131.html; Noor Zahid, 'Afghan Civilians Bear Brunt of Taliban, IS Clashes in Eastern Nangarhar', Voice of America, October 20, 2017 https://www. voanews. com/a/afghan-civilians-bear-brunt-of-taliban-is-clashes-in-eastern-nangarhar/4079720. html'; Zeerak Fahim, '31 Taliban, Daesh fighters killed in Nangarhar', Pajhwok Afghan News, July 14, 2017 http://www.pajhwok.com/en/2016/07/14/31-taliban-daesh-fighters-killed-nangarhar;

168 'Humanitarian Bulletin Afghanistan, Issue 70, 1–30 November 2017', United Nations Office for the Coordination of Humanitarian Affairs, December 12, 2017 https://www.humanitarianresponse.info/system/files/ documents/files/20171218_ocha_afghanistan_monthly_humanitarian_bulletin_november_2017_en.pdf

169 Khogyani, Sherzad and PachirWaAgam are separate districts but often referred to as part of a wider 'Khogyani' area, which includes some other districts as well. Global Witness interview with a credible source from Khogyani, January 2018; Christian Parenti, 'Tropic of Chaos: Climate Change and the New Geography of Violence,' Hachette, 2011 Chapter 9, endnote 1; 'IS, Taliban fight for key towns in Nangarhar', Dawn, November 29, 2017 https://www. dawn.com/news/1373507; Yousuf Zarifi, 'Clashes between Taliban, Daesh resume in Nangarhar's Khogyani district', Pajhwok Afghan News, October 28, 2017 https://www.pajhwok.com/ en/2017/10/28/clashes-between-taliban-daesh-resume-nangarhar%E2%80%99s-khogyani-district; Khyber Sarban, 'Islamic State Khorasan Province: Pakistan's New Foreign Policy Tool?', The Diplomat, November 15, 2016 http://thediplomat.com/2016/11/ islamic-state-khorasan-province-pakistans-new-foreign-policy-tool/;

170 Borhan Osman, 'Another ISKP leader "dead": Where is the group headed after losing so many amirs?', Afghanistan Analysts Network, July 23, 2017 https:// www.afghanistan-analysts.org/another-iskp-leaderdead-where-is-the-group-headed-after-losing-somany-amirs/ ; Rod Nordland and Fahim Abed, 'ISIS Captures Tora Bora, Once Bin Laden's Afghan Fortress', New York Times, June 14, 2017 https://www.nytimes. com/2017/06/14/world/asia/isis-captures-to-

ra-bora-afghanistan.html; ZiarYaad, 'Tora Bora Completely Cleared of Daesh: MoD', Tolo News, June 25, 2017 http://www.tolonews.com/afghanistan/tora-boracompletely-cleared-daesh-mod

171 Noor Zahid, 'Clashes Between IS, Taliban Displace Hundreds in Eastern Afghanistan', Voice of America, November 26, 2017 https://www.voanews.com/a/ afghanistan-nangarhar-province-taliban-islamic-state-clashes/4137455.html

172 The source suggested that unlike the Taliban, ISKP would not allow locals any rights to the mines they controlled (although at the time he was interviewed, around two months later, he said ISKP had not yet started exploit them). See lower in the main text for references to the Taliban controlling the Ghunday mines. Global Witness interview-C, late 2017

173 Source W directly said the WaziroTangai mines were active; Source X said that WaziroTangai and Tora Bora were under ISKP control and that "none of the dealers can extract mine until they pay to the Taliban or Daesh."Global Witness interview with Source W, early 2018; Global Witness interview with Source X, early 2018

174 Global Witness interview with Source Z, early 2018

175 Global Witness interview with a former senior police officer from Nangarhar, early 2018

176 The quote is a paraphrase based on the notes of the individual who carried out the interview. Global Witness interview with Taliban commander, early 2018

177 The source said ISKP gave up the project as the government was preparing an operation against it. It is likely that the only reason to build such a road would indeed be to transport minerals, given people and weapons already flowed over the southern border relatively easily. Global Witness interview with a former senior police officer from Nangarhar, early 2018; Borhan Osman, 'The Battle for Mamand: ISKP under strain, but not yet defeated'

178 'Caliphate [based] on the Prophetic Methodology', in 'The Isis papers: a masterplan for consolidating power', The Guardian, December 7, 2105 https:// www.theguardian.com/world/2015/dec/07/islamic-state-document-masterplan-for-power

179 The document specifically talks about barring those who had not pledged allegiance from a stake in an oil or gas field, or from excavating gold or antiquities.

180 Michael Weiss and Hassan Hassan, 'ISIS: inside the army of terror', Regan Arts, New York, 2015, p 227

181 An American journalist held hostage by the Al Nusra Front (the Al Qaeda franchise in Syria) reported that: "The real issue between the Nusra Front and the Islamic State was that their commanders, former friends from Iraq, were unable to agree on how to share the revenue from the oil fields in eastern Syria that the Nusra Front had conquered." William McCants, 'The ISIS Apocalypse: The History, Strategy, and Doomsday Vision of the Islamic State' St. Martin's Press, New York, 2015 pp 136, 90

182 Oil was also used for other strategic goals apart from revenue, like rewarding cooperative tribes and individuals (somewhat similar to the use of ISKP sympathisers as workers reported in Achin). In 2013 for example, ISIS offered a share of oil revenues (among other incentives) to younger tribal leaders if they would turn on their elders in Syria, and gave oil as a reward for cooperative tribes. The tribes that cooperated received various goods as well as oil, and the right to handle their own security and gain advantage over other rival tribes. Those who did not cooperate found their children kidnapped and their tribal members killed. This is the IS version of plato o plomo ("silver or lead" in Spanish) – a tactic often used by Latin American drug cartels to ensure compliance by journalists, government officials etc. The person is offered to either take an offered bribe (the silver) or be killed (the lead). The quote is sometimes attributed to Colombian drug lord Pablo Escobar, but is also used by various Mexican drug syndicates. Finally, as well as providing a lever for influence, the Islamic State also saw attacking critical oil infrastructure as a way to tie down security forces, using oil as bait: an influential 2004 treatise (The Management of Savagery by Abu Bakr Naji) encourages jihadists to carry out "vexation operations" against important targets like oil pipelines, forcing the diversion of local forces to protect those sites. But it is unclear if ISIS, not to mention ISKP, has actually followed this strategy. McCants, The Isis Apocalypse, pp 83, 136; Weiss and Hassan, 'ISIS: Inside the Army of Terror, p 206

183 American classified reports from November 2006 estimated that \$25m-\$100m per year was going to insurgents in Iraq from oil smuggling and other criminal activity associated with the state owned oil industry there. In 2008 an Iraqi official estimated the Al Qaeda was making as much as \$2 million a month by setting up "quasi-legitimate gas stations and fuel-trucking companies, demands "protec-

tion" payments from legitimate businesses, and hijacks trucks carrying gasoline and kerosene, then resells the fuel." Phil Williams, 'Criminals, Militias, and Insurgents: Organized Crime in Iraq', Strategic Studies Institute, June 2009; Lennox Samuels, 'Al Qaeda in Iraq Ramps Up Its Racketeering', Newsweek, Ma20, 2008 http://www.newsweek.com/ al-qaeda-iraq-ramps-its-racketeering-89733

184 As Michael Weiss and Hassan Hassan note, "ISIS is a terrorist organization, but it isn't only a terrorist organization. It is also a mafia adept at exploiting decades-old transnational grey markets for oil and arms trafficking." Weiss and Hassan, 'ISIS: Inside the Army of Terror', pp xv, 234

185 Stefan Heißner, Peter R. Neumann, John Holland-McCowan, and Rajan Basra, 'Caliphate in Decline: An Estimate of Islamic State's Financial Fortunes', The International Centre for the Study of Radicalisation (ICSR), February 2017, p8 http://icsr.info/wp-content/uploads/2017/02/ICSR-Report-Caliphate-in-Decline-An-Estimate-of-Islamic-States-Financial-Fortunes.pdf

186 Rukmini Callimachi, 'The ISIS files', New York Times, April 4, 2018 https://www.nytimes.com/ interactive/2018/04/04/world/middleeast/isis-documents-mosul-iraq.html?hp&action=click&pgtype=Homepage&clickSource=story-heading&module=span-ab-top-region&region=top-news&WT. nav=top-news

187 This, too, originates at least with ISIS' predecessor, the Islamic State of Iraq, who also had a Ministry of Oil. The term diwan can be translated as ministry or bureau – but ministry if perhaps more appropriate given the creation was part of a 'cabinet structure' which surely reflected ISIS concerns to bolster their claims to statehood. The "Cabinet" reported to the Islamic State supreme leader Ibrahim Awwad Ibrahim Ali al-Badri al-Sammarai (better known by his nom de guerre as Abu Bakr al-Baghdadi), although it is unclear if this individual is still alive. The Minister of Oil was a fighter who used the nom de guerre Abu Ahmad al Janabi. Global Witness interview with Caitlin Forrest, March 2017; Williams, 'Criminals, Militias, and Insurgents', p 232; 'Letter dated 11 January 2017 from the Chair of the Security Council Committee'

188 There are, however, at least two other ministries which could control mining-related operations and revenues: the Ministry of Agriculture or the Ministry of War Spoils. Global Witness interview with Caitlin Forrest, March 2017

189 For regularly updated maps, see https://isis.liveuamap.com/ Louisa Loveluck and Liz Sly, 'Islamic State defeated in de facto Syrian capital Raqqa,' Sydney Morning Herald, October 17, 2017 http://www.smh.com.au/world/islamic-state-defeated-in-de-facto-syrian-capital-raqqa-20171017-gz2x34.html

190 Their estimated oil revenue had already fallen by more than half in 2016. 'Letter dated 11 January 2017 from the Chair of the Security Council Committee', p 9

191 The media report dates from October 2017, but does not make clear when exactly the $4m figure relates to. The implication is that it was current at the time of publication. Jim Michaels, 'U.S. coalition slashes ISIS oil revenue by more than 90%', USA Today, October 2, 2017 https://www.usatoday.com/story/news/ world/2017/10/02/u-s-coalition-slashes-isis-oil-revenue-more-than-90/717303001/

192 It is unclear where those gems originated or if they were mined by an Islamic State affiliate. The local affiliates in South East Asia have not been declared full-fledged wilayats yet by senior ISIS leaders. Attacks by Islamic State associated groups have occurred in the Philippines, Malaysia, and Indonesia, with one affiliate made up of the remnants of the Abu Sayyaf group in the Philippines. 'Letter dated 11 January 2017 from the Chair of the Security Council Committee', pp 18-19

193 Aside from oil, another core Islamic State model that may have relevance for Afghanistan is how they have treated antiquities. In Syria, antiquities have been exploited in a variety of ways that can bring money into the organization. First, ISIS has issued excavation licenses and taxed antiquities that have been excavated or were being smuggled out. In Manbij, Syria, ISIS had even established an office to handle antiquities issues and ran a market for antiquities-related exploitation such as metal detectors and digging equipment. They had also imposed taxes on excavation teams and may have had direct relations with some antiquities buyers. It is possible that IS-K could use a similar model for natural resource exploitation in Afghanistan as well – or simply turn to targeting Afghan antiquities. Humud, Pirog, and Rosen, 'Islamic State Financing and US Policy Approaches', p 7

194 Global Witness interview with Source V, a credible source with local connections in Paktia, mid-2015

195 Global Witness interview with Source V, mid-2015

196 He claimed ISKP had brought in an antenna to block mobile phone signals across Shahikot – while this is very likely no more than local rumour, it demonstrates the sense that ISKP were keeping a tight grip on the area. Global Witness interview with Source V, mid-2015

197 According to Source V, the smuggling was carried out by a cousin of Jalaluddin Haqqani called Jalali. He said: "Before a camel was 50,000 – now it is up to 150,000 to 300000." However, he admitted he had not seen camels carrying the minerals himself. Global Witness interview with Source V, mid-2015

198 A well-informed source from the province reported that ISKP no longer controlled the mines. There is some mention of ISKP activity in Paktia in media reports, but no indication that they still control the mine. Global Witness interview-A, mid 2018; Antonio Giustozzi, 'Taliban and Islamic State: enemies or brothers in jihad?', Center for Research and Policy Analysis, December 14, 2017 https://www.crpaweb. org/single-post/2017/12/15/Enemies-or-Jihad-Brothers-Relations-Between-Taliban-and-Islamic-State

199 Jean MacKenzie and Aziz Ahmad Tassal, 'ISIS in Afghanistan is like the boogeyman under the bed', The Week, January 27, 2015 http://theweek.com/articles/534830/ isisin-afghanistan-like-boogey-man-under-bed; Mirwais Adeel, 'ISIS promotes training camp in Logar province of Afghanistan'. Khaama Press, April 29, 2015 http://www.khaama.com/isis-promotes-trainingcamp-in-logar-province-of-afghanistan-9403

200 Global Witness interview with Source U, a senior official in the Logar provincial government, late 2016

201 Sayed Sharif Amiri, 'ANSF Nabs Foreign Militants In Logar As Daesh Infiltrates North', Tolo News, December 10, 2017 http://www.tolonews.com/index.php/ afghanistan/concerns-grow-over-daesh-activities-logar%E2%80%99s-azra-district; GulabuddinGhubar, 'Concerns Grow Over Daesh Activities in Logar'sAzra District', Tolo News, November 27, 2017 http://www. tolonews.com/afghanistan/ansf-nabs-foreign-militants-logar-daesh-infiltrates-north

202 Global Witness interview with Source T, late 2016

203 This was far higher than the 20,000 ($294) the source said the Taliban offered. The UN said one member-state reported high salaries for ISKP of around $600 which then fell to a lower level after period. Global Witness interview with Source T, late 2016; 'Letter dated 9 May 2017 from the Chair of the Security Council Committee estab-

lished pursuant to resolution 1988 (2011) addressed to the President of the Security Council', United Nations, May 25, 2017, p 12 http:// www.un.org/en/ga/ search/view_doc.asp?symbol=S/2017/409

204 Global Witness interview with Source T, late 2016

205 Global Witness interview with Source T, late 2016

206 Global Witness interview with an international diplomatic source, early 2018

207 'War in the Treasury of the People', Global Witness, June 2016 pp 22-23 https://www.globalwitness.org/en/ reports/war-treasury-people-afghanistan-lapis-lazuli-and-battle-mineral-wealth

208 'War in the Treasury of the People', Global Witness

209 Global Witness interview with Franz Marty, a freelance journalist who visited the mines in late 2016, January 2017; Franz Marty, 'Afghanistan's lapis lazuli trade at a standstill', The Third Pole, December 15, 2016 https:// www.thethirdpole.net/en/2016/12/15/afghanistans-lapis-lazuli-trade-at-a-standstill/

210 Ali M. Latifi and Mohsin Khan Mohmand, 'When Islamic State Showed up in a Corner of Afghanistan, "Nothing Was Safe, Not Even the Cows"'; Hamid Shalizi, 'In Afghan province, government woos allies against Islamic State', Reuters, December 6, 2016 http:// www.reuters.com/ article/us-afghanistan-nuristan-islamicstate-ins-idUSKBN13U2WA; Shadi Khan Saif, 'Gun fight in northeastern Afghanistan kills 27', Anadolu Agency, January 9, 2018 http:// aa.com.tr/en/middle-east/gun-fight-in-northeastern-afghanistan-kills-27/1026164; Lalit K Jha, 'Death of Abu Syed disrupts ISIS-K expansion: Pentagon', Pajhwok Afghan News, July 18, 2017 https:// www. pajhwok.com/en/2017/07/18/death-abu-syed-disruptsisis-k-expansion-pentagon

211 'ISIL raises funds in Afghanistan by taxing illegal timber trade', The National, January 21, 2018 https://www. thenational.ae/world/ asia/isil-raises-funds-in-afghanistan-by-taxing-illegal-timber-trade-1.697436; Khalid Zerai, 'Illegal logging, mining help bankroll militants in Kunar Province', Salaam Times, October 18, 2017 http:// afghanistan.asia-news.com/en_GB/articles/cnmi_st/ features/2017/10/18/feature-01; Rohullah Anwari and Abubakar Siddique, 'Illegal Logging Boosts Taliban, IS Revenues In Eastern Afghanistan', Radio Free Europe/ Radio Liberty, October 5, 2017 https://gandhara.rferl. org/a/afghanistan-kunar-forest/28775967. html;

212 'Study on Political Economy of Mineral Extraction in Afghanistan – Kabul, Khost, Kunar, and Samangan', The Liaison Office, 2016 pp 29-41 http://www.tloafghanistan.org/Study_on_Political_Economy_of_Mineral_Extraction_in_Afghanistan_Final_Report.pdf; Harry Bader, Clint Hanna, Clint Douglas, and John Fox, 'Illegal Timber Exploitation and Counterinsurgency Operations in Kunar Province of Afghanistan: A Case Study Describing the Nexus Among Insurgents, Criminal Cartels, and Communities Within the Forest Sector', Journal of Sustainable Forestry, Vol. 32, 2013, pp 329-352 https://calhoun.nps.edu/bitstream/handle/10945/48942/Hanna_Illegal_Timber_2013a.pdf?sequence=1

213 Zia-U-Rahman, 'IS Runs Timber Smuggling Business in Afghanistan, Officials Say', Voice of America, February 8, 2016 https://www.voanews.com/a/islamic-state-timber-smuggling-afghanistan/3182282.html

214 Global Witness interview with an elder originally from Achin district, mid-2017

215 Global Witness interview with a former senior police officer from Nangarhar, early 2018

216 ZabihullahJehanmal, 'MoMP Worries Daesh Might Extract Mineral Riches', Tolo News, December 12, 2017 http://www.tolonews.com/business/mompworries-daesh-might-extract-mineral-riches; ArefMusawi,' Daesh 'Could Exploit' Mineral Resources In Jawzjan', Tolo News, December 9, 2017 http://www. tolonews.com/business/daesh-%E2%80%98could-exploit%E2%80%99-mineral-resources-jawzjan

217 Borhan Osman, 'Descent into chaos: Why did Nangarhar turn into an IS hub?', Afghanistan Analysts Network, September 27, 2016 https://www.afghanistan-analysts.org/descent-into-chaos-why-did-nangarhar-turn-into-an-is-hub/

218 Global Witness interview, late 2016

219 Heather Barr, 'From the Taliban Frying Pan to the Islamic State Fire'; Borhan Osman, 'Descent into chaos: Why did Nangarhar turn into an IS hub?'

220 Global Witness interview with a senior official of the United Nations Assistance Mission to Afghanistan, October 2017

221 The source reported that: "There was an old man who had a car and [so] he came and went [from the area] and they killed him for spying." Global Witness interview, mid-2016

222 Two of the sources mentioned this story. In late 2015 Noor Mohammad, a man from the village of Surobi, who had several daughters, had finally been blessed with a son. In celebration, he had fired his rifle (which many people in Nangarhar keep for self defense) in the air. ISKP reacted by arresting him and using the mosque loudspeakers to call all the local inhabitants together. While Global Witness found significant corroboration for this account, the story is so exceptionally brutal as to prompt some scepticism, and ISKP has denied it. Borhan Usman reported that: "I have heard this story about the baby. People talking about it in the solid details. A woman came and said she had talked to the wife of the Malek – but there was some inconsistency. At the end of the day my impression was that this was made very skilfully. I was never able to trace it to a real thing. IS came out and said we did not do it." Global Witness interview, mid-2016; Global Witness interview, mid-2017; Global Witness interview with Borhan Osman, November 2017

223 ISKP in fact reportedly imposed restrictions on all children going to school, not just girls, but it is not clear if this has been maintained. Heather Barr, 'From the Taliban Frying Pan to the Islamic State Fire'

224 Heather Barr, 'From the Taliban Frying Pan to the Islamic State Fire'

225 Ali M. Latifi and Mohsin Khan Mohmand, 'When Islamic State Showed up in a Corner of Afghanistan, "Nothing Was Safe, Not Even the Cows"'; Mujib Mashal, 'Afghan ISIS Branch Makes Inroads in Battle Against Taliban', New York times, October 13, 2015 https://www.nytimes.com/2015/10/14/world/asia/afghan-isis-branch-makes-inroads-in-battle-against-taliban.html

226 Ali M. Latifi and Mohsin Khan Mohmand, 'When Islamic State Showed up in a Corner of Afghanistan, "Nothing Was Safe, Not Even the Cows"'

227 Global Witness interview, late 2016

228 Global Witness interview, late 2016

229 Global Witness interview, mid-2016

230 David Mansfield, 'The Devil is in the Details: Nangarhar's Continued Decline into Insurgency, Violence and Widespread Drug Production', Afghanistan Research and Evaluation Unit (AREU), February

2016, p 13 http:// areu.org.af/wp-content/uploads/2016/02/1602E-TheDevil-is-in-the-Details-Nangarhar-continued-declineinto-insurgency.pdf

231 Global Witness interview, mid 2016

232 Global Witness interview, late 2016

233 Based on the limited information available, the talc trade does not seem to have especially tight margins once the stone leaves the mines. See section in Chapter 8 on supply chain and associated endnotes for a brief discussion on the talc value chain. But another source also reported that the Taliban in this period took nothing from the local people at all, just from traders who paid in Peshawar. Global Witness interview with an elder originally from Achin, mid-2017

234 Global Witness interview, mid-2016

235 Global Witness interview with a local source from Shadal, mid-2017; Julien Bouissou, 'Comment uneentreprisefrançaise se fourniten talc au pays des talibans', Le Monde, February 13, 2017 http://www. lemonde.fr/asie-pacifique/article/2017/02/13/ un-talc-tout-en-douceur-dans-la-guerre-des-talibans_5078682_3216.html

236 Global Witness email correspondence with Borhan Osman, November 2017

237 Global Witness interview with Taliban commander, early 2018

238 The source said that the rent was 3m rupees a month, and 10m every 3 months – implying that it was a little higher than 3m a month. But it was not clear if this was paid daily, monthly, or quarterly. Global Witness interview with Source M, early 2018

239 The source said that the rent was 3m rupees a month, and 10m every 3 months – implying that it was a little higher than 3m a month. But it was not clear if this was paid daily, monthly, or quarterly. Global Witness interview with Source M, early 2018

240 Global Witness interview with Source Z, early 2018

241 See Annex B for a discussion of talc prices.

242 The Taliban official we interviewed said that the mines were divided up by the Finance Committee of the Quetta Shura, though it was not clear what this meant in practice. A former senior police officer from Nangarhar similar said that the Taliban's revenue from the mines was "divided to different parts, one part for weapons in Sherzad and Achin districts, one part to the Quetta shura and the other

part to the Peshawar shura." Global Witness interview with a Taliban official, early 2018; Global Witness interview with a former senior police officer from Nangarhar, early 2018

243 Global Witness interview with Source M, early 2018

244 There is a Zakhel area in the district of Rodat, immediately south of Jalalabad, and this could be what the source was referring to. Global Witness interview with Source G, early 2018

245 At least one other source also mentioned the Taliban extracting more directly. Matt DuPée also mentioned the Taliban mining directly, but said he had heard of it only in Helmand. Global Witness interview with Taliban commander, early 2018; Global Witness interview with Source H, early 2018; Global Witness interview with Matt DuPée, November 2017

246 The Taliban official and another source suggested locals would also mine informally, but only in their own areas. See Chapter 8 for more discussion of this. Global Witness interview with Source H, early 2018; Global Witness interview with Taliban commander, early 2018

247 A leading talc trader put the load at about 42-45 metric tons, while a truck driver put it at between 40-50 tons. Global Witness interview with a leading talc trader, mid-2017; Global Witness interview with Source G, early 2018; Global Witness interview with Source J, early 2018

248 Global Witness interview with Source G, early 2018

249 Global Witness interview with Source M, early 2018. One individual (Source J) had direct information on one trader who he said never paid any transit tax – but that trader had unusually good contacts with the Taliban, including with "someone in the Quetta Shura," and they still provided a share of profits as well as other assistance. Global Witness interview with Source J, early 2018

250 The former police officer from Nagarhar mentioned that when the Taliban took money on the road: "They give [the driver or trader] an official document to say that we took this much money. Once [the driver] takes the document [they go forward]. Another source specifically mentioned that the Taliban provided a letter which allowed safe passage through their territory, as did Le Monde. It seems very likely this was the general rule. Global Witness interview with a former senior police officer from Nangarhar, early 2018; Global Witness interview with Source J, early 2018; Julien Bouissou, 'Comment

l'industriemondiale du talc finance les talibans et l'Etatislamiqueen Afghanistan'

251 Global Witness interview with Source K, early 2018

252 The source said traders rented these small trucks for around Rs30,000 ($285) per trip. They also mentioned that if the load was wood, the charge would be Rs1,000 ($9.50). Global Witness interview with Source Q, late 2017

253 Global Witness interview with Source H, early 2018

254 Global Witness interview with source L, early 2018

255 The source said that the Taliban were charging Rs100,000 per truck, but that this was an increase from 'before', when they had charged Rs50,000-Rs60,000 ($476-$571). (Presumably this reflected a tighter grip on the trade or a better understanding of how much could be charged.) Given this, it is perhaps sensible to treat the Rs100,000 figure as the top end of a wider range – especially since at Rs100,000 per truck, Rs30m would only be equivalent to just 300 trucks a month, much less than our estimates indicate. See Annex C for further discussion. Global Witness interview with a former senior police officer from Nangarhar, early 2018

256 The source reported that the Taliban would take 50,000 rupees from a 10-wheeler truck with capacity of around 60 tons; from a Kamaz truck with a 22 ton capacity the toll was 40,000 rupees; and from a 16-ton truck it was 30,000. These figures appear high both in terms of the tolls and in terms of the cited capacities. Global Witness interview with Source O, late 2017

257 See figures cited higher in the main text and in the preceding endnote. Our calculations were based on taking the mid-range of load and tax amount estimates. For our eight sources, these were in order Rs700, Rs700, Rs1000, Rs1666, Rs900, Rs1125, Rs2,222 and Rs1,417 (the last is an average of the four figures cited by that one source, so as not to give them too much weight, especially as there was some reason for caution on his estimates). The overall average is about Rs1,216, but to weight the more conservative end of the scale (and the two more credible sources who were discussing the largest trucks, which we assume carry the large part of the trade) we ignore the highest figure and reduce the resulting average by 30%. This gives us a figure of around Rs750.

258 The royalties vary between Afs606 and Afs673 ($5.77$6.40) per ton. 'An analysis and review of talc sector value chain', Ministry of Mines and Petroleum, 2017, copy on file with Global Witness

259 Global Witness interview with Source O, late 2017. The figure for the rental of a Mazda came from another source. Global Witness interview with Source Q, late 2017

260 Global Witness interview with Source O, late 2017

261 Global Witness interview with Source P, late 2017

262 The other checkpostswere described as being in a place called Miyonkhel or Myagon, and in a place called Kurtar or Gortargar. Global Witness interview with Source P, late 2017

263 Global Witness interview with Source Z, early 2018

264 Global Witness interview with an influential local elder from Khogyani, mid-2017

265 The quote was from source W. Global Witness interview with Source W, early 2018; Global Witness interview with Source X, early 2018

266 Global Witness interview with Source X, early 2018

267 Source A-E confirmed the mine was active, with about 15 trucks a day leaving the area with various minerals (although they specifically mentioned only talc and marble mines being in the area). Satellite imagery also showed vehicles at sites in Ladabagh (see main text). Global Witness interview-E, mid 2017

268 Global Witness interview with Source W, early 2018; Global Witness interview with Source X, early 2018

269 Julien Bouissou, 'Comment l'industriemondiale du talc finance les talibans et l'Etatislamiqueen Afghanistan' Another source also mentioned payments being made 'on the ring road of Peshawar'. Global Witness interview with Source X, early 2018

270 The source cited in Le Monde recounted that a colleague who had tried to stop talc trucks in Nangarhar was attacked and had to flee. Julien Bouissou, 'Comment l'industriemondiale du talc finance les talibans et l'Etatislamiqueen Afghanistan'

271 Global Witness email correspondence with Matt DuPée, April 2018

272 Matt DuPée reported a rate ranging from Rs25,000 ($239) to Rs60,000 ($572) per ton charged by the Taliban on marble in Helmand, depending on the type of marble. Another researcher, former

UN political officer Graeme Smith, said one Nangarhar businessmen reported that for every truckload of white marble exported from Khogyani, "the Taliban receive fifty thousand Pakistani Rupees (...) from a money exchanger in the Notyah area of Pakistan." This would imply a much lower rate of tax than Matt DuPée reported from Helmand, though part of the difference may be due to differences in the type and quality of marble between the two parts of the country. Matt DuPée, 'The Taliban Stones Commission and the insurgent windfall from illegal mining', Combatting Terrorism Center, March 10, 2017 https://ctc.usma.edu/ posts/the-taliban-stones-commission-and-the-insurgent-windfall-from-illegal-mining; Global Witness email correspondence with Matt DuPée, April 2018; Global Witness email correspondence with Graeme Smith, May 17, 2018

273 William Byrd and JavedNoorani, 'Industrial-Scale Looting of Afghanistan's Mineral Resources', p 8

274 It seems likely that the Kadikhel the District Governor mentioned refers to Khadakhel, where some activity can be seen at 34.24763 N 69.96281 E and 34.25218 N 69.95767 E. It is perhaps significant that this is around the area referred to as Tutu by another source (see lower in main text), where the Taliban had a checkpost. But there is also a Katikhel listed at 34.21218 N 70.02621 E, which is within or adjacent to Markikhel – the Soviet maps appear list Markikhel as an area rather than a village, although the iMMAP OASIS database records a spot location under that place name. The maps also list a Merkekhel village (with different transliteration but similar pronunciation) south of Ghunday – on our map we have listed it as Markikehl for consistency. On balance, it seems likely the Markikhel the District Governor mentioned simply refers to a wider area or to the valley that Ghundayis located in – there is a 'MerkekhelTangai' (Merkekhel Narrows or Gorge) referenced in that area. Given all this, it is quite possible that the District Governor was generally talking about the Taliban taxing talc and marble mining around Ghunday – but the possibility he was also referring to Tutu/Khadakhel as a second area should not be discounted. We were not able to contact the District Governor to clarify the situation. Zeerak Fahim, 'Precious stones being smuggled to Pakistan from Sherzad', Pajhwok Afghan News, December 27, 2017 https://www.pajhwok.com/en/2015/12/27/precious-stones-being-smuggled-pakistan-sherzad

275 The Taliban themselves claim to control 75% of Khogyani and 95% of Sherzad and Hesarak, but more neutral sources generally re-

port a similar picture. A former police officer from Nangarhar said it had taken around 1,000 government troops three days to travel just 25-30km to reach the district center. LandInfo reported that the "southwestern [Nangarhar] districts of Hesarak, Sherzad and Khogyani have long been the heartland of [the] Taliban in Nangarhar." They said that in April 2016 a local journalist "considered that the authorities had very little presence in Sherzad. Here the rebels had almost full freedom of movement, and the government's presence was limited to their own buildings in the district centre. He further claimed that the population largely supported the Taliban." The same source (it appears) said that "the authorities had greater control in Khogyani district than in Sherzad and Hesarak. According to the source, this means that there are many people who support the government. At the same time, he stressed that the conflict dynamic is complicated." But this contrasts with the more recent report from Matt DuPée, who said that: "I have been told a number of times that all of the [Khogyani] district apart from the centre is under Taliban control – except the centre plus 2km round it. Sources have been consistent with that in late 2017." Multiple sources claim extraction was ongoing when the Islamic State took over in mid-2015 (see start of Chapter 7 for more details). DuPée reported that the Taliban's taxation of mines in those districts began as early as 2004 or 2005. The New York Times similarly reports that the "Afghan government's authority in Khogyani, in a remote region of Nangarhar Province, has long been confined to the district compound and the immediate surroundings." 'Percent of Country under the control of Mujahideen of Islamic Emirate', Voice of Jihad, March 26, 2017 https://alemarah-english.com/?p=12443; Global Witness interview with Matt DuPée, January 2018; Global Witness correspondence with Matt DuPée, April 2018; 'Afghanistan: The security situation in Nangarhar province', LandInfo, October 13, 2016 pp 17, https:// landinfo.no/asset/3493/1/3493_1.pdf; Mujib Mashal, 'In Tangled Afghan War, a Thin Line of Defense Against ISIS', New York Times, December 25, 2017 https://www. nytimes.com/2017/12/25/world/asia/eastern-afghanistan-isis.html? _r=0; Global Witness interview with a former senior police officer from Nangarhar, early 2018

276 See discussion of this point in the main text and endnotes of Chapter 8.

277 Corruption Bouissou, 'Comment l'industriemondiale du talc finance les talibans et l'Etatislamiqueen Afghanistan'

278 The report, from the Afghanistan Anti-Corruption Network (AACN), alleged that 500 trucks of talc were exported from Khogyani every day, creating revenues for insurgents (both Taliban and ISKP) of $46m a year. The report is cited in media articles, but the actual research is not published on the AACN website or apparently anywhere else, and so must be treated with a good deal of scepticism. FarhadNaibkhel, 'Bootie of natural riches; Insurgents earns $46m from illegal mining to continue war in Afghanistan: Survey', Afghanistan Times, February 1, 2017 http://afghanistantimes.af/ bootie-of-natural-riches-insurgents-earns-46m-from-illegal-mining-to-continue-war-in-afghanistan-survey/

279 Global Witness interview with Franz Marty, January 2017

280 One source recounted how that in late 2015, a local militia commander called Sabz Ali had been killed by the Taliban after a disagreement over the mines: allegedly he had taken a 20 per cent cut on local mining revenue to allow passage through the checkpoints he controlled, and the Taliban wanted to reduce this to 5 per cent. Global Witness interview with Source T, late 2016; Global Witness interview with Source U, late 2016

281 Matt DuPée, 'The Taliban Stones Commission and the insurgent windfall from illegal mining', Combatting Terrorism Center, March 10, 2017 https://ctc.usma.edu/ posts/the-taliban-stones-commission-and-the-insurgent-windfall-from-illegal-mining

282 'Letter dated 18 August 2015 from the Chair of the Security Council Committee established pursuant to resolution 1988 (2011) addressed to the President of the Security Council', United Nations, August 26, 2015, p 15 http://www.securitycouncilreport.org/ atf/cf/%7B65BFCF9B-6D27-4E9C-8CD3-CF6E4FF96FF9%7D/s_2015_648.pdf

283 The UN report in fact also described mining as the second highest source of revenue for the Taliban, but there is some uncertainty about how much revenue comes from other sources (notably taxes on local business) and this could be substantial. Matt DuPée, 'The Taliban Stones Commission and the insurgent windfall from illegal mining', Combatting Terrorism Center, March 10, 2017; 'Letter dated 18 August 2015 from the Chair of the Security Council Committee established pursuant to resolution 1988 (2011) addressed to the President of the Security Council', United Nations, August 26, 2015, p 15; Gabriel Dominguez and Masood Saifullah, 'How the Tal-

iban get their money', Deutsche Welle, January 21, 2016 http://www.dw.com/en/howthe-taliban-get-their-money/a-18995315

284 'War in the Treasury of the People', Global Witness, pp 6-9 There are other examples like this. In Paktika province for example, one source said he had visited a laal (garnet or ruby) mine located in Urgun district. The source identified a Commander Jabar, a former follower of the notorious local militia leader Commander Azizullah, whose forces have been implicated in significant human rights abuses. The source believed the mine was under Azizullah's control. Interview with Source A-D, an inhabitant of Paktia province, late 2016; '"Today We Shall All Die": Afghanistan's Strongmen and the Legacy of Impunity'; Human Rights Watch, March 2015, pp 31-36 https://www.hrw.org/sites/default/ files/report_pdf/afghanistan0315_4up.pdf

285 As described above, a large talc stockpile of talc was systematically removed from the village of Shadal in early 2017. The fact that the mineral was held in Shadal an extended time makes it more plausible that there was not another way to remove it apart from the route through government-controlled territory to Shadal. Global Witness interview, late 2016; Global Witness interview with Source G, early 2018; Global Witness interview with Source J, early 2018; Global Witness interview with Source K, early 2018; Julien Bouissou, 'Comment uneentreprisefrançaise se fourniten talc au pays des talibans', Le Monde, February 13, 2017 http://www.lemonde.fr/asie-pacifique/article/2017/02/13/un-talc-tout-en-douceur-dans-laguerre-des-talibans_5078682_3216.html

286 A USIP report put the date the ban was imposed as early 2015, but an Imerys official reported that the "border was indeed closed to talc trade between the third quarter of 2015 and the third quarter of 2016. Then the border reopened before closing again at the end of 2016. Talc export resumed in the first quarter of 2017." [sic] This may be a reference to border closings caused by tensions between the Afghan and Pakistani governments rather than by attempts to restrict the talc trade. The USIP dates in any case seem more reliable given there is a media confirmation of the ban being partially lifted in September 2015. 'Minister of Mines and Petroleum meets the members of the union of talc', Ministry of Mines and Petroleum, September 21, 2015 http://mom.gov.af/en/news/minister-ofmines-and-petroleum-meets-the-members-of-theunion-of-talc; Global Witness email correspondence with Vincent Gouley, Head of Financial Communica-

tion & Investor Relations, Imerys, April 18, 2018; William Byrd and JavedNoorani, 'Industrial-Scale Looting of Afghanistan's Mineral Resources', United States Institute for Peace, June 2017, p 8

287 The figure of a million tons comes from an unnamed Afghan government official cited in the USIP report – it is not known where they obtained the figure from or how exact it is. But Matt DuPée also reported that between 850,000 and 1m tons of talc was taken out after the ban was lifted. Global Witness interview with Matt DuPée, November 9, 2017; Julien Bouissou, 'Comment l'industriemondiale du talc finance les talibans et l'Etatislamiqueen Afghanistan'; 'Minister of Mines and Petroleum meets the members of the union of talc', Ministry of Mines and Petroleum, September 21, 2015 http://mom.gov.af/en/news/minister-of-mines-and-petroleum-meets-the-members-of-the-union-of-talc; Global Witness interview with Afghan researcher, early 2018

288 It was difficult to fully confirm what restrictions were in place. But a government presentation also references the ban on unprocessed talc. It gives the Afghan year 1392 (2013) as its start date, but this may be an error. An official from Imerys, the international talc traders, said the requirement that talc be processed had been in place from the third quarter of 2016. The precise legal status of both the bans is unclear: while presumably they are the result of presidential decrees, Global Witness could not find a reference to them. Global Witness email correspondence with Vincent Gouley, Head of Financial Communication & Investor Relations, Imerys, April 18, 2018; Global Witness email correspondence with a Ministry of Mines advisor, March 2018; 'An analysis and review of talc sector value chain', Ministry of Mines and Petroleum, 2017, copy on file with Global Witness

289 It is unclear exactly how 'semi-processed bulk form' is defined, but it is differentiated in the government report from raw talc. One trader said 21 processing plants had been established near Jalalabad. Global Witness interview with Source Y, early 2018; 'An analysis and review of talc sector value chain', Ministry of Mines and Petroleum, 2017, copy on file with Global Witness

290 Global Witness interview with a former senior police officer from Nangarhar, early 2018; trade data from resourcetrade.earth, accessed April 14, 2018 https:// resourcetrade.earth/data?year=2016&exporter=4&category=1151&units=value

291 The first of these sources put the figure at Rs6,000Rs7,000 ($57-$66), the second at Rs6,000, and the third at Rs5,000 ($48). There is a slight possibility that the third source was referring to the price for smaller vehicles. Global Witness interview with Source G, early 2018; Global Witness interview with Source J, early 2018; Global Witness interview with Source K, early 2018

292 The source suggested those who were unfamiliar with the system might pay Rs8,000 ($76), and said described a diver paying twice on one occasion "because the person of the customs had been changed." Global Witness interview with Source G, early 2018

293 Global Witness interview with Source K, early 2018 294 Global Witness interview with Source J, early 2018 295 Global Witness interview with Source W, early 2018

296 Global Witness interview with Source G, early 2018

297 Bouissou, 'Comment l'industriemondiale du talc finance les talibans et l'Etatislamiqueen Afghanistan'

298 One source reported that in Achin as well two local tribes (the Rahimdadkhel and Haiderkhel) controlled the rights to the mines in the time when the Taliban still held the area. Meanwhile, a media report suggested communities in Sherzad had clashed over control of minerals, which indicates they must have been of some benefit to them. Global Witness interview with a local source from Shadal, mid-2017; Yousuf Zarifi, 'Taliban seen behind tribal clash over Nangarhar stone deposit', Pajhwok Afghan News, August 21, 2017 https:// www.pajhwok.com/en/2017/08/21/taliban-seen-behind-tribal-clash-over-nangarhar-stone-deposit

299 Global Witness interview with a former senior police officer from Nangarhar, early 2018

300 Global Witness interview with a former senior police officer from Nangarhar, early 2018

301 The former senior police officer from Nangarhar reported that one politically-connected individual involved in the trade had "30 to 40" armed men. Another credible and informed source also said that this individual "has a militia." Global Witness interview with a former senior police officer from Nangarhar, early 2018; Global Witness interview with Source O, early 2018

302 The government's own talc study suggested a figure of $151. The average price of unprocessed talc exported from Pakistan in 2016 was

about $190, and one trader reported buying talc at $130 and selling it at $170-$200 in Peshawar. Internationally, processed Afghan talc is advertised on the trading website Alibaba.com at around $150-$300. Semi-processed talc lumps (purportedly originating in Pakistan) was advertised at $168-$222. 'Talc lumps', Alibaba.com, https://www. alibaba.com/product-detail/talc-lumps_115510779. html?spm=a2700.7724838.2017115.9.317e2977x7fkQD; "Talcum Powder Brands Mineral Talc Lumps Importers Talc Afghanistan', Alibaba.com https://www.alibaba. com/product-detail/Talcum-Powder-Brands-MineralTalc-Lumps_60557892546.html?spm=a2700.7724838.2017115.1.317e2977x7fkQD; Global Witness interview with Source X, early 2018; 'An analysis and review of talc sector value chain', Ministry of Mines and Petroleum, 2017, copy on file with Global Witness; trade data from resourcetrade.earth, accessed April 14, 2018 https://resourcetrade.earth/data?year=2016&exporter=586&category=1152&units=value

303 The export tax revenue figure was cited in the government's own analysis for the year 1396 according to the Afghan calendar, but it is unclear if it refers to all of that period or just the first three quarters. The 5% rate was found in the Ministry of Finance's list of customs tariffs. 'An analysis and review of talc sector value chain', Ministry of Mines and Petroleum, 2017, copy on file with Global Witness; 'Customs Tariff – 2010/1390', Islamic Republic of Afghanistan Ministry of Finance, General Directorate of Customs, p 75 http://mof.gov.af/Content/files/Tariff_English_final.pdf

304 Global Witness requested the revenue figures from the Minister of Mines and one of her key advisors, but they were not able to provide the data. Global Witness correspondence with Nargis Nehan, March 2018; 'An analysis and review of talc sector value chain', Ministry of Mines and Petroleum, 2017, copy on file with Global Witness

305 Mansfield notes that: The magnesium silicate business does not generate income just in RS 11 [one of Mansfield's research sites in southern Nangarhar] and the Mahmand [sic] valley but provides revenue across a much wider area, including to the government of Afghanistan and Pakistan. The value chain for magnesium silicate, known locally as shawkanay, begins in the hills to the north and east of RS11 where it is mined by people from the Mahmand valley. It is estimated that one miner collects around 100 seer [an Afghan unit of weight equivalent to 7kg) of shawkanay in a day and sells it for 8 PR in the Mahmand valley. The shawkanay is subsequently transported

across the bridge at the mouth of the Mahmand valley to Shadal bazaar where it is stored and purchased by traders for around 12 PR per seer. The shawkanay is then transported onwards to Pakistan where it is sold on the Peshawar ring road for around 6,000 to 6,500 PR per metric ton. Some of the final product is said to be transported to Karachi port and then on to Italy. While the government of Afghanistan is no longer present in the Mahmand valley it still generates a revenue stream from the production and subsequent trade in Shawkanay. Firstly, the government raises a revenue by issuing licenses to traders. These costs 50,000 PR and are issued by the Ministry of Trade following approval by the Directorate of Mines. Secondly, the government then taxes the trade, weighing the trucks transporting the shawkanay in Kahi, and charging 650 Afs per metric ton to be paid in the bank in Jalalabad. The final beneficiary of the trade is the Pakistani government which is said to charge a tax of 150 PR per metric ton on exports and 1,600 PR per metric ton when the shawkanay is sold in Pakistan. It is alleged that in the recent past the Taliban have also approached the traders of shawkanay looking for a financial contribution. It is said that the traders declined this request on the basis that there are insufficient profit margins in the business. [sic] The prices he cites seem very low: Rs12 per ser ($0.11) amounts to just $16.32 a ton. While this echoes the export records showing an average price of $14 per ton, we have already discussed why those appear artificially low. So does the price he quotes for sales in Pakistan of $57$61 a ton. If the traders are paying Af650 ($9.56) per ton to the government (which seems highly unlikely), that increases the plausibility of our reports that an average of around this much per ton was taken by the Taliban in Sherzad, with bribes of a few thousand rupees going to the government in place of the bulk of royalties. There might be some on the supply chain – the labourers for example – who would indeed struggle with any extra burden, but Mansfield specifically cites the traders. David Mansfield, 'David Mansfield, 'Examining the Impact of IDEA-NEW on Opium Production – Nangarhar: A Case Study', Alcis Ltd, January 11, 2015 p 60 https://www.alcis.org/media/102697/idea-new_nangarhar_evaluation_2015-report.pdf; 'An analysis and review of talc sector value chain', Ministry of Mines and Petroleum, 2017, copy on file with Global Witness

306 Le Monde makes a similar point, quoting a "source well informed on the supply chain to the Afghan frontier" saying that: "Talc costs between $40 and $60 a ton when it leaves the Afghan mine, and $150 a ton when it arrives at the depot of North West Minerals, on the

other side of the frontier. Between the two, between $50 and $100 go on official taxes, transport...and into nature." Part of the money is in fact taken by corrupt officials and by the insurgents. The same applies for traders moving stone all the way to Pakistan. One trader with a mine in Nangarhar said that "in general with all custom duties and expenses [presumably including bribes], one [ton] of talc costs us about $130, and we sell it from $170 to $200." Julien Bouissou, 'Comment uneentreprisefrançaise se fourniten talc au pays des talibans', Le Monde, February 13, 2017 http://www.lemonde.fr/asie-pacifique/article/2017/02/13/un-talc-tout-en-douceur-dans-la-guerre-des-talibans_5078682_3216.html; Global Witness interview with Source X, early 2018

307 Another source reported that while they did not have exact information, the belief among those in a position to know was that the talc "goes to China and [other places] abroad, some say it is used in Pakistani factories." Global Witness interview, mid-2016; Global Witness interview, late 2016

308 One trader confirmed that "most of the talc mining areas are under control of the Taliban. The Taliban send their agent to collect taxes in some areas which are not under [their] control." Global Witness has not come across any report of talc extraction outside of Nangarhar in our extensive research, apart from one report of two talc mines in Kandahar being put up for tender in early 2015. No corresponding contracts appear on the Ministry of Mines list. If we take the government's talc contracts as a proxy for the location of all talc mines, all are in districts that are either under effective Taliban control, or highly contested (see below). Our research did not uncover any reports of talc mines in other districts, and mIndat.org does not list any deposits in the province outside of Achin and Sherzad. 'Talc', Mindat.org, accessed May 1, 2018 https://www.mindat. org/min-3875.html; Global Witness interview with Source W, early 2018 'An analysis and review of talc sector value chain', Ministry of Mines and Petroleum, 2017, copy on file with Global Witness; Ahmad Bashir Naadem, 'Kandahar puts 4 minerals deposits on offer', Pajhwok Afghan News, February 3, 2015 https://www. pajhwok.com/en/2015/03/10/kandahar-puts-4-mineral-deposits-offer

309 Of the 47 talc contracts (active and expired) listed on the Ministry of Mines website, all are in Nangarhar, and all but nine are in Achin and Sherzad (with 14 and 24 respectively). Of those nine, three are in Hesarak, which is largely Taliban-controlled, and two each are in Haska

Mena and PachirWaAgam, which are heavily contested. The location of the other contracts could not be determined: only 10 of the contacts had GPS coordinates, with the rest having place names. Interestingly, there are no contracts for any mineral listed for Khogyani. In terms of active contracts (i.e. within their period of validity and not listed as cancelled), in Achin district 10 of the 14 contracts were registered as active as of April 2017, according to the Ministry of Mines lists, with another 21 out of 24 listed as active in Sherzad. A Ministry of Mines report from late 2017 listed 21 contracts as active, 15 of them in Sherzad. Our research produced no indication that contracts had been cancelled or suspended because of the presence of insurgents. 'Small mines contracts', Ministry of Mines and Petroleum of the Islamic Republic of Afghanistan, http://mom.gov. af/en/page/momp-contracts/104421; 'An analysis and review of talc sector value chain', Ministry of Mines and Petroleum, 2017, copy on file with Global Witness 'Small mines contracts', Ministry of Mines of the Islamic Republic of Afghanistan, http://mom.gov.af/en; 'Percent of Country under the control of Mujahideen of Islamic Emirate', Voice of Jihad, March 26, 2017 https:// alemarah-english.com/?p=12443; 'Afghanistan: The security situation in Nangarhar province', LandInfo, October 13, 2016, pp 16-19 https://landinfo.no/asset/3493/1/3493_1.pdf; Yousuf Zarifi, "Civilian deaths only outcome of Haska Mena operation", Pajhwok Afghan News, August 12, 2017 https://www.pajhwok. com/en/2017/08/12/%E2%80%98civilian-deaths-only-outcome-haska-mena-operation%E2%80%99; Rod Nordland and Fahim Abed, 'ISIS Captures Tora Bora, Once Bin Laden's Afghan Fortress', New York Times, June 14, 2017 https://www.nytimes.com/2017/06/14/ world/asia/isis-captures-tora-bora-afghanistan.html; ZiarYaad, 'Tora Bora Completely Cleared of Daesh: MoD', Tolo News, June 25, 2017 http://www.tolonews. com/afghanistan/tora-bora-completely-cleareddaesh-mod

310 A former senior police officer from Nangarhar with knowledge of the trade told Global Witness that "Pakistani companies do not work in Afghanistan. They have represenatives who come to Afghanistan." Le Monde's research on the work of IMI Omar suggests that occasionally Pakistani companies may be more directly involved, although it was somewhat unclear if did more than sourcing from Afghan sellers. In terms of numbers. according to resourcetrade.earth, of 561,430 tons of Afghan exports to all countries, 561,286 tons went to Pakistan – all of it unprocessed. The Ministry of Mines study on talc supply chains meanwhile found that "Afghanistan has

exported 100 percent of its talc in bulk to Pakistan and China." Talc bound for China presumably exists via Pakistan, given the difficulty of alternative routes. Global Witness interview with a former senior police officer from Nangarhar, early 2018; 'An analysis and review of talc sector value chain', Ministry of Mines and Petroleum, 2017, copy on file with Global Witness; trade data from resourcetrade.earth, accessed April 14, 2018 https://resourcetrade.earth/data?year=2016&exporter=4&category=1152&units=value; trade data from resourcetrade.earth, accessed April 2, 2018 https://resourcetrade.earth/data?year=2016&exporter=4&-category=1151&units=value

311 Pakistan's share was 37%, with Canada and China the other two major sources. 'Talc and Pyrophyllite', United States Geological Survey, January 2017 https:// minerals.usgs.gov/minerals/pubs/commodity/talc/ mcs-2018-talc.pdf

312 A 2014 report on talc from Pakistan's export promotion bureau lists 12 other major exporting companies in Pakistan. Mustansar Mehmood, Sajid Hussain, 'A Report on Talc (Soap Stone)', Trade Development Authority of Pakistan, November 2014 https://www.tdap.gov.pk/ doc_reports/TDAP_Report_on_Talc_(Soap_Stone).pdf; SA, 'MINERALS LINE, Minerals, soapstone, natural Talc, on EUROPAGES.' http://www.europages.co.uk/ MINERALS-LINE/00000004642402-452335001.html

313 'World Mineral Production 2012-2016', British Geological Survey, February 2018, p 72 http://www. bgs.ac.uk/downloads/start.cfm?id=3396; trade data from resourcetrade.earth, accessed April 17, 2018 https://resourcetrade.earth/data?year=2016&exporter=586&category=1151&units=value; trade data from resourcetrade.earth, accessed April 17, 2018 https:// resourcetrade.earth/data?year=2016&exporter=586&category=1152&units=value

314 There is one import of about 8,400 tons from China in 2016, but no other imports above 5,000 tons apart from those coming from Afghanistan. Trade data from resourcetrade.earth, accessed April 14, 2018 https://resourcetrade.earth/data?year=2016&importer=586&category=1151&units=value; Trade data from resourcetrade.earth, accessed April 14, 2018 https:// resourcetrade.earth/data?year=2016&importer=586&category=1152&units=value

315 An Afghan government report refers to Pakistan accounting to 2% of global talc consumption in 2016. A separate source lists global talc consumption as 6m tons in that year, giving a figure of 120,000 tons for Pakistani consumption. 'An analysis and review of talc sec-

tor value chain', Ministry of Mines and Petroleum, 2017, copy on file with Global Witness; 'Global Talc Market to Cross US$ 1.6 Billion by 2022', Cision PR Newswire, December 12, 2016 https://www.prnewswire.com/news-releases/global-talc-market-to-crossus-16-billion-by-2022-606049696.html

316 The calculation here is that of 305,970 tons of Pakistani talc exports, 125,330 originate in Pakistan (the entirety of Pakistani production) and the remaining 180,640 tons in Afghanistan (41% and 59% of the total). If we assume that domestic consumption of 120,000 tons is equally supplied by Pakistani and Afghan talc (60,000 tons each), then the figures are 65,330 and 240,640 tons – 21% and 79% of the total.

317 In 2016, out of a total of 305,970 tons of total Pakistani talc exports (both processed and unprocessed) 128,542 tons, or 42%, went to the United States. Trade data from resourcetrade.earth, accessed April 17, 2018 https://resourcetrade.earth/data?year=2016&exporter=586&category=1151&units=value; trade data from resourcetrade.earth, accessed April 17, 2018 https:// resourcetrade.earth/data?year=2016&exporter=586&category=1152&units=value; Ian Wilson, 'Global Talc Markets'

318 The calculation here is that of the 35% of US imports of talc that come from Pakistan, at least 60% (and more realistically 80%) of those come from Afghanistan, so between 21% and 28% of US imports come from Afghanistan. (35%x60%=21%; 35%x80%=28%). 'Talc and Pyrophyllite', United States Geological Survey, January 2017 https://minerals.usgs.gov/minerals/ pubs/commodity/talc/mcs-2018-talc.pdf

319 In 2016 the Netherlands imported 40,279 tons of talc from Pakistan, while Italy imported 39,034 tons, making them the second and third largest markets after the USA, respectively accounting for 13.2% and 12.8% of Pakistani exports. In the Netherlands Pakistani talc accounted for 17.6% of all talc imports (processed and unprocessed), although is accounted for 88.6% of unprocessed talc imports. In Italy Pakistan accounted for 29.7% of all talc imports, and 50.2% of unprocessed talc imports. Other European countries (Germany, Portugal, Belgium, Greece, Spain, Slovenia, and Poland) accounted for 10.5% of Pakistani exports, meaning that a total of 78.5% of Pakistani export went to the US and EU. Trade data from resourcetrade.earth, accessed April 14, 2018 https://resourcetrade.earth/data?year=2016&exporter=586&category=1151&units=value; Trade data from

resourcetrade.earth, accessed April 14, 2018 https://resourcetrade.earth/data?year=2016&exporter=586&category=1152&units=value; Trade data from resource trade.earth, accessed April 20, 2018 https://resourcetrade.earth/data?year=2016&importer=381&category=1151&units=weight; Trade data from resource trade.earth, accessed April 20, 2018 2018https://resourcetrade.earth/data?year=2016&importer=381&category=1152&units=weight; Trade data from resource trade.earth, accessed April 20, 2018 https://resourcetrade.earth/data?year=2016&importer=528&category=1151&units=weight; Trade data from resource trade.earth, accessed April 20, 2018 https:// resourcetrade.earth/data?year=2016&importer=528&category=1152&units=weight

320 Using the same data sources, we can work out that other European countries (Poland, Germany, Portugal, Belgium, Greece, Spain, Slovenia, in ascending order by weight of exports) accounted for 10.5% of Pakistani exports, meaning that a total of 78.5% of Pakistani exports went to the US and EU combined.

321 The basis for this estimate is as follows. If we take the total of Pakistani exports and Pakistani domestic consumption we get a total of (305,970+120,000 =) 425,970 tons of talc being used in total (this is assuming there is no significant net stockpiling). From this we deduct the amount produced in Pakistan (125,330 tons): the remainder (300,640 tons) we assume must be supplied by Afghan talc. If we then assume that half of the domestic consumption of 120,000 tons is supplied by domestic talc and half by Afghan talc, this means that 240,640 tons of Afghan talc is going to export, along with 65,330 tons of Pakistani talc – a roughly 80%-20% split. So of the 128,542 tons going to the US, 80% (102,834 tons) are Afghan. That is 34% of the total amount of Afghan talc (300,640 tons). Total EU imports are 111,600 tons, of which 80% is 89,280 tons, or 30% of the total. This would mean 64% of Afghan talc goes to the US and EU together. However, the major problem with this calculation is that we know the figure for the total amount of Afghan talc does not match the resourcetrade.earth export data, which shows Afghan exports to Pakistan of 561,286 tons. There is a fundamental discrepancy in the data, as noted in the main text, with the figures for Afghan exports (even without adding in Pakistani production) far exceeding Pakistani consumption and exports. We can try to compensate for this by taking the Afghan export figure as the correct total, then the amount going to the US (102.834 tons) is 18%, and to the EU (89,280 tons) is 16% - a total of 34%. We can take this as the lower end of our

range. But there is clearly an error somewhere in the data, which it is important to acknowledge as it casts a certain question over the overall process. Incidentally, our calculations are based on volume of exports, but an analysis by value produces very similar figures.

322 Trade data from resourcetrade.earth, accessed April 14, 2018 https://resourcetrade.earth/data?year=2016&exporter=4&category=1152&units=value; trade data from resourceTrade.Earth, accessed April 2, 2018 https://resourcetrade.earth/data?year=2016&exporter=4&category=1151&units=value

323 Trade data from resourcetrade.earth, accessed April 14, 2018 https://resourcetrade.earth/data?year=2016&exporter=586&category=1388&units=value; 'Dynamics of chrome trading', Dawn, October 1, 2012 https://www.dawn.com/news/753264; 'Pakistan chromite production by year', Index Mundi https:// www.indexmundi.com/minerals/?country=pk&product=chromite&graph=production; 'World Mineral Production 2012-2016', British Geological Survey, February 2018, p 13 http://www.bgs.ac.uk/downloads/ start.cfm?id=3396

324 Abdul Maqsod Azizi' 'Illegal mining, smuggling of chromites continue unabated', Pajhwok Afghan News, April 23, 2017 https://www.pajhwok.com/en/2017/04/23/ illegal-mining-smuggling-chromites-continue-unabated; Matt DuPée, 'The Taliban Stones Commission and the insurgent windfall from illegal mining', Combatting Terrorism Center, March 10, 2017 https://ctc.usma.edu/ posts/the-taliban-stones-commission-and-the-insurgent-windfall-from-illegal-mining; Luis de la Corte and HristinaHristova, 'The Role of Illicit Trafficking in the Af-Pak Context', Instituto Español de EstudiosEstratégicos (IEEE), April 11, 2012 p7 http://www. ieee.es/en/Galerias/fichero/docs_marco/2012/ DIEEEM03-2012_PapelTraficosIlicitosAF-PAK_ENGLISH.pdf; 'World Mineral Production 2012-2016', British Geological Survey, February 2018, p 13 http:// www.bgs.ac.uk/downloads/start.cfm?id=3396; trade data from resourcetrade.earth, accessed April 17, 2018 https://resourcetrade.earth/data?year=2016&exporter=4&category=1388&units=value; 'Chromite extraction in Kunar, factor of [in]stability', Integrity Watch Afghanistan, 2013 https://iwaweb.org/wp-content/uploads/2015/11/05-chromite_extraction_in_kunar_factor_of_instability.pdf

325 Legal imports into Pakistan registered at resourcetrade.earth amount to less than 2,500 tons in 2012 – and even lesser amounts in subsequent years. It is of course possible that there is production in Pakistan that is not registered, but no reports of illegal chromite mining

there were found in a short review of online sources. See endnote above for references to illegal chromite mining outside of Nangarhar. 'Pakistan chromite imports', trade data from resourcetrade. earth, accessed April 14, 2018 https://resourcetrade. earth/data?year=2016&importer=586&category=1388&units=value 'Afghanistan chromite production by year', 'World Mineral Production 2012-2016', British Geological Survey, February 2018, p 12; Index Mundi, https://www.indexmundi.com/minerals/?country=af&product=chromite&graph=production

326 'Afghanistan marble exports', trade data from resourcetrade.earth https://resourcetrade.earth/data?year=2016&exporter=4&category=1184&units=value; 'Marbles of Afghanistan', Ministry of Mines and Petroleum http://mom.gov.af/Content/files/Marble%20in%20Afghanistan%20Brochure.pdf

327 Bouissou, 'Comment uneentreprisefrançaise se fourniten talc au pays des talibans'

328 Global Witness correspondences with Imerys, April 2018 IMI Fabi did not respond to an email inquiry from Global Witness on this question.

329 'USA Import Customs Data: Price of Talc', USA Import, accessed April 17, 2018 https://www.usaimportdata. com/usa-import-product-talc.aspx; Julien Bouissou, 'Comment uneentreprisefrançaise se fourniten talc au pays des talibans

330 Bouissou, 'Comment uneentreprisefrançaise se fourniten talc au pays des talibans'

331 Ghunday is in fact in Sherzad district, but part of the wider area often referred to as Khogyani. 'Small contracts', Ministry of Mines and Petroleum, www.mom. gov.af

332 Shamshir Zamir appears to have also paid significant taxes to the government, though the data raises some questions. Afghanistan's 5th EITI Reconciliation Report records zero tons of production for Shamshir Zamir in 1393 (2014) and 1394 (2015), but revenue of Afs51,523,007 ($757,691) and Afs4,544,373 ($66,829). The figures suggest there is an inaccuracy in the data, and the company claimed that a legal dispute among its leadership prevented it from filing EITI data, which could explain why it is listed as not having production. The royalty rate on the company's Sherzad contract is Afs673 ($9.89) per ton, and on its Sherzad contract Afs606 ($8.91) per ton. Taking an average of these tow rates would indicate that the company

extracted at most 80,567 tons in 2014 and 7,106 tons in 2015. This would be consistent with the ban on talc exports in 2015. 'Inception Report and Fifth Reconciliation Report', Afghanistan Extractive Industries Transparency Initiative, April 29, 2017 pp 40, 62, 71, 72 https://eiti.org/ sites/default/files/documents/5threconciliationfinal report_1393-1394_21052017440572255533253225.pdf

333 Bouissou, 'Comment l'industriemondiale du talc finance les talibans et l'Etatislamiqueen Afghanistan'

334 'Afghanistan: The security situation in Nangarhar province', p 17

335 Global Witness email correspondence with Vincent Gouley, Head of Financial Communication & Investor Relations, Imerys, April 10, 2018

336 As early as 2011, around the time Imerys began sourcing talc originating in Afghanistan, a report described Khogyani district as a "disputed zone, controlled neither by the authorities or by the insurgents" Julien Bouissou, 'Comment uneentreprisefrançaise se fourniten talc au pays des talibans'

337 Global Witness email correspondence with Vincent Gouley, Head of Financial Communication & Investor Relations, Imerys, April 18, 2018

338 It is notable that these do not appear in the supposedly comprehensive list of contracts published by the Ministry of Mines.

339 It is not clear not clear why the head of the Omar Group only referred to buying from local concession holders if he had concessions himself. Julien Bouissou, 'Comment l'industriemondiale du talc finance les talibans et l'Etatislamiqueen Afghanistan', Le Monde, October 4, 2016 http://www.lemonde.fr/ asie-pacifique/ article/2016/10/04/comment-l-industrie-mondiale-du-talc-finance-les-talibans-et-l-etat-islamique-en-afghanistan_5007632_3216.html#lJiUGyWP5Xd4oiRx.99

340 Julien Bouissou, 'Comment l'industriemondiale du talc finance les talibans et l'Etatislamiqueen Afghanistan', Le Monde, October 4, 2016

341 Julien Bouissou, 'Comment l'industriemondiale du talc finance les talibans et l'Etatislamiqueen Afghanistan'

342 IMI Fabi CEO CorradoFabi confirmed the joint venture was still active, and the IMI Fabi website also listed "IMI Omar PTV. Ltd – Karachi, Pakistan" as one of the company's worldwide locations. Global

Witness correspondence with CorradoFabi, Chief Executive Officer of IMI Fabi, April 12, 2018; 'Worldwide locations', IMI Fabi https://www.imifabi.com/52-Worldwide-locations.html; 'Talc', IMI Fabi, https://www.imifabi. com/53-Talc.html

343 Global Witness emails to IMI Fabi, April 2018

344 Global Witness correspondence with CorradoFabi, Chief Executive Office of IMI Fabi, April 12, 2018

345 'Mission and Vision', IMI Fabi, https://www.imifabi. com/46-Mission-Vision.html

346 A 2014 report on talc from Pakistan's export promotion bureau lists 12 major producers. Mustansar Mehmood, Sajid Hussain, 'A Report on Talc (Soap Stone)', pp 26-28

347 When U.S. President Donald Trump and Afghan President Ashraf Ghani met in New York City in the autumn of 2017, they too discussed the extractive sector. A Sep tember White House statement said the two presidents agreed that tapping Afghan mineral resources "would help American companies develop materials critical to national security while growing Afghanistan's economy and creating new jobs in both countries, therefore defraying some of the costs of United States assistance as Afghans become more self-reliant." President Ghani said "The economic development and prosperity of Afghanistan depend on its mining sector, which will enable Afghanistan to pay its military expenditure and achieve self-reliance." 'Quarterly report to the United State Congress', Special Inspector General for Afghanistan Reconstruction, January 30, 2018 pp 3-4 https:// www.sigar.mil/pdf/quarterlyreports/2018-01-30qr-intro-section1.pdf

348 'Press Release – Afghanistan to announce Strategy for Extractives at PDAC 2018', Ministry of Mines and Petroleum, March 3, 2018 http://mom.gov.af/en/news/ press-release---afghanistan-to-announce-strategyfor-extractives-at-pdac-2018

349 'Islamic Republic of Afghanistan: Mining Sector Roadmap', Ministry of Mines and Petroleum, December 2017

350 Many of them were displaced by arrivals from Pakistan, including the families of ISKP members.

351 Borhan Osman, 'Descent into chaos: Why did Nangarhar turn into an IS hub?', Afghanistan Analysts Network, September 27, 2016

https://www.afghanistan-analysts.org/descent-into-chaos-why-did-nangarhar-turn-into-an-is-hub/

352 CDCs are local elected councils charged with developing and implementing economic programs in their area as part of the Afghan National Solidarity Program. Each council is ideally comprised of about 25 families. 'Community Development Councils in Afghanistan – A Social Capital', United Nations Post-Conflict Reconstruction Programme, July 2011 http://www. unitar.org/hiroshima/sites/unitar.org.hiroshima/ files/19_Case_Study_CDCs_as_Social_Capital.pdf

353 Community Based Monitoring of Extractives (CBM-E) program mobilize communities to monitor extraction processes to avoid negative social and environmental impacts and to ensure socio-economic development of local communities around extraction areas. 'CBM – Extractives', Integrity Watch Afghanistan, December 29, 2017

354 These include for example the PBIM tourmaline contract in Badakhshan. In January 2018, the Afghan government released many contracts, a positive step – but it is possible that further contracts remain hidden in provincial offices of the Ministry of Mines. 'War in the Treasury of the People', Global Witness, pp 41-45

355 William Byrd and JavedNoorani, 'Industrial-Scale Looting of Afghanistan's Mineral Resources', pp 2, 5-9

356 Global Witness correspondence with Imerys, April 2018

357 Both the British ambassador and the US acting ambassador visited the Minister of Mines around May 2017, but the primary purpose of the meetings was to discuss the 'resolution' of two contracts, the Badakhshan gold contract and the Balkhab copper contract. Preferred bidders had been named for the contracts in 2012 but they had not been finalised. So far as Global Witness is aware (and based on our discussions with the two embassies) no ambassador level meeting with the Minister of Mines has recently taken place with a specific focus on governance. Global Witness meetings with British and US embassy officials, and officials of the Ministry of Mines, May 2017; 'Preferred bidder for current mineral tenders', Ministry of Mines and Petroleum of the Islamic Republic of Afghanistan, December 8, 2012 http://mom.gov.af/en/announcement/15333

358 James Mackenzie, 'The victor, the spoils? Trump eyes Afghanistan's elusive mineral riches', Reuters, August 21, 2017 https://www.reuters.

com/article/us-usa-afghanistan-minerals/the-victor-the-spoils-trump-eyes-afghanistans-elusive-mineral-riches-idUSKCN1B102L

359 The Brussels Conference produced a set of Deliverables which included this: "To operationalize the government's commitment to the Extractive Industries Transparency Initiative (EITI), amendments to the Mining Law submitted to the parliament include measures such as publication of mining contracts, identification of the mining contracts beneficial ownership, assignment of mineral rights for funding of mining projects, suspension for Force Majeure, rights of private land owners' enforcement of mining contracts being linked to their publication, by first half 2018 and the mineral fiscal regime developed by 2018." Self-Reliance Through Mutual Accountability Framework - Smart Deliverables 2017/2018', Brussels Conference on Afghanistan, October 5, 2016 http://mfa.gov.af/Content/Media/Documents/agreed_smaf_smart_deliverables_final26102016113033613553325325.pdf

360 'Afghanistan's Oil, Gas, and Minerals Industries: $488 Million in U.S. Efforts Show Limited Progress Overall, and Challenges Prevent Further Investment and Growth', Special Inspector General for Afghanistan Reconstruction, January 2016 https://www.sigar.mil/ pdf/audits/SIGAR-16-11-AR.pdf

361 A good example of this is that the performance indicators for the main USAID project with the Ministry of Mines did not include any which directly related to improved transparency or governance (such as publication of contracts or implementation of audits). 'Afghanistan's Oil, Gas, and Minerals Industries: $488 Million in U.S. Efforts Show Limited Progress Overall, and Challenges Prevent Further Investment and Growth', Special Inspector General for Afghanistan Reconstruction, January 2016, p 8

362 For a full discussion of the weaknesses in the Ministry of Mines and the wider extractive sector, see for example 'Quarterly report to the United State Congress', Special Inspector General for Afghanistan Reconstruction, January 30, 2018 pp 3-4 https://www.sigar.mil/ pdf/quarterlyreports/2018-01-30qr-intro-section1.pdf

363 'Extractives, Corruption, And Conflict in Afghanistan: Avoiding The Resource Curse', Global Witness, November 2017 https://www.globalwitness.org/en-gb/ campaigns/afghanistan/extractives-policy-briefing-avoiding-resource-curse-afghanistan/

364 'Proposed Amendments to the Afghan Mining Law: December 2015 draft', Global Witness, December 2015, https://www.globalwitness.org/en/campaigns/afghanistan/suggested-amendments-afghan-mining-law/

365 Other useful documents include a report on the Afghan Mining Law, A Shaky Foundation; the policy document Building for the Long Term, and the policy report 'A Citizens' Checklist'. 'A Shaky Foundation?: Analysing Afghanistan's Draft Mining Law', Global Witness, November 2013 http://www.globalwitness.org/sites/ default/files/library/SHAKEY_FOUNDATION_GW.pdf; 'Building for the Long Term: Avoiding the Resource Curse in Afghanistan', Global Witness, February 2014 http://www.globalwitness.org/sites/default/ files/ library/LONG-TERM_BUILDING_Report.pdf; 'A Citizens' Checklist: Preventing corruption in the award of oil, gas and mining licenses', Global Witness, January 2012 https://www.globalwitness.org/sites/default/ files/A%20citizens%20checklist%20EN%20 Jan%20 2012.pdf

366 See for example Integrity Watch Afghanistan Community Based Monitoring Project, http://iwaweb.org/cbm. html

367 See http://www.open-contracting.org/global_principles

368 The figure was based on extrapolation from incomplete official figures for that year, which showed 443,594 tons of exports. An adjacent sentence talks about 2m tons of exports – but there is no explanation for the contradiction, so we have taken the more conservative figure. 'An analysis and review of talc sector value chain', Ministry of Mines and Petroleum, 2017, copy on file with Global Witness

369 Global Witness interview with a leading talc trader , mid-2017

370 The trader was source Y. Another Global Witness source (source A-E) reported around 15 trucks as day from the Ladabagh mines (though this may have been other minerals as well as talc – especially marble). Another (Source Z) talked of 2,000 to 2,500 trucks a year going from two mines in Ghunday (equivalent to 80,000 to 100,000 tons if the load was 40 tons a truck). If there were 8-10 such mines as the source suggested, that would be up to a half a million tons just from Ghunday. But they also spoke of those mines generating 10 trucks a week – about a fifth as much – which suggests that there was some misunderstanding or that his information was incorrect (their testimony was otherwise credible, and they had plausible reasons to have access to accurate information). As noted above in the

main text, production at Achin at best was around 10,000 tons a year, so the overall export picture is about the same. Global Witness interview with Source Y, early 2018; Global Witness email correspondence with Matt DuPée, April 23, 2017; Global Witness interview-E, early 2018 Global Witness interview with Source Z, early 2018

371 All but 96 tons of this was unprocessed talc, and all but 114 tons went to Pakistan. Trade data from resourcetrade.earth, accessed April 14, 2018 https:// resourcetrade.earth/data?year=2016&exporter=4&category=1152&units=value; trade data from resourcetrade.earth, accessed April 2, 2018 https:// resourcetrade.earth/data?year=2016&exporter=4&category=1151&units=value

372 The government's figures showed 198,157 tons of exports in 2016-2017 and 73,438 tons in 2015-2016, but the resourcetrade.earth data shows 60,524 tons of export in 2015 (doubtless because of the ban on the talc trade). 487,256 tons in 2014, 223,246 tons in 2013, and 23,644 in 2012. If Ian Wilson's 2012 assessment of that there could be more than 300,000 tons of Afghan talc output is correct, the lower figures may just reflect under-declared exports or poor records. Jack Elliott, 'Pakistan, Afghanistan talc production vastly underestimated', Industrial Minerals, April 11, 2012 http:// www.indmin.com/Article/3009828/Pakistan-Afghanistan-talc-production-vastly-underestimated.html; Ian Wilson, 'Global Talc Markets', powerpoint presentation to the 21st Industrial Minerals Congress & Exhibition, Budapest, Hungary, March 2012 http://www.indmin. com/events/download.ashx/document/speaker/6517/ a0ID000000X0jN2MAJ/Presentation; trade data from resourcetrade.earth, accessed April 2, 2018 https:// resourcetrade.earth/data?year=2016&exporter=4&category=1152&units=value

373 'An analysis and review of talc sector value chain', Ministry of Mines and Petroleum, 2017, copy on file with Global Witness

374 USIP reported that: "Concerned about the uncontrolled exploitation of talc and associated funds going to the Taliban, the Afghan government declared a blanket ban on the extraction and export of talc, precipitating a sudden disruption of supply across the border and a buildup of talc stocks in Nangarhar. According to an MoMP official who personally inspected stocks of talc, about 375,000 tons were piled up in Sherzad district alone. Estimates of the total amount of talc stockpiled after the ban were as high as 750,000 tons, worth perhaps $40 million within Afghanistan." William Byrd and JavedNoorani, 'Industrial-Scale Looting of Afghanistan's Mineral

Resources', United States Institute for Peace, June 2017, p 8 https://www.usip.org/sites/default/ files/2017-05/sr404-industrial-scale-looting-of-afghanistan-s-mineral-resources.pdf

375 Julien Bouissou, 'Comment l'industriemondiale du talc finance les talibans et l'Etatislamiqueen Afghanistan'

376 'An analysis and review of talc sector value chain', Ministry of Mines and Petroleum, 2017, copy on file with Global Witness

377 Trade data from resourcetrade.earth, accessed April 14, 2018 https://resourcetrade.earth/data?year=2016&exporter=4&category=1152&units=value

378 Julien Bouissou, 'Comment uneentreprisefrançaise se fourniten talc au pays des talibans', Le Monde, February 13, 2017

379 One trade is listed at $54.64, but it seems to be exceptional. Trade data from resourcetrade.earth, accessed April 14, 2018 https://resourcetrade.earth/data?year=2016&exporter=586&category=1152&units=value

380 Talc lumps', Alibaba.com, https://www.alibaba.com/ product-detail/talc-lumps_115510779.html?spm=a 2700.7724838.2017115.9.317e2977x7fkQD; "Talcum Powder Brands Mineral Talc Lumps Importers Talc Afghanistan', Alibaba.com https://www.alibaba.com/ product-detail/Talcum-Powder-Brands-Mineral-TalcLumps_60557892546.html?spm=a2700.7724838.20171 15.1.317e2977x7fkQD

381 Trade data from resourcetrade.earth, accessed April 14, 2018 https://resourcetrade.earth/data?year=2016&exporter=4&category=1388&units=value

382 Global Witness interview with local source from Shadal, mid-2017

383 Global Witness interview with an elder originally from Achin district, mid-2017

384 The source was cited by AAN researcher Borhan Osman. Global Witness email correspondence with Borhan Osman, November 2017

385 Global Witness interview, mid-2016

386 Global Witness interview, late 2016

387 The source mentioned that Mazda six-wheel trucks were normally rated to carry 6 tons. Global Witness interview, mid-2016

388 The source spoke of 8-9 mines in the area in total, but only specifically mentioned one of them as having talc. At least one marble and one chromite mine were also among that number, but it is not clear what the others produced. Global Witness interview, mid 2016; Global Witness interview, mid 2017

389 One source mentioned that the mines were worked every day except for Friday, so this is conservative. Global Witness interview, mid-2016

390 The calculation here for talc is: 2.5 trucks x 6 tons load x 4 days a week of mining x 52 weeks a year equals 3,120 tons a year or 260 tons a month. For chromite it is: 2 trucks x 6 tons x 4 days a week of mining x 52 weeks a year equals 2,496 tons a year or 208 tons a month.

391 The calculation here is 4 trucks a day x 6 tons load x 4 days a week of mining x 52 weeks a year equals 4,992 tons a year or 416 tons a month.

392 Trade data from resourcetrade.earth, accessed April 14, 2018 https://resourcetrade.earth/data?year=2016&exporter=586&category=1388&units=value One of our sources reported a price of about Rs40,000-Rs50,000 ($380-$475) for a ton, with chromite worth about Rs80,000 ($760) a ton – but this clearly seems to be inaccurate given the global prices for those commodities. Global Witness interview, late 2016 and mid-2017; Global Witness interview, mid-2017

393 Julien Bouissou, 'Comment uneentreprisefrançaise se fourniten talc au pays des talibans', Le Monde, February 13, 2017

394 Global Witness interview, mid-2017. This was based on extraction from the single site where our source said marble mining was taking place, with 10-12 trailer a day being extracted with a load of around 6 tons each.

395 In Afghanistan miners often pay 20% of the value of production to the Taliban. Matthew DuPée, 'Afghanistan's Conflict Minerals: The Crime-State Insurgent Nexus,' CTC Sentinel, February 16, 2012 https://www. ctc.usma.edu/posts/afghanistans-conflict-minerals-the-crime-state-insurgent-nexus; Michael Renner, 'The Anatomy of Resource Wars', WorldWatch Institute, October 2002 http://www.worldwatch.org/system/ files/EWP162.pdf; 'Afghanistan's Fabulous Ruby Mines Plundered by Thieves,' BBC News, May 25, 2012 http://www.bbc.co.uk/news/world-asia-18070571

396 See discussion of the number of ISKP fighters higher in the main text.

397 Corruption Bouissou, 'Comment l'industriemondiale du talc finance les talibans et l'Etatislamiqueen Afghanistan'

398 Zeerak Fahim, 'Precious stones being smuggled to Pakistan from Sherzad', Pajhwok Afghan News, December 27, 2017

399 Global Witness interview with an Afghan researcher, early 2018. If we assumed similar income from marble and chromite, the total would be $4.2m a year.

400 Global Witness interview with a former senior police officer from Nangarhar, early 2018

401 If the toll was really Rs100,000 ($952) per trailer, the Rs30m ($285,714) a month that the source reported in revenue for the Taliban would be equivalent to only 300 trucks a month, or just 162,000 tons of talc a year if the average load was 45 tons. That is far less than our estimate of the size of the talc trade, which comes in at around 500,000 tons of production (see Annex A). But if the average toll was only Rs35,000 ($333), as two credible sources indicated (see main text), then it would be equivalent to around 463,000 tons, much closer to our estimate. If on the other hand the toll really was Rs100,000 per truck, 500,000 tons would generate more that $10.5m. Global Witness interview with a former senior police officer from Nangarhar, early 2018

402 The fact that the upper range of the second figure is exactly a tenth of the first figure it may lead to suspicion that one or the other is off by a single zero, but there was no indication of this from the sources. Global Witness interview with Source M, early 2018; Global Witness interview with Source Z, early 2018

403 We take Matt Duppee's rate of $8333 a month ($10,000 a year/12) and our other data point of $1190 a month, and the higher data point of $14,285 a month. We then give the lower data points five times as much weight in the calculation of the overall average – as follows: [(5x833)+(5x1190)+14,284]/11 = $2,218.

404 'Small mines contracts', Ministry of Mines and Petroleum of the Islamic Republic of Afghanistan, http://mom. gov.af/en/page/momp-contracts/104421; 'An analysis and review of talc sector value chain', Ministry of Mines and Petroleum, 2017, copy on file with Global Witness

405 Source Z guessed that tolls of Rs5,5000 to Rs20,000 might be paid by trucks that did not have road passes from mine owners, but this was not based on direct knowledge. Sources W and X both said that

road tolls were 6,000 per truck regardless of load. Global Witness interview with Source Z, early 2018; Global Witness interview with Source W, early 2018; Global Witness interview with Source X, early 2018

406 This is based on the resourcetrade.earth figures of 561,430 tons of exports, at an average price of about $60 a ton. See endnote on Taliban take from mines elsewhere in Annex B.

407 A tax of $571 a ton for the highest quality marble would be broadly consistent with a media report of taxes $300-$500 per ton for Helmand marble. A price of up to $3,000 for onyx was cited by one Afghan involved in the stone trade: while it is certainly at the high end of the range, green Afghan onyx is listed on Alibaba.com for up to $3,500 per ton. Sune Engel Rasmussen, 'Afghan government money reaching Taliban through marble trade', The Guardian, June 3, 2016; Global Witness interview-B, mid 2018; 'Afghan Green Onyx', Alibaba. com, accessed April 22, 2018 https://www.alibaba. com/product-detail/Afghan-Green-Onyx_157650743. html?spm=a2700.7724838. 2017115.277.145e66e2EfMZ1E;

408 See endnote on this in Annex B.

Chapter 2: The Sun cannot be hidden by two fingers: Illicit Drugs and the Discussions on a Political Settlement in Afghanistan. *David Mansfield*

1 Orzala Ashraf Nemat is an Afghan scholar and civil society activist.

2 Ahmed Rashid, 'One step closer to an elusive peace in Afghanistan', The New York Review of Books, 27 March 2019, https:// www.nybooks.com/daily/2019/03/27/one-step-closer-to-an-elusive-peace-in-afghanistan/

3 SIGAR, "2019 High Risk List", 2019, page 34-39 https://www.sigar.mil/pdf/spotlight/2019_High-Risk_List.pdf

4 Islamic Republic of Afghanistan, National Statistics and Information Authority, "Afghanistan Statistical Yearbook 2017-2018", Issue No, 39, August 2018, page 111.

5 William Byrd and David Mansfield, 'Licensing Afghan Opium for Medicinal Use: Why it won't work' United States Institute for Peace, Peace Brief, No 179, September 2014, https://www.usip.org/sites/default/files/PB179-Licensing%20Afghan%20 Opium%20for%20 Medicinal%20Use.pdf

6 David Mansfield and Paul Fishstein, 'Eyes Wide Shut: Counternarcotics in Transition' AREU Briefing paper, September 2013, https://www.ecoi.net/en/file/local/1217493/1226_1382354119_opium-20bp.pdf

7 SIGAR, 'Counternarcotics: Lessons from the US experience in Afghanistan' June 2018, https://www.sigar.mil/pdf/lessonslearned/SIGAR-18-52-LL.pdf

8 Islamic Republic of Afghanistan, National Statistics and Information Authority, "Afghanistan Statistical Yearbook 2017-2018", Issue No, 39, August 2018, page 111.

9 This figure is derived from a model created by David Mansfield and used in the World Bank Agricultural Strategy 2014

10 UNODC estimates that Afghanistan produces 250-300 mt of heroin base and 360-610 mt of heroin. At a price of around US$ 1,000/kg for heroin base and US US$ 2,000 for heroin this production would be worth up to US$ 1.2 billion. See UNODC Afghanistan Opium Survey 2018, page 43

11 The Afghan government estimated GDP including opium at US$ 21.4 billion in 2017-2018. See Islamic Republic of Afghanistan, National Statistics and Information Authority, "Afghanistan Statistical Yearbook 2017-2018", Issue No, 39, August 2018, page ii.

12 Islamic Republic of Afghanistan, National Statistics and Information Authority, "Afghanistan Statistical Yearbook 2017-2018", Issue No, 39, August 2018, page 218.

13 David Mansfield, "Denying Revenue or Wasting Money: Assessing the impact of the air campaign against 'drugs labs' in Afghanistan" IDPU, LSE, April 2019, page 45.

14 William Byrd and Richard Brittan, 'Can Technology Help Afghanistan Avoid the Resource Curse?' 13 February 2019, https:// www.usip.org/publications/2019/02/can-technology-help-afghanistan-avoid-resource-curse

15 Interview with Afghan Government official, August 2011.

16 Anatol Lieven "It's time to trust the Taliban" Foreign Policy, 31 January 2019 https://foreignpolicy.com/2019/01/31/itstime-to-trust-the-taliban/

17 Transcript of speech delivered by the delegation of the Islamic Emirate at Moscow conference, 09 November 2018, https:// alemarahenglish.com/?p=37316

18 Vanda Felbab-Brown, Shooting Up: Counterinsurgency and the War on Drugs Washington DC, Brookings Institute Press, 2010, pages 125-126; Johnson, Chris & Leslie, Jolyon, Afghanistan: the Mirage of Peace London: Zed Books, 2004, page 293; Alex Strick Van Lindschoten and Felix Kuehn, 'An Enemy We Created: The Myth of the Taliban - Al Qaeda Merger in Afghanistan, Hurst: London, 2012, page 156

19 See UNODC, Afghanistan Annual Opium Poppy Survey 1995. UNODC: Islamabad. Page 23-24.

20 See US Department of State, 'International Narcotics Control Strategy Report 1995'.

21 The USG statistics show a decrease in cultivation between 1995 and 1996 from 38,740 ha to 27,950 ha. In Helmand cultivation was estimated to have fallen by 5%. During the same period UNODC reported that cultivation increased from 53,759 ha to 56, 824 ha with cultivation falling in Helmand (19,753 ha to 24,909 ha) and rising in Kandahar (2,461 ha to 3,160 ha) and Uruzgan (2,573 ha to 7,777 ha). See US Department of State, 'International Narcotics Control Strategy Report 1996' and UNODC, Afghanistan Annual Opium Poppy Survey 1997. UNODC: Islamabad. Page 5.

22 On November 10 1996 the Taliban declared "their opposition to the production, processing and trafficking and abuse of opium and pledged their determination to take all necessary measures, in the context of regional and international cooperation and assistance to deal with the drug phenomenon in accordance with the international drug control conventions" cited in UNODC, 'Strategy Paper for the Implementation for the Poppy Crop Reduction Project (C28) Afghanistan, 1997-2000', UNODC/ROSWA Unpublished Paper, August 1997, page 10.

23 'On 10 September 1997, the State High Commission for Drug Control stated that: "The Islamic State of Afghanistan informs all compatriots that as the use of heroin and hashish is not permitted in Islam, they are reminded once again that they should strictly refrain from growing, using and trading in hashish and heroin. Anyone who violates this order shall be meted out a punishment in line with the lofty Mohammed and Sharia Law and this shall not be entitled to

launch a complaint." This declaration was subsequently amended by a clarification issued on October 1997 which specifically banned the cultivation and trafficking of opium'. See UNODC, Afghanistan Annual Opium Poppy Survey 1998. UNODC: Islamabad. Page 6.

24 Cited in Farrell, G. & Thorne, J. (2005). Where have all the flowers gone?: Evaluation of the Taliban crackdown against opium poppy cultivation in Afghanistan. International Journal of Drug Policy 16(2005):81-91, page 85 http://www.unawestminster.org.uk/pdf/drugs/UNdrugsfarrell_IJDP16.pdf

25 World Food Programme, '1.5 million Afghans face severe' food shortages' WFP News Release, 11 February 2000.

26 Bureau Report, 'Ban on movement of wheat creates flour crisis in NWFP', 23 March 2000, https://asianstudies.github.io/ area-studies/SouthAsia/SAserials/Dawn/2000/mar25.html#bano

27 David Mansfield, A State Build on Sand: How Opium Undermined Afghanistan

28 Johnson, C & Leslie, J. (2004) Afghanistan: the Mirage of Peace. London: Zed Books, page 145; Crews, R. D. and Tarzi A. (Ed.,) (2008). The Taliban and the crisis of Afghanistan. Cambridge: Harvard University Press page 111-112.

29 FrancescVendrell, personal communication 24 April 2001; Crews, R. D. and Tarzi A. (Ed.,) (2008). The Taliban and the crisis of Afghanistan. Cambridge: Harvard University Press pages 262 & 265.

30 Rashid, A. (2001). Taliban Islam, Oil and the New Great Game in Central Asia. London: IB Tauris, page 212; Johnson, C & Leslie, J. (2004). Afghanistan: the Mirage of Peace. London: Zed Books, pages 152-153; Donini, A., Niland, N. &Wermester, K. (Ed.,) (2004). Nation-building unravelled? Aid, peace and justice in Afghanistan. Connecticut: Kumarian Press, page 190; and Marsden, P. (1998) The Taliban War, Religion and the New Order in Afghanistan. London: Zed Books, page 93.

31 Maley, W. (2002). The Afghanistan Wars. London: Palgrave Macmillan.

32 Barfield, T. (2010). Afghanistan A Cultural and Political History Princeton, U.S.A.: Princeton University Press.

33 Rashid, A. (2001). Taliban Islam, Oil and the New Great Game in Central Asia. London: IB Tauris; Crews, R. D. and Tarzi A. Ed.,)

(2008). The Taliban and the crisis of Afghanistan. Cambridge: Harvard University Press; pages 259-268.

34 Vendrell, personal communication 24/04/01; Crews, R. D. and Tarzi A. (Ed.,) (2008). The Taliban and the crisis of Afghanistan. Cambridge: Harvard University Press, pages 262, 265.

35 Crews, R. D. and Tarzi A. (Ed.,) (2008). The Taliban and the crisis of Afghanistan. Cambridge: Harvard University Press, page 262, Mansfield D. Mansfield, D. (2001, May). The Impact of the Taliban Prohibition on Opium Poppy Cultivation in Afghanistan. Unpublished paper prepared for the Donors Mission to Afghanistan, 23 April – 4 May 2001, page 28.

36 'At the time of the fieldwork for the Taliban ban, a Taliban commander was killed in the Pekhar valley in Achin and the Taliban advised team members not to go to the area'

37 Goodson, L. P. (2001) Afghanistan's Endless War: State failure, regional Politics, and the Rise of the Taliban. Seattle: University Of Washington Press, page 107.

38 Crews, R. D. and Tarzi A. (Ed.,) (2008). The Taliban and the crisis of Afghanistan. Cambridge: Harvard University Press, page 238-273; Nojumi, N. (2002) The rise of the Taliban in Afghanistan: Mass mobilization, civil war, and the future of the region. New York: Palgrave, pages 179-181; Gannon, K. (2005). I is for Infidel: from Holy War to Holy terror: 18 years inside Afghanistan. New York, USA: Public Affairs, pages 51-65; Donini, A., Niland, N. &Wermester, K. (Ed.,) (2004). Nationbuildingunraveled? Aid, peace and justice in Afghanistan. Connecticut: Kumarian Press, page 190.

39 FransescVendrell, personal communication 24 April 2001.

40 Special Inspector General Afghanistan Reconstruction, Counternarcotics: Lessons from the US Experience in Afghanistan, June 2018, page 108-109 https://www.sigar.mil/pdf/lessonslearned/SIGAR-18-52-LL.pdf

41 Margot Kelly and Laurissa Smith, 'Opium poppy industry causing headaches for Tasmanian farmers with crop no longer considered lucrative' ABC Rural, 23 June 2018, https://www.abc.net.au/news/rural/2018-06-24/pain-for-pharmaceuticalpoppy-industry-in-tasmania/9881084

42 Madeline Clark, 'State's first opium crop harvest under way in Riverina', The Land, 2 January 2018, https://www.theland. com.au/

story/5146391/states-first-opium-poppy-crop-harvest-under-way-in-riverina/

43 Department of Primary Industries, Parks, Water and Environment & Poppy Growers Tasmania, 'Factors Influencing Farmers Decisions to Grow Poppies', January 2013, page 15 https://dpipwe.tas.gov.au/Documents/Poppy-Report-220213.pdf

44 William Byrd and David Mansfield, Licensing Afghan Opium for Medicinal Use: Why it Won't Work. USIP, Peace Brief, September 2014, page 3. https://www.usip.org/sites/default/files/PB179-Licensing%20Afghan%20Opium%20for%20 Medicinal%20Use.pdf

45 William Byrd and David Mansfield, Licensing Afghan Opium for Medicinal Use: Why it Won't Work. USIP, Peace Brief, September 2014, page 3. https://www.usip.org/sites/default/files/PB179-Licensing%20Afghan%20Opium%20for%20 Medicinal%20Use.pdf

46 Divya Rajagopal, 'Opium trade sluggish as norms, infra beg for upgrade', The Economic Times, 18 May 2019, https:// economictimes.indiatimes.com/news/economy/foreign-trade/opium-trade-sluggish-as-norms-infra-beg-for-upgrade/articleshow/69382400.cms

47 International Narcotics Control Board, 'Supply of opiate raw material and demand for opiates for medical and scientific purposes', 2013, pages 93-100, http://www.incb.org/documents/Narcotic-Drugs/Technical-Publications/2013/Part_3_ supply_E.pdf

48 Margot Kelly and Laurissa Smith, 'Opium poppy industry causing headaches for Tasmanian farmers with crop no longer considered lucrative' ABC Rural, 23 June 2018, https://www.abc.net.au/news/rural/2018-06-24/pain-for-pharmaceuticalpoppy-industry-in-tasmania/9881084

49 Jamie Smyth 'US opiod crisis bites for Tasmania's poppy farmers' Financial Times, 22 March 2018 https://www.ft.com/content/76e9d486-25bc-11e8-b27e-cc62a39d57a0 ; Margot Kelly and Laurissa Smith, 'Opium poppy industry causing headaches for Tasmanian farmers with crop no longer considered lucrative' ABC Rural, 23 June 2018, https://www.abc.net. au/news/rural/2018-06-24/pain-for-pharmaceutical-poppy-industry-in-tasmania/9881084

50 Special Inspector General Afghanistan Reconstruction, Counternarcotics: Lessons from the US Experience in Afghanistan, June 2018, https://www.sigar.mil/pdf/lessonslearned/SIGAR-18-52-LL.pdf

51 David Mansfield 'Truly Unprecedented: How the Helmand Food Zone supported an increase in the provinces capacity to porduce opium' AREU, October 2017 https://areu.org.af/wp-content/uploads/2017/10/1728E-TRULY-UNPRECEDENTED-Howthe-Helmand-Food-Zone-supported-an-increase-in-the-province%E2%80%99s-capacity-to-produce-opium.pdf

52 US Department of Defense, Department of Defense Press Briefing by General Nicholson via teleconference from Kabul, Afghanistan: General John W. Nicholson Jr., commander, Resolute Support and U.S. Forces Afghanistan, 20 November 2017, https://dod.defense.gov/News/Transcripts/Transcript-View/Article/1377753/department-of-defense-press-briefing-bygeneral-nicholson-via-teleconference-fr/

53 David Mansfield, "Denying Revenue or Wasting Money: Assessing the impact of the air campaign against 'drugs labs' in Afghanistan" IDPU, LSE, April 2019.

54 David Mansfield, "Denying Revenue or Wasting Money: Assessing the impact of the air campaign against 'drugs labs' in Afghanistan" IDPU, LSE, April 2019.

55 David Mansfield, 'Stirring up the Hornet's Nest: How the population of central Helmand view the current counterinsurgency campaign' AREU, October 2018 https://areu.org.af/wp-content/uploads/2018/11/1814E-STIRRING-UPTHE-HORNET%E2%80%99S-NEST.pdf

Chapter 3: The Myth of 'Afghan Black': A Cultural History of Cannabis Cultivation and Hashish Production in Afghanistan.
Fabrizio Foschini and Jelena Bjelica

1 Nikolay Ivanovich Vavilov, Origin and Geography of Cultivated Plants, Cambridge, Cambridge University Press, 1992

2 The United Nations' Commission on Narcotic Drugs and the Economic and Social Council, established in 1946, decided around 1949 "that it would be desirable to disseminate authoritative information" on the subject of narcotics drugs "in a bulletin published by the Secretariat of the United Nations." The bulletins that have been published between 1949 and 2006 provide a rich and indispensable source of information, available here.

3 See Mitch Earleywine, Understanding Marijuana: A new look at the scientific evidence, New York, Oxford University Press, 2002. Ear-

leywine refers to a number of references in Chinese and Sanskrit on the use of cannabis for medical purposes, recorded as early as 2737 BC in China and around 1400 BC in India. See also an in-depth analysis for the UN narcotics bulletin in 1965 about the use of opium and cannabis in the traditional systems of medicine in India, by an adviser in indigenous systems of medicine for the Government of India, Shri C. Dwarakanath. He argued in his paper that the traditional use of cannabis in the Ayurvedic and Unani practices should be allowed.

4 Vavilov, for example, mentions cannabis references by Varro, a Roman author who lived between 127 and 116 BC and authored books on agriculture; Columella, who published a book on agriculture in 65 AD; Pliny the Elder, a Roman scholar (23 to 79 AD) on natural phenomena and; Dioscorides a known physician and herbalist from the first century AD. Vavilov said that Herodotus, the famous Greek historian, mentioned that hemp was not known in ancient Greece before 484 BC Herodotus' Histories mentions hemp clothing in the land of the Scythian (nomadic people of Iranian origin that inhabited territories north of the Black Sea) and offer an account of a Scythian funeral rite that included inhaling the smoke of cannabis seeds.

5 See for example: Nikolay Ivanovich Vavilov, Origin and Geography of Cultivated Plants, Cambridge, Cambridge University Press, 1992; Mitch Earleywine, Understanding Marijuana: A new look at the scientific evidence, New York, Oxford University Press, 2002; Robert Connell Clarke, Hashish!, Los Angeles, Red Eye Press, 1998.

6 In historiography, the term 'black legend' refers to what is produced in historical writing by deliberately misreporting on a class of people in order to present them as uniquely inhuman or immoral. It would use false facts or take facts out of context, or exaggerate events to do this.

7 See also Chapter 7 "Drug Use in Afghanistan's History" in Macdonald, D., Drugs in Afghanistan, New York, Pluto Press, 2007.

8 It also included a number of famous French writers like Alexandre Dumas (1802–1870); Honoré Daumier (1808–1879); Honoré de Balzac (1799–1850); Gustave Flaubert (1821–1880) and Victor Hugo (1802–1885) who participated occasionally (see here).

9 Benjamin's experiments were inspired by Baudelaire's writings and life and were documented in his book, published posthumously, entitled On Hashish.

10 For more details, see also this bulletin from 1962, entitled "The cannabis problem: A note on the problem and the history of international action" which offers a historical overview of the international legal regimes on cannabis. For a historical overview, see this 1966 bulletin published on the occasion of twenty years of narcotics control under the United Nations: For the Commission on Narcotic Drugs' resolutions and decisions from 1946 until 2014, see here.

11 See for example this ORF 2 (Austrian TV) documentary from 2016 about the hippie movement, entitled: "Afghanistan on the hippie trail in the 1960s and 1970s – A lost paradise"; (with English subtitles here). See also this documentary from 1977, entitled "Road to Kathmandu" (here).

12 Nikolay Ivanovich Vavilov, Origin and Geography of Cultivated Plants, Cambridge, Cambridge University Press, 1992

13 The United Nations' Commission on Narcotic Drugs and the Economic and Social Council, established in 1946, decided around 1949 "that it would be desirable to disseminate authoritative information" on the subject of narcotics drugs "in a bulletin published by the Secretariat of the United Nations." The bulletins that have been published between 1949 and 2006 provide a rich and indispensable source of information, available here.

14 See Mitch Earleywine, Understanding Marijuana: A new look at the scientific evidence, New York, Oxford University Press, 2002. Earleywine refers to a number of references in Chinese and Sanskrit on the use of cannabis for medical purposes, recorded as early as 2737 BC in China and around 1400 BC in India. See also an in-depth analysis for the UN narcotics bulletin in 1965 about the use of opium and cannabis in the traditional systems of medicine in India, by an adviser in indigenous systems of medicine for the Government of India, Shri C. Dwarakanath. He argued in his paper that the traditional use of cannabis in the Ayurvedic and Unani practices should be allowed.

15 Vavilov, for example, mentions cannabis references by Varro, a Roman author who lived between 127 and 116 BC and authored books on agriculture; Columella, who published a book on agriculture in 65 AD; Pliny the Elder, a Roman scholar (23 to 79 AD) on natu-

ral phenomena and; Dioscorides a known physician and herbalist from the first century AD. Vavilov said that Herodotus, the famous Greek historian, mentioned that hemp was not known in ancient Greece before 484 BC Herodotus' Histories mentions hemp clothing in the land of the Scythian (nomadic people of Iranian origin that inhabited territories north of the Black Sea) and offer an account of a Scythian funeral rite that included inhaling the smoke of cannabis seeds.

15 See for example: Nikolay Ivanovich Vavilov, Origin and Geography of Cultivated Plants, Cambridge, Cambridge University Press, 1992; Mitch Earleywine, Understanding Marijuana: A new look at the scientific evidence, New York, Oxford University Press, 2002; Robert Connell Clarke, Hashish!, Los Angeles, Red Eye Press, 1998.

17 In historiography, the term 'black legend' refers to what is produced in historical writing by deliberately misreporting on a class of people in order to present them as uniquely inhuman or immoral. It would use false facts or take facts out of context, or exaggerate events to do this.

18 See also Chapter 7 "Drug Use in Afghanistan's History" in Macdonald, D., Drugs in Afghanistan, New York, Pluto Press, 2007.

19 It also included a number of famous French writers like Alexandre Dumas (1802–1870); Honoré Daumier (1808–1879); Honoré de Balzac (1799–1850); Gustave Flaubert (1821–1880) and Victor Hugo (1802–1885) who participated occasionally (see here).

20 Benjamin's experiments were inspired by Baudelaire's writings and life and were documented in his book, published posthumously, entitled On Hashish.

21 For more details, see also this bulletin from 1962, entitled "The cannabis problem: A note on the problem and the history of international action" which offers a historical overview of the international legal regimes on cannabis . For a historical overview, see this 1966 bulletin published on the occasion of twenty years of narcotics control under the United Nations: For the Commission on Narcotic Drugs' resolutions and decisions from 1946 until 2014, see here.

22 See for example this ORF 2 (Austrian TV) documentary from 2016 about the hippie movement, entitled: "Afghanistan on the hippie trail in the 1960s and 1970s – A lost paradise"; (with English subtitles here). See also this documentary from 1977, entitled "Road to Kathmandu" (here).

23 A local militia commander called Abdullah Charsi even became a high-ranking officer of the Afghan National Border Police in western Afghanistan in 2012, showing the possibility of a career even with such a strongly-flavoured sobriquet.

24 During the anti-Soviet war, Logar also had a famous local mujahedin check post, on a hill west to the road to Paktia, the fighters at which were known as charsian. It was a famous weekend hang out spot for the local youth who had not much choice where to spend their spare time.

25 The same sorts of jokes and gossip are reported from the Tribal Areas of Pakistan. For example, the Afridi Pashtuns inhabiting those parts of the Khyber Agency where hashish is extensively grown are said to be the world's most skilled people at recognising varieties of chars by its smell: these 'human hounds' are able to tell not just the variety but even the specific field where a particular hemp plant is grown, just by smelling a piece of its hashish.

26 Saqi is the cup-bearer of Persian classical poetry, a symbol for the serving of substances, which offer a pleasant intoxication that allow one to forget personal or worldly troubles.

27 The lexicon here is important: Mrech Agha 'held court' like some sort of secular or religious authority; Zabar Ali also styled himself a padsha, a king, showing the status recognition that this unique class of people enjoyed in the eyes of at least part of Afghan society.

28 David B. Edwards, Heroes of the Age: Moral Fault Lines on the Afghan Frontier, University of California Press, 1996; Nile Green, "Tribe, Diaspora and Sainthood in Afghan History", Journal of Asian Studies, Vol. 67, n°1, 2008.

Chapter 4: Money Laundering, Terrorist Financing, and Hawala's Damage to the Afghan Economy. ***Michael Kelvington***

1 "Afghanistan," The World Bank, accessed 20 December 2016, http://data.worldbank.org/country/afghanistan.

2 "Afghanistan | Economic Indicators," Trading Economics, updated 20 December 2016, accessed 20 December 2016, http://www.tradingeconomics.com/afghanistan/indicators.

3 See Annex A and Annex B.

4 Javid Ahmad, "Dirty Money in Afghanistan," Foreign Affairs, published 07 September 2016, accessed 20 December 2016, https://www.

foreignaffairs.com/articles/afghanistan/2016-09-07/dirty-money-afghanistan.

5 Edwina Thompson, "The Nexus of Drug Trafficking and Hawala in Afghanistan," UNODC, accessed 20 December 2016, http://siteresources.worldbank.org/SOUTHASIAEXT/Resources/Publications/448813-1164651372704/UNDC_Ch6.pdf, 155.

6 Ibid., 184.

7 Gretchen Peters, Seeds of Terror: How Heroin is Bankrolling the Taliban and al Qaeda, (New York: St. Martin's Press, 2009), 177.

8 See Annex C.

9 "The Money Laundering Cycle," United Nations Office on Drugs and Crime, accessed 19 December 2016, https://www.unodc.org/unodc/en/money-laundering/laundrycycle.html.

10 Ibid.

11 "The Money Laundering Cycle," United Nations Office on Drugs and Crime.

12 Thompson, 155.

13 Ibid.

14 Ahmad, "Dirty Money in Afghanistan," Foreign Affairs.

15 "Afghanistan | Economic Indicators."

16 Ahmad, "Dirty Money in Afghanistan."

17 Ibid.

18 "Islamic Republic of Afghanistan: Poverty Reduction Strategy Paper," International Monetary Fund, IMF Country Report No. 08/153, (Washington, D.C.: IMF, 2008), 46.

19 John McDowell, et al., "The Consequences of Money Laundering and Financial Crime," Economic Perspectives: An Electronic Journal of the U.S. Department of State, Vol. 6, No. 2, May 2001, accessed 20 December 2016, https://www.hsdl.org/?view&did=3549, 6.

20 "Islamic Republic of Afghanistan: Poverty Reduction Strategy Paper," International Monetary Fund, IMF Country Report No. 08/153, (Washington, D.C.: IMF, 2008), 49.

21 McDowell, et al., "The Consequences of Money Laundering and Financial Crime," 7.

22 SIGAR Office of Special Projects, "Afghanistan's High Office of Oversight: Personal Asset Declarations of High Ranking Afghan Government Officials are Not Consistently Registered and Verified," Special Inspector General for Afghanistan Reconstruction, SP-16-60-SP, published September 2016, accessed 19 September 2016, https://www.sigar.mil/pdf/special%20projects/SIGAR-16-60-SP.pdf, 2.

23 "Afghanistan | Economic Indicators."

24 McDowell, et al., "The Consequences of Money Laundering and Financial Crime," 8.

25 "Afghanistan Economic Indicators." See also Annex D.

26 McDowell, et al., "The Consequences of Money Laundering and Financial Crime," 7-8.

Bibliography (Chapter 4)

"Afghanistan." The World Bank. Accessed 20 December 2016, http://data.worldbank.org/ country/afghanistan.

"Afghanistan | Economic Indicators." Trading Economics. Updated 20 December 2016.Accessed 20 December 2016. http://www.tradingeconomics.com/afghanistan/indicators.

Ahmad, Javid. "Dirty Money in Afghanistan." Foreign Affairs. Published 07 September 2016.Accessed 20 December 2016. https://www.foreignaffairs.com/articles/afghanistan/2016-09-07/dirty-money-afghanistan."Islamic Republic of Afghanistan: Poverty Reduction Strategy Paper." International MonetaryFund. IMF Country Report No. 08/153. Washington, D.C.: IMF, 2008.

McDowell, John, et al. "The Consequences of Money Laundering and Financial Crime."

Economic Perspectives: An Electronic Journal of the U.S. Department of State. Vol. 6, No. 2, May 2001. Accessed 20 December 2016. https://www.hsdl.org/?view&did=3549, 6-8.

Peters, Gretchen. Seeds of Terror: How Heroin is Bankrolling the Taliban and al Qaeda. NewYork: St. Martin's Press, 2009.

SIGAR Office of Special Projects. "Afghanistan's High Office of Oversight: Personal Asset

Declarations of High Ranking Afghan Government Officials are Not Consistently Registered and Verified." Special Inspector

General for Afghanistan Reconstruction. SP-16-60-SP. Published September 2016. Accessed 19 September 2016. https://www.sigar.mil/pdf/special%20projects/SIGAR-16-60-SP.pdf.

“The Money Laundering Cycle.” United Nations Office on Drugs and Crime. Accessed 19December 2016. https://www.unodc.org/unodc/en/money-laundering/laundrycycle.html.

Thompson, Edwina. “The Nexus of Drug Trafficking and Hawala in Afghanistan,” UNODC,accessed 20 December 2016, http://siteresources.worldbank.org/ SOUTHASIAEXT/ Resources/ Publications /448813-1164651372704/UNDC_Ch6.pdf.

Chapter 5: War on drugs for peace in Afghanistan: Lessons from South America. By SADF

1 The Constitution of Afghanistan, ratified on 26 January 2004, retrieved from http://www.afghanembassy.com.pl/afg/images/pliki/TheConstitution.pdf.

2 Afghan National Drug Action Plan, published on 14 October 2015, retrieved from http://mcn.gov.af/Content/files/Afghan%20National%20Drug%20Action%20Plan%20(1).pdf.

References

Ahmed, D. (2015, August 17). Heroin and extremism in Pakistan. Retrieved fromhttps://foreignpolicy.com/2015/08/17/heroin-and-jihad-in-pakistan/

Asmann, P. &Yagoub, M. (2018, September 14). Wavering of ELN peace talks could cause further criminalization. Retrieved from https://www.insightcrime.org/news/brief/wavering-eln-peace-talks-could-cause-further-criminalization/

Avila Ceron, C.A., De los Rios-Carmenado, I. & Martín Fernández, S. (2018). Illicit crop substitution and rural prosperity in armed conflict areas: A conceptual proposal based on the WORKING WITH PEOPLE model in Colombia. LAND USE POLICY, 42, 118-120.

Blanchard, C. (2009, August 12). Afghanistan: Narcotics and U.S. Policy. Retrieved from https://fas.org/sgp/crs/row/RL32686.pdf

Bonner, A. (1986, June 18). Afghan rebels' victory garden: Opium. Retrieved from https://www.nytimes.com/1986/06/18/world/afghan-rebel-s-victory-garden-opium.html

Browne, D. (2014, March 23). How Pakistan succumbed to a hard-drug epidemic. Retrieved from https://www.telegraph.co.uk/news/worldnews/asia/pakistan/10705585/How-Pakistan-succumbed-to-a-hard-drug-epidemic.html

Burns, J.F. (1989, November 19). U.S. cuts off arms to Afghan faction. Retrieved from https://www.nytimes.com/1989/11/19/world/us-cuts-off-arms-to-afghan-faction.html

Casaca, P. & Wolf, S.O. (2017, June 29). Waging jihad by other means: Iran's drug business and its role within the international crime-terror nexus. Retrieved from https://www.sadf.eu/wp-content/uploads/2017/06/5WORKING-PAPER.N.5.Waging-Jihad-by-Other-Means_-Iran_s-Drug-Business-and-its-Role-within-the-International-Crime-Terror-Nexus.pdf

Cerdá, M. & Kilmer, B. (2017). Uruguay's middle-ground approach to cannabis legalization. INTERNATIONAL JOURNAL OF DRUG POLICY, 42, 118-120.

Daniels, J.P. (2018, August 23). Colombian activists face 'extermination' by criminal gangs. Retrieved from https://www.theguardian.com/world/2018/aug/23/colombian-activists-face-extermination-by-criminal-gangs

De Danieli, F. (2014). Beyond the drug-terror nexus: Drug trafficking and the state-crime relations in Central Asia. INTERNATIONAL JOURNAL OF DRUG POLICY, 25(6), 1235-1240.

Felbab-Brown, V. (2009, October 26). Narco-belligerents Across the Globe: Lessons from Colombia for Afghanistan? Retrieved from http://www.realinstitutoelcano.org/wps/wcm/connect/da0e7a80401cec18ab82eb1ecbd00d37/WP55-2009_Felbab-Brown_Narco-belligerants_Lessons_Colombia_Afghanistan.pdf?MOD=AJPERES

Forero, J. (2018). Drug gang's battle in old rebel lands: In Colombia trafficking groups fight to control cocaine-growing regions once home to the FARC. WALL STREET JOURNAL, 2018, July 17, A9.

Global Commission on Drug Policy (GCDP). (2011, June). War on drugs: Report of the Global commission on Drug Policy. Retrieved from https://drugscouts.de/sites/default/files/image/pdfs/Global_Commission_Report_English.pdf

Goodhand, J. (2009). Bandits, borderlands and opium wars: Afghan state-building viewed from the margins. Retrieved from https://www.econstor.eu/bitstream/10419/44703/1/615075703.pdf

Goodhand, J. (2008). Corrupting or consolidating the peace? The drugs economy and post-conflict peacebuilding in Afghanistan. INTERNATIONAL PEACEKEEPING, 15(3), 405-423.

Green, M. (2012, September 5). Special report: Murder spotlights Pakistan's 'heroin kingpin'. Retrieved from https://www.reuters.com/article/us-pakistan-kingpin/special-report-murder-spotlights-pakistans-heroin-kingpin-idUSBRE88401R20120905

Hall, W. (2018). The future of the international drug control system and national drug prohibitions. ADDICTION, 113(7), 1210-1223.

Hudak, J., Ramsey, G. & Walsh, J. (2018, March). Uruguay's cannabis law: Pioneering a new paradigm. Retrieved from https://www.brookings.edu/wp-content/uploads/2018/03/gs_032118_uruguaye28099s-cannabis-law_final.pdf

Kazmi, S.K.H. (2017). Commodity updates: Colombia coca producers defy new crop substitution plan. ADDICTION, 112(7), 1128-1135.

Kilmer, B. &LiccardoPacula, R. (2017). Understanding and learning from the diversification of cannabis supply laws. ADDICTION, 112(7), 1128-1135.

Kreutzmann, H. (2007). Afghanistan and the Opium World Market: Poppy Production and Trade. IRANIAN STUDIES, 40(5), 605-621.

LeGrand, C.C., van Isschot, L. &RiañoAlcalá, P. (2017). Land, justice, and memory: Challenges for peace in Colombia. CANADIAN JOURNAL OF LATIN AMERICAN AND CARRIBEAN STUDIES, 42(3), 259-276.

Maass, C.D. (2011). Afghanistan's Drug Career: Evolution from a War Economy to a Drug Economy. Retrieved from https://

www.afghanistan-analysts.org/wp-content/uploads/downloads/2012/10/20110401CithaM-Afghanistans_Drug_Career-FINAL.pdf

Majidyar, A. (2017). Iran's double game in drug war. http://www.mei.edu/content/io/iran-s-double-game-drug-war

Mancini, A. & Sati, S. (2017). Afghanistan and Colombia, A common struggle against narcotics. Retrieved from https://www.ispionline.it/sites/default/files/pubblicazioni/wp_65_2017.pdf

Mansfield, D. (2018). Turning desert into flowers: Settlement and poppy cultivation in southwest Afghanistan. THIRD WORLD QUARTERLY, 39(2), 331-349.

McCoy, A. (2018, January 9). How the heroin trade explains the US-UK failure in Afghanistan. Retrieved from https://www.theguardian.com/news/2018/jan/09/how-the-heroin-trade-explains-the-us-uk-failure-in-afghanistan

McDermott, J. (2018, March 15). The 'Invisibles': Colombia's New Generation of Drug Traffickers. Retrieved from https://www.insightcrime.org/investigations/invisibles-colombias-new-generation-drug-traffickers/

Norman, S.V. (2017). NARCOTIZATION as security dilemma: The FARC and drug trade in Colombia. STUDIES IN CONFLICT & TERRORISM, 41(8), 638-659.

Organization of American States (OAS). (2012). Scenario of the drug problem in the Americas 2013-2025. Retrieved from https://globalexchange.org/wp-content/uploads/2013/11/Scenarios_Report.pdf

Osman, B. (2018, September 5). As new US envoy appointed, turbulent Afghanistan's hopes for peace persist. Retrieved from https://www.crisisgroup.org/asia/south-asia/afghanistan/new-us-envoy-appointed-turbulent-afghanistans-hopes-peace-persist

Paoli, L., Rabkov, I., Greenfield, V. & Reuter, P. (2007). Tajikistan: The rise of a narco-state. JOURNAL OF DRUG ISSUES, 37(4), 951-979.

Peters, G. (2009). How Opium Profits the Taliban. Retrieved fromhttps://www.usip.org/ sites/default/files/resources/taliban_opium_1.pdf

Quigley, J.T. (2014, March 24). Pakistan: The most heroin addicted country in the world. Retrieved from https://thediplomat.com/2014/03/pakistan-the-most-heroin-addicted-country-in-the-world/

Ríos, J. (2015). Del Caguán a La Habana. Los diálogos de paz con las FARC en Colombia: una cuestión de correlación de fuerzas. REVISTA DE ESTUDIOSENSEGURIDADINTERNACIONAL, 1(1), 63-83.

Rubin, B.R. (2000). The political economy of war and peace in Afghanistan. WORLD DEVELOPMENT, 28(10), 1789-1803.

Rudaw. (2018, June 23). Kermanshah: Iran's drug addiction capital? Retrieved from http://www.rudaw.net/english/middleeast/iran/230620182

Shenk, J. & Kugelman, M. (2017, December 23). What Peace in Colombia Teaches Us About War in Afghanistan. Retrieved from https://thediplomat.com/2017/12/what-peace-in-colombia-teaches-us-about-war-in-afghanistan/

Siddique, A. & Salih, S.M. (2007, October 10). Afghanistan: Poor Helmand farmers find themselves in eye of drug storm. Retrieved from https://www.rferl.org/a/1078915.html

Sulaiman. (2018, April 11). Iran teams up with Taliban narcotics ring in Western Afghanistan. Retrieved fromhttp://afghanistan.asia-news.com/en_GB/articles/cnmi_st/features/2018/04/11/feature-01

The Asia Foundation. (2017). Afghanistan in 2017: A Survey of the Afghan People. Retrieved from https://asiafoundation.org/wp-content/uploads/2017/11/2017_AfghanSurvey_report.pdf

The Associated Press (2018, September 10). Colombian rebels reject conditions for resuming peace talks. Retrieved from https://www.nytimes.com/aponline/2018/09/10/world/americas/ap-lt-colombia-peace-talks.html

The Economist. (2018a, June 21). Colombia's president will struggle to heal his country's divisions. Retrieved from https://www.economist.com/the-americas/2018/06/21/colombias-new-president-will-struggle-to-heal-his-countrys-divisions

The Economist. (2018b, February 20). Colombia's two anti-coca strategies are at war with each other. Retrieved fromhttps://www.economist.com/the-americas/2018/02/20/colombias-two-anti-coca-strategies-are-at-war-with-each-other

The Economist. (2016). Regulating cannabis: The right way to do drugs. THE ECONOMIST, 418(8976), 9.

The World Bank. (2017, December 28). Implementation completion and results report: Grants to the Islamic Republic of Afghanistan for the National Solidarity Program III. Retrieved fromhttp://documents.worldbank.org/curated/en/984941514909801500/pdf/ICR00003688-12282017.pdf

Third Eye Photojournalism Center. (2013, July). Celebrating 10 years of the National Solidarity Programme: A glimpse of the rural development story in Afghanistan. Retrieved from http://documents.worldbank.org/curated/en/155731467993744166/pdf/819840WP0FINAL0Box0379855B00PUBLIC0.pdf

Transparency International (2018, February 21). Corruption perception index 2017. Retrieved from https://www.transparency.org/news/feature/corruption_perceptions_index_2017

United Nations Institute for Training and Research (UNITAR). (2011). Community Development Councils in Afghanistan: A social capital. Retrieved from http://www.unitar.org/hiroshima/sites/unitar.org.hiroshima/files/19_Case_Study_CDCs_as_Social_Capital.pdf

United Nations Office on Drugs and Crime (UNODC). (2018). World drug report: Analysis of drug markets: opiates, cocaine, cannabis, synthetic drugs. Retrieved from https://www.unodc.org/wdr2018/prelaunch/WDR18_Booklet_3_DRUG_MARKETS.pdf

United Nations Office on Drugs and Crime (UNODC) & Afghanistan Ministry of Counter Narcotics (MCN). (2018). Afghanistan Opium Survey 2017: Cultivation and Production. Retrieved from https://www.unodc.org/documents/crop-monitoring/Afghanistan/Afghan_opium_survey_2017_cult_prod_web.pdf

United States Department of Justice, United States Attorney's Office, Southern District of New York. (2018, May 31). Head of Pakistani drug trafficking network pleads guilty in Manhattan Federal Court to conspiring to import heroin into the United States. Retrieved from https://www.justice.gov/usao-sdny/pr/head-pakistani-drug-trafficking-network-pleads-guilty-manhattan-federal-court

United States Department of the Treasury. (2012, March 7). Treasury designates Iranian Qods Force general overseeing Afghan heroin trafficking through Iran. Retrieved from https://www.treasury.gov/press-center/press-releases/Pages/tg1444.aspx

United States Drug Enforcement Administration (DEA). (2017). 2015 heroin domestic monitor program. Retrieved fromhttp://www.aidac.org/uploads/2015%20Heroin%20Domestic%20Monitor%20Program.pdf

Vick, K. (2005, September 23). Opiates for the Iranian people. Retrieved fromhttp://www.washingtonpost.com/wp-dyn/content/article/2005/09/22/AR2005092202287.html

Von Hoffmann, J. (2016). The international dimension of drug policy reform in Uruguay.INTERNATIONAL JOURNAL OF DRUG POLICY, 34, 27-33.

Walsh, N.P. (2018, August 17). Trump's strategy is failing and the Taliban is winning. Retrieved fromhttps://edition.cnn.com/2018/08/16/asia/afghan-analysis-npw-intl/index.html

Warrick, J. (2012, November 1). In Iran, drug trafficking soars as sanctions take a bigger bite. Retrieved from https://www.washingtonpost.com/world/national-security/in-iran-drug-trafficking-soars-as-sanctions-take-bigger-bite/2012/10/31/12ff0930-1d81-11e2-b647-bb1668e64058_story.html?noredirect=on&utm_term=.d5c86861a162

Index

About the Author

Musa Khan Jalalzai is a journalist and research scholar. He has written extensively on Afghanistan, terrorism, nuclear and biological terrorism, human trafficking, drug trafficking, and intelligence research and analysis. He was an Executive Editor of the Daily Outlook Afghanistan from 2005-2011, and a permanent contributor in Pakistan's daily The Post, Daily Times, and The Nation, Weekly the Nation, (London). However, in 2004, US Library of Congress in its report for South Asia mentioned him as the biggest and prolific writer. He received Masters in English literature, Diploma in Geospatial Intelligence, University of Maryland, Washington DC, certificate in Surveillance Law from the University of Stanford, USA, and diploma in Counter terrorism from Pennsylvania State University, California, the United States.